"This is a fresh look at the university in the twenty-first century. The book focuses on the potential of digital distance education to improve university teaching and learning so that it provides a more personalised and effective service for learners. Mark Nichols' fundamental premise is that the university as a system must cater for digitally enriched teaching and learning, and the book sets out eleven core principles for creating such a system. Essential reading for university administrators and educational policymakers."

—Tony Bates, *Distinguished Visiting Professor in the G. Raymond Chang School of Continuing Education, Ryerson University, Canada, and President & CEO of Tony Bates Associates Ltd*

"This provocative book, written unashamedly in Dr Nichols' voice, draws on his decades of experience and knowledge of UK, NZ, and Australian models of Higher Education to offer a clearly articulated vision for a new model of provision. It is not, as he says, for the administratively squeamish, and it challenges unease with a systems approach to universities as business organisations. Explicitly countering slow models of change, these bold recommendations will elicit lively discussions regarding the purposes and strategies for universities of the future."

—Laura Czerniewicz, *Professor and Director of the Centre for Innovation in Learning and Teaching (CILT) at the University of Cape Town, South Africa*

"This book provides a thoughtful analysis of the impact of technology on higher education. By examining the potential of digital technology and the demands for saleable, personalised education, Nichols argues for a restructured education system around distance education as the priority. For those considering the structural and educational challenges of new technology, this book will offer a coherent position, which can be accepted or refuted, but should be considered."

—Martin Weller, *Professor of Educational Technology at The Open University, United Kingdom*

"One of the most revolutionary ideas about education to emerge in the 20th century was the application of systems methods to teaching as well as resource management, most notably in the open universities. In response, traditional universities have focused attention on the adoption of revolutionary technologies while deflecting attention from structural and pedagogical reform. Mark Nichols has added his voice to the (short) list of those in higher education who have acknowledged the dysfunctionality of the traditional university. In a very personal and sometimes passionate argument, he lays out his vision of a systems approach to higher education. As a long-time advocate of the systems approach in distance education, I am delighted to welcome this fresh, expansive elaboration of both the imperative for reform in higher education and the systems approach as the only viable solution."

—Michael G. Moore, *Distinguished Professor Emeritus of Education at The Pennsylvania State University, USA; Editor of the* American Journal of Distance Education; *and co-author of* Distance Education: A Systems View of Online Learning

Transforming Universities with Digital Distance Education

Transforming Universities with Digital Distance Education explores the ways in which higher education stakeholders can apply and leverage the benefits of online learning. Systems-wide access, scale and quality are achievable goals but require forms of teamwork and financial modelling beyond those at the instructor or programme level. This book's organisational view tackles the systems and practices that will help senior managers and decision-makers guide an entire institution away from dysfunction – incremental progress, insufficient capacity, high costs and generic products— and towards the macro-level implementation and operations of effective online pedagogies.

Mark Nichols is Executive Director of Learning Design & Development at The Open Polytechnic of New Zealand. Before returning to Open Polytechnic, he was previously Director of Technology Enhanced Learning at The Open University, UK.

Transforming Universities with Digital Distance Education

The Future of Formal Learning

Mark Nichols

NEW YORK AND LONDON

First published 2020
by Routledge
52 Vanderbilt Avenue, New York, NY 10017

and by Routledge
2 Park Square, Milton Park, Abingdon, Oxon, OX14 4RN

Routledge is an imprint of the Taylor & Francis Group, an informa business

© 2020 Taylor & Francis

The right of Mark Nichols to be identified as author of this work has been asserted by him in accordance with sections 77 and 78 of the Copyright, Designs and Patents Act 1988.

All rights reserved. No part of this book may be reprinted or reproduced or utilised in any form or by any electronic, mechanical, or other means, now known or hereafter invented, including photocopying and recording, or in any information storage or retrieval system, without permission in writing from the publishers.

Trademark notice: Product or corporate names may be trademarks or registered trademarks, and are used only for identification and explanation without intent to infringe.

Library of Congress Cataloging-in-Publication Data
A catalog record for this title has been requested

ISBN: 978-1-138-61471-0 (hbk)
ISBN: 978-1-138-61470-3 (pbk)
ISBN: 978-0-429-46395-2 (ebk)

Typeset in Bembo
by Wearset Ltd, Boldon, Tyne and Wear

Printed in the United Kingdom
by Henry Ling Limited

To my Mum, who would have been proud; to my Dad, who is; and, though I never met him, to Charles Wedemeyer who so plainly heralded this many decades before I did and whose influence is oft taken for granted. And, of course, thanks Sweet.

Contents

Preface		x
Acknowledgements		xi
1	Introduction	1
2	On Learning and Formal Education	16
3	Models of University Education	35
4	The Digital Distance Education (DDE) Model	48
5	Module Narratives	70
6	Teaching Roles	90
7	Module Development: Context, Direction and Practice	113
8	Operating Models and Organisational Change	143
	Appendix: Am I Ready for Distance Learning?	168
	Index	172

Preface

In this book I propose a simple model for making education more accessible, scalable and personalised. The model, termed 'digital distance education' (DDE), is based on a sound understanding of what a university is and what it does. It draws on over 15 years of change experience in higher education and a deep engagement with distance and digital education theory, practice and thinking.

This book is also about change. It is unfortunate that the term 'transformation' these days is rather a hackneyed one that promises much but delivers little. I've tried to angle this book towards real transformation, not as an abstract ambition but as a tangible objective. I haven't provided a complete set of change tools, but there's enough between these covers for anyone to get the right conversations started and develop the requisite vocabulary for getting things underway.

Two disclaimers before you get started. First, I use the term 'university' generically in this book. The model and discussion apply equally as well to other institutions involved in higher education; polytechnics, TAFEs, small private education providers and others, I invite you to see yourselves alongside your university contemporaries. Second, while the 11 principles of the DDE model are generic, no example is. Do not be constrained by how I have illustrated the principles in action. Any core is possible, so be creative in your own application mindful that the principles are integrated.

I wrote this book because I believe the sort of education I'm advocating is inevitable. Cracks in the supply-centred paradigm that is contemporary university education can only be plastered over for so long. We can't simply continue to overinvest in costly, inaccessible campuses as a means of securing places for the many thousands of aspirational learners seeking to improve themselves and society. I'm no alarmist; instead, I'm surprised that political and university decision-makers are not already *insisting* on the form of education described in this book. I invite the reader to discern the model, visualise the potential and advocate for change. Real change. Transformative change. Education-centred change.

Before everyone else does.

Acknowledgements

So many people's ideas and perspectives have enriched mine for this book, both before and during its development. Digital distance education (DDE) is a consolidation of encounters with many precious colleagues, each of whom will no doubt see their thinking reflecting and overlapping in these pages. A few stand out for me and deserve special mention. Caroline Seelig, Chief Executive of Open Polytechnic, New Zealand, whose example and leadership have illustrated the level of change movement toward DDE requires; Bart Rienties, Simon Cross, Wayne Holmes and others of The Open University, United Kingdom, acknowledging those few short weeks of intensive design where we dreamed big; Bill Anderson, acknowledging your wonderful and generous affinity for energetic chats about distance education that always fill my tank; the teams I've worked with at Laidlaw College, Open Polytechnic, The Open University, acknowledging the richness of the challenges, changes and opportunities; colleagues in Ascilite, EDEN, FLANZ and additional professional communities worldwide that have linked me to new ideas and practices; each Leader & Legend of Online Learning (both interviewed and yet to be interviewed) for the podcast, acknowledging the incredible generosity, innovation and expertise across the international distance and digital education community. Such fullness.

Acknowledgement

Chapter 1

Introduction

> Thirty years from now the big university campuses will be relics. Universities won't survive. It's as large a change as when we first got the printed book.
>
> (Drucker, as cited in Lezner & Johnson, 1997, para. 70)

> Education is on the brink of being transformed through learning technologies; however, it has been on that brink for some decades now ... never before has there been such a clear link between the needs and requirements of education, and the capability of technology to meet them. It is time we moved education beyond the brink of being transformed, to let it become what it wants to be.
>
> (Laurillard, 2008, para. 2)

My mother and father were determined: my sister and I would go to university. I remember both of us understanding this before we were 10 years old. We simply assumed we would go to university as we advanced through the New Zealand compulsory schooling system. Neither of my parents went on to higher education, yet they saw the opportunities it could unlock. They wanted their children to benefit from the choices and lifestyle they saw university graduates had access to. I remain very, very grateful. My sister and I were among the first of our extended family on both sides to graduate with degrees; her in law, mine in business. For me, the bachelor's degree would be only a first step into a very interesting, rich, diverse, rewarding and often challenging career in education.

Higher education continues to provide opportunity, but access to it has changed radically between my generation and my children's. In the United Kingdom, as in New Zealand, Australia and various other nations, the proportional cost of education paid by the student relative to public subsidy has dramatically increased. Yet, demand continues to be strong. In 2018 it was estimated that an additional capacity for a further 300,000 new students will be required across the United Kingdom university sector by 2030 (Bekhradnia & Beech, 2018), raising serious questions about how universities will be able to cater for this extra demand. Without rethinking the dynamics of how universities work, future options are threefold: turning less-qualified students away, placing excessive demands on the public purse for new campuses, or compromising personalisation through massification. None of these options is desirable, nor inevitable.

2 Introduction

The foundation of this book is the notion that higher education can be accessible, scalable and highly personalised all at once, without compromising quality or student outcomes. Its thesis is that digital distance education (DDE), linked to online learning, holds the solution. If we were looking today to invest money into a university sector where accessibility, scalability and personalisation were characteristic, we would start with the same *educational outcomes (substance)* but would seek to design a different *educational system (means of facilitation)*. We would seek to achieve the same things but would pursue them differently.

Education in Context

Education changes lives. It provides opportunity, perspective and prospects to the individuals who experience it, and economic and social benefits to the societies that nurture it. A 2013 report by the Department for Business Innovation & Skills in the United Kingdom summarises a wide range of market and non-market benefits for both society and the individual that result from higher education (Figure 1.1). It is these benefits that continue to drive and justify the massive social investment in higher education. In 2016, excluding R&D costs, New Zealand spent some US$11,910 per full-time equivalent student and the United Kingdom US$18,405. Australia was close to New Zealand, at US$10,791 per student (OECD, 2019). Yet while costs are readily quantifiable, the returns of education tend to be indirect and intangible. It is difficult to quantify the benefits of developing social cohesion, human potential and self-actualisation, even if the average economic benefit per graduate is calculable. Education is both a public and social service, and a private and personal experience. Finding the best ways of sharing the costs for these benefits across public and personal budgets is an enduring political problem.

The OECD report *Education at a Glance 2019: OECD Indicators* observes that graduates with higher-order skills earn more, are more likely to be in good health, take care of the environment and participate in public life (2019). However, the same report states that between 2005 and 2016 "spending on tertiary institutions increased at more than double the rate of student enrolments ... private sources have been called on to contribute more" (2019, p. 10). Costs, particularly directly to students, continue to increase.

Over the past two decades, funding for higher education has increased at a disproportionate rate to student volumes. Data from HESA (the Higher Education Statistics Agency) shows that 2017/18 higher education provider income in the United Kingdom was 114% of what it was in 2014/15, even though the volume of students was only 103% of 2014/15 levels.[1] Perhaps this relative increase in income is in response to the situation faced by the sector at that time, where 'overall the sector is predicting lower surpluses, a fall in cash levels and a rise in borrowing, signalling a trajectory that is not sustainable in the long term' (HEFCE, 2015, p. 28). It is not all bad news: across the same period access to higher education has improved for disadvantaged groups, and there is a greater proportion of new students entering the system. Nevertheless, costs continue to increase relative to student volumes.

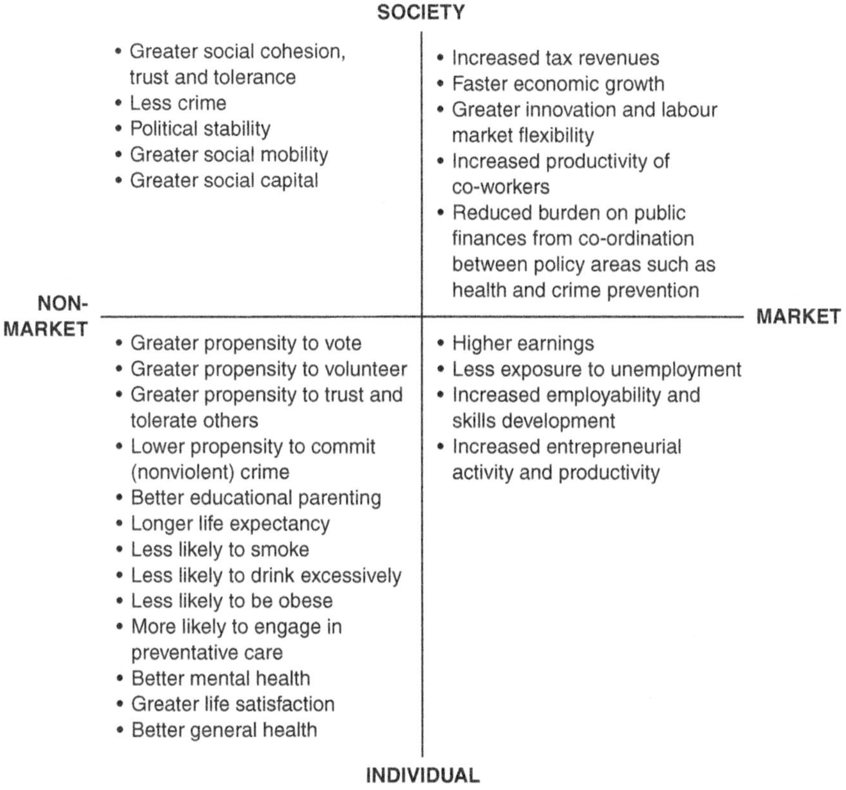

SOCIETY

• Greater social cohesion, trust and tolerance • Less crime • Political stability • Greater social mobility • Greater social capital	• Increased tax revenues • Faster economic growth • Greater innovation and labour market flexibility • Increased productivity of co-workers • Reduced burden on public finances from co-ordination between policy areas such as health and crime prevention

NON-MARKET ———————————————————————— **MARKET**

• Greater propensity to vote • Greater propensity to volunteer • Greater propensity to trust and tolerate others • Lower propensity to commit (nonviolent) crime • Better educational parenting • Longer life expectancy • Less likely to smoke • Less likely to drink excessively • Less likely to be obese • More likely to engage in preventative care • Better mental health • Greater life satisfaction • Better general health	• Higher earnings • Less exposure to unemployment • Increased employability and skills development • Increased entrepreneurial activity and productivity

INDIVIDUAL

Figure 1.1 The Market and Wider Benefits of Higher Education to Individuals and Society.

Source: Department for Business Innovation & Skills, 2013, p. 6. Re-used under the terms of the Open Government Licence, www.nationalarchives.gov.uk/doc/open-government-licence/version/3/.

My first degree left me with no debt. In fact, I first went to the University of Waikato campus in Hamilton, New Zealand with about NZ$20 in my pocket. I signed up with a local bank, received an immediate NZ$500 overdraft capacity, paid all my fees, bought all my textbooks and had plenty of credit to spare. I received a student allowance that mostly covered my living costs. My undergraduate years were the last in New Zealand for fee-free tertiary education; since then student fees have regularly ratcheted up, as has student debt from loans. As I write, the typical university student in the United Kingdom will incur somewhere around £40k in personal debt as they earn their degree. No wonder many are questioning the viability of a university degree, and no wonder politicians are seeking to extend competition, encourage efficiency and grow capacity.

4 Introduction

Education as a Wicked Problem

Education is key to advancing civilisation, economic development and self-actualisation. It is also a wicked problem prone to shifting priorities, practices and expectations. All elements of education – from access to it, what it is concerned with, how it is taught; from the suitability of various subject areas to the ethics of changing someone's perspective; from its overall objectives to its epistemological emphases – are open to debate and disagreement. Given the importance and controversy associated with education, it is vital that decisions related to how it is funded and expressed be made deliberately and transparently. The difficulty is that all views about all aspects of education will inevitably have an element of truth to them. This is characteristic of all wicked problems: any and every position will have both adherents and opponents, with associated agreement and disagreement. One person's enlightenment is another's indoctrination; providing massive student choice across multiple subject areas provides valuable variety in the eyes of some, yet is viewed as a pointless waste of limited funds by others; effective teaching in the eyes of one person is dismissed as excessive, unnecessary or overly contextualised by the next.

Debate, constant and open, ensures that no destructive extremes dominate but also inoculates against systematic innovation. It the nature of a wicked problem that it will never be solved, never be settled. This could be why educational philosophy suffers from what Siegel calls 'a benign neglect' (2009, p. 5): it is risky to propose solutions to education's many maladies, because biting and accurate critique will always follow.

Yet we must continue to look for solutions. At the time of writing most university students studying in the United Kingdom pay £9,250 a year in tuition fees. These figures ignore the costs to each individual graduate in terms of their living costs, debt servicing and opportunity cost as they study. If we were able to completely start designing universities from scratch today, mindful that it costs each student well over £30k in private funds and opportunity cost to become a graduate, I suspect the system we would design to cater for student volumes close to two and a quarter million would be rather different to that incumbent today. While much would remain recognisable, most would be radically different. In my view, the core elements – accredited qualifications, valid learning outcomes, quality criteria, assessment, the parts that constitute the *substance* of education – are well worth carrying forward. Other parts – timetables, attendance, academic responsibilities, campuses, lectures, formal exams, the *facilitative* aspects of education – require substantial critique and revision.

Redesigning Higher Education

If we were developing a higher education system from scratch, what would it aim to achieve? I propose the system would be designed to provide accessible, scalable and personalised education, shaped to the interests of society and students.

- By *accessible*, I mean a system that welcomes those new to it and is flexible enough to make ready allowances for individual circumstances.
- By *scalable*, I mean a system that can dynamically cater for changing student numbers, above a break-even number, in cost-effective ways.

Introduction 5

- By *personalised*, I mean a system that offers more support where more is needed, that draws on each individual's experiences and perspectives, and emphasises feedback.
- By being shaped by the interests of *society*, I mean a genuine attempt to meet the reasonable demands of society for publicly funded graduates to participate in the economy and community.
- By being shaped by the interests of *students*, I mean the opportunity for students to be engaged, enlightened and empowered as elements characteristic of education.

The terms *engaged, enlightened* and *empowered* add up to education (as outlined in the next chapter); ultimately it is these things that students and society reasonably expect to be characteristic of their investment in education. Tempting though it often is for advocates of digital change to promote the trinity of technology, online and learning, this is to mistake means for ends. Engaged, enlightened and empowered are the three terms that define education in this book, as it is these three things that education is uniquely concerned with.

I also propose that a redesigned system would not settle for any compromise to quality standards or student completion rates. Any worthwhile higher education system must be able to demonstrate the integrity of its activities and its contribution towards society in the form of developing work-ready graduates and free-thinking citizens. Speaking personally and with the benefit of hindsight, if I were a fee-paying student in formal education today, I would anticipate learning about ideas that surprise me, challenge me, change me and prepare me for a professional career. I would anticipate *engaging* with these ideas, not merely being expected to simply acknowledge or later recall them. I would anticipate feedback that insightfully informed me about my understanding, not just my knowledge, and that directed me into personalised advice for self-improvement as to how I think and express myself. So, I would expect to be *enlightened* as to how I think. I would appreciate learning activities that were clever, that led me to new ways of understanding and that drew on innovative approaches. I would expect my university to learn about me as I studied, and for the people I interacted with to know who I was. Of course, I would also expect my educators to know their stuff and to apply the best of pedagogical knowledge to their task. Ultimately, I would expect to be *empowered* as a graduate, to be able to interact confidently and competently within the social and employment milieu I aspired to be a part of. I would expect my qualification to give me opportunities to flourish in the ways that best align with my life orientation. A major part of this would be, economy permitting, the ability to get work in a profession related to my interests and be able to contribute to activities in my chosen sphere.

In other words, I would expect my fees to provide me with an effective *education*.

Also, with the benefit of hindsight, I would seek to study part-time alongside a substantial part-time job. During my undergraduate years distance study was an option, but it lacked popular reputation as a viable alternative to the campus. There is no reason why this should be the case now.

6 Introduction

A Twenty-First Century Higher Education System: Would We Start Where We Are?

If we were seeking a higher education sector characterised by accessible, scalable and personalised education, shaped by the interests of society and students, and aiming to provide an engaging, enlightening and empowering educational experience, would we start from where we are? On the one hand, yes: we would do well to start with the rich legacy of formal quality and compliance systems. We would see to continue the exchange of ideas between experts and learners and maintain the status of graduates. However, in another sense, the answer is no. We would not necessarily choose to start with a system designed around attendance and physical proximity, which come at a considerable cost and constrain supply – particularly where physical proximity is not necessary for education to take place.

Ultimately, though, when it comes to starting place we have little choice. We *must* start from where we are. As discussed, the problem isn't with the core elements of accredited qualifications, valid learning outcomes, quality criteria or the fact of assessment. The problem is that, fatally, most universities are hardwired to facilitate a form of education that is generally[2] already unsustainable in terms of public expenditure. As this chapter's epigraph from Laurillard indicates, we have known for well over a decade how technology might utterly transform our models of higher education. In the intervening years, we have also learned a lot about why it is so difficult for higher education to utterly transform.

It is not as if technology has not already had a fair chance to improve things. Massive Open Online Courses (MOOCs) and their multiple variants are a recent example. Micro-credentialing, or the adding up of discrete, usually small, learning encounters into an ad hoc qualification, is one of the more contemporary approaches MOOCs seek to exploit. Neither MOOCs nor micro-credentials can offer the sort of education universities are expected to provide. I don't believe the solution is videocasting lectures, providing content online, or training faculties to design online courses. To date, these activities have merely increased the costs of education. The solution I propose has its roots in traditional distance education – which has also had good opportunity to demonstrate its superiority but is yet to fully do so.

The reasons behind traditional distance education's apparent failure are threefold. First, traditional distance education is easily done, *poorly*. Much distance education is an add-on by campus-based universities keen to extend their reach, yet such an approach tends to provide students with resources designed for lectures, rather than for dedicated interdependent study. Second, many successful distance education providers find it extremely difficult to disentangle themselves from the print-based workflows that have so well served them historically. Seldom do traditional distance education universities have real opportunity to express digital education in a systematic way so as to realise its true potential. Third, many approaches to distance education serve to take the subject-matter expert direct to the student without a serious design element in place. The delicate balance between an academic teaching the way they know how and having an educational designer determine the student experience is not easy to find. An effective digital and collaborative approach to education is sorely needed.

Introduction   7

What I propose in this book is a digital distance education *system*, designed to provide the benefits of an accessible, scalable and personalised student experience within the framework of education that is engaging, enlightening and empowering – and all this while maintaining academic standards of quality and promoting student success. As I hope to demonstrate, such a system will continue to provide the multiple benefits in Figure 1.1.

Besides *having* to start from where we are, I believe we are *best* to start from where we are. There is a precious soul to the university endeavour, even if that soul might appear to be enclosed in an elderly, stubborn and massively unfit body! It is my conviction that universities have, at the core of their identity, something infinitely precious that continues to justify the vast volume of investment placed in them each year. It's not that people *learn* through universities; it's that people are *educated* by them. Universities encourage the sort of mental work that culminates in an education. Learning opportunities abound in public libraries, websites, MOOCs and short courses. It is easy to provide opportunities for people to learn. But it takes something much more to provide an *education*. Various challengers and new entrants to the HE sector tend to misunderstand what it is universities do, mistaking learning and access to knowledge for education. Universities take learning further. Universities build on the activity of learning to improve not only what people know, but also how they think and who they are. Universities *already* engage, enlighten and empower. The qualifications universities offer continue to provide opportunity to graduates, just as they did for my sister and me. If we are looking to redesign higher education, it is vital that their ability to engage, enlighten and empower is not lost.

So, our starting point is an appreciation of what universities accomplish. From here, we must boldly explore how we might reflect this core activity of education that engages, enlightens and empowers students in ways that are accessible, scalable and personalised. Digital distance education is our means to this end.

The Last Bastion of the Pre-Internet Economy

The observation that someone walking into any lecture hall 100 years ago and then today would not notice much that is different is not *entirely* true. PowerPoint has replaced chalk boards; laptops and tablets now complement pen and paper. Perhaps the lecture hall is somewhat emptier, as some students opt to stream recordings rather than attend the live event. But these are merely aesthetics. In truth, not much has *really* changed. Higher education is largely still organised around the notion of students meeting in large lecture halls, listening to a subject expert explain the key elements of his or her academic discipline. Generally, the lecturer's interest in the subject and the students are sincere, the subject knowledge of the lecturer is sharp, and the ideas themselves are intellectually stimulating. For the most part lecturers do a great job of lecturing, yet the format remains exceptionally inefficient and inflexible. Lecture attendance requires an investment of student time and travel, and there are better alternatives for learning. Why has this format not yet been completely disrupted by the internet?

In their book *Blown to Bits*, Evans and Wurster (2000) propose that the internet offers three strategic opportunities to organisations: affiliation, richness and reach.

8 Introduction

These three means of interacting with 21st-century customers online are evident across most sectors of society with the frustrating (though perhaps admirable) exception of higher education. If *Encyclopaedia Britannica* can be brought to its knees by Encarta (itself now long irrelevant because of Wikipedia), local record and video stores can be closed across a decade because of downloadable media (more recently displaced by Spotify and Netflix) and high street shops are struggling because of Amazon, why is it that we still have physical campuses burgeoning with eager enrolees? Not much has changed in the lecture hall, and the overall sector is ripe with supply-side systems, high costs, a largely generic product and, overall, insufficient capacity. Large campuses, building programmes, semesters and lectures still dominate how things are done.

Universities are apparent exceptions to the online economy. One of the reasons universities appear immune to disruption from the internet is that they are concerned with education, not solely learning (and certainly not with the distribution of information!). But this is only part of the story.

Education as an Industry

The higher education sector has one very unusual customer dynamic: customers pay so that they can work. Ultimately, though, customers of higher education are motivated by the attainment of knowledge and expertise resulting in a qualification that evidences their new understanding and ability. The end is primarily achieved through the students' own sheer tenacity, which could be summed as the winning combination of late nights, frustration and bloody-mindedness interspersed with aha moments, inspired thinking and personal triumph! The pain is part of the process, the persistence in learning leads to an education and the degree is testimony to the achievement. Strangely, there is a certain inelasticity of demand to this dynamic: even if the price of education increases, customers are still prepared to pay to work to learn. The market forces of higher education are unusual and defy simple explanation.

It is perfectly possible and wise to consider higher education as an industry and universities as economic entities. Dismissing the concept of a university as an economic entity is an academic privilege, not a valid truth. Yet universities are also far from solely being economic entities. The value universities bring cannot be easily quantified in ways that reflect the ways in which they grow potential. How are we best to consider the identity of the university?

Universities face the dynamics of competition, return on investment (often in the shape of a 'surplus'), economies of scale, the workings of supply and demand and the necessity of a customer focus. They exist because what they do is valued. When it comes to providing value, though, universities are projections of conflicting aspiration. It has been said that, when you consider education, 'what you see tends to reflect where you sit' (Archibald & Feldman, 2011, p. 7). Students see opportunities to learn, grow and receive recognition of their achievement. Academics see opportunities to inspire students, develop scholarly reputation through research and improve thinking in their field and in society. Administrators see opportunities to

Introduction 9

enhance the university's reputation, strategic viability and graduation rate. Greater society sees opportunities for economic growth, innovation and self-actualisation. Each of these groups is motivated by the success of students, yet their projections do not often align to form a unanimous way of doing things. What upsets the potential for unity is intense disagreement as to whether universities should emphasise private or public interests.

Universities serve both private and public interests at the same time. To assume one is more important than the other is to grossly misunderstand the higher education sector and simplify the challenges it faces. Higher education is an easy target for anyone trying to emphasise private over public interests and vice versa. If considered more of a private service, education is expected to provide more choice towards subjects of interest, more engaging teaching and more individualised attention; all of these imply specific spending priorities. If education is viewed as a public service, more focused subject choice, more flexibility in study, better accessibility, more efficiencies and more qualifications leading directly to employable graduates are demanded; anything else is considered sheer academic indulgence or mismanagement. That universities are also economic entities adds a further, somewhat darker hue to the picture. As economic entities, universities come under constant pressure to reduce spend on academic reflection and research, increase student to staff ratios, reduce curriculum towards employment relevance and, as a result of these activities, lower fees. As explained earlier, however, the costs of higher education are actually *rising* despite cost-cutting efforts across most universities – creating an urgent problem and defying the disruption potential of the internet.

Education's Resistance to Internet Disruption

There are three reasons identified by Archibald and Feldman (2011) for why higher education models seem resistant to technological change. Primarily, they point out, education functions as if it were a professional service limited to the productivity of a qualified specialist. The authors observe that the education industry follows similar cost dynamics to those of physicians, dentists and lawyers. The actual practice and efficiency of these specialists are not seriously influenced by the application of technology because they are knowledge-based professions, requiring the time of specialised people with limited availability. The second cause of resistance: there is no crisis of demand. Increases in technology across society have increased the demand for skilled labour, which in turn increases the demand for higher education. There is no crisis to spur efficiency in universities and, because on-campus education does not easily benefit from economies of scale, the cost of catering for additional students actually increases the overall price of tuition. Finally, there is the way in which technology is frequently applied to higher education, complementing rather than transforming the existing service offering. This third characteristic has the effect of increasing cost rather than introducing efficiencies. As an example, lectures are still the primary means of tuition; the additional costs of technology enable them to also be streamed and revised.

That universities are not transformed by technology should not surprise us. At the heart of the problem is not that universities lack the will to innovate, are

10 Introduction

pedagogically short-sighted or even academically resistant. The reason is that the incumbent operating model of campus-based universities is incompatible with technological efficiency. Technology is leveraged to complement rather than transform practice. This is because all universities have deep-set systems and processes *that reinforce incumbent practice*. For an on-campus university, the model of education as a professional service limited to the productivity of a qualified specialist is completely ingrained across the entire institution. The setting of budgets, the conditions of accreditation, enrolment services, student support functions, timetabling and the campus itself all reflect and further serve to reinforce the lecture as the basis of teaching. In such a context, technology can, at best, only hope to *ever* make incremental adjustments to practice.

Incumbent practice can also limit the digital transformation of traditional distance universities. As with campus-based universities, it is processes that are ultimately at fault; in distance education those processes that serve a print-based approach designed for module *authorship* (as in 'writing a module') tend to limit the role digital technologies might play. The path towards digital transformation is not merely to transfer print output to digital output, because the real issue is how the incumbent medium of print *has shaped the entire way things are done*. In print-based distance universities, course materials are typically produced according to a schedule timed to hard semester dates. Print-based editing requirements drive the writing process, and requirements that materials be printable limit learning activities and make digital elements optional. In both campus-based and print-based distance universities, digital approaches are typically applied peripherally rather than centrally.

Ultimately, technology fails to transform education and adds cost rather than efficiency because the effective, innovative application of technology requires changes to how a university functions, across all its most important departments. So, rather than determining the way in which the university operates, technology is bolted on to how things are already done. This is why Peter Drucker, an otherwise profound and insightful management theorist across the mid- to late twentieth century, was entirely wrong in his 1997 prediction cited at the opening of this chapter: he both misunderstood education to be the dissemination of knowledge, and underestimated the rigidity of how universities operate in support of their predominant way of teaching (be it the lecture or the printed manual). Somewhat ironically, it is also not easy for new players to enter and shake up the higher education sector. Weighty compliance activities, reputation and established student volumes are key to success, and so incumbents typically have exceptional competitive advantages over new university brands.

So, given that education is a specialised service limited by the activities of qualified gatekeepers (academics), there is no crisis in demand, the economic and social contribution by the incumbent university system is widely accepted, there is systematic resistance to technological change, universities are apparently already successful in their educational endeavour and it's very hard for new entrants to shake things up, why would I bother writing this book? Simply because I believe that transformed universities offering digital distance education can provide much more educational value in so many ways. Alongside all the affirmation the current system ought to be provided with, it can be – indeed, *ought* to be – much more accessible, scalable and personalised through the sound application of technology. There is a moral, social, economic and educational imperative to the wise distribution of public funds towards the personal and social outcomes universities are concerned with. I am also of the view that the model presented in this book is inevitable, even if most universities operate as if it were not.

Supply- and Demand-Orientated Education

Most universities tend to operate in a supply-oriented rather than demand-oriented way, which is to say that university operations are typically designed to be internally convenient. There are three main reasons for this somewhat parochial self-centredness. First, as we have seen, there are inadequate incentives to become more demand-orientated; there is no crisis. Second, perhaps more insidiously, universities' operating models work against a true demand orientation. Universities tend to work within rigid structures and annualised processes that are difficult to change, particularly with no crisis at hand. Third, compliance in the form of academic and administrative standards does not require a demand orientation.

Quality in universities tends to be formally measured in terms of compliance (supply-orientated) rather than the student experience (demand-orientated). Compliance is vitally important to the integrity of higher education. However, accreditation standards provide a very narrow and supply-sided definition of quality that misses the critical, demand-oriented dimension of personalisation (as stated earlier, by personalised I mean offering more support where more is needed, drawing on each individual's experiences and perspectives, and emphasising feedback). The quality thinking of many universities does not go far enough, in that it does not seek to transcend compliance requirements towards a more personalised student experience.

Part of education's apparent resistance to internet disruption is that universities see little wrong with the quality of what they do, and that their compliance requirements tend to encourage a supplier-oriented view to quality in which the actual student experience is represented by proxy. One of my main motivations for writing this book is that universities tend to only take tentative steps towards providing overall service quality *from a demand perspective*, and I believe that the demand perspective will become a vital means of competing in the future.

Personalisation is one of the three main objectives I consider central to what society should expect from its universities. Universities are simply not encouraged under current formal compliance (quality) regimes to meet the service expectations of a digitally empowered consumer. If the purpose of the university is to educate, then those accessing university are legitimately termed students. However, with fees increasing and student expectations towards service legitimately changing, the perspective of students *as consumers* also becomes more important. As a paying purchaser of a product and service, the student is a consumer entitled to the respect and demand orientation all institutions ought to provide. However, the consumer *is also a student*: required to work hard towards the ultimate objective of graduation, often

12 Introduction

through conditions and activities they may not value at the time. Universities must intentionally navigate this potentially constructive tension, not relying on compliance to be their sole determinant of quality.

Personalisation provides a means of differentiation of service and a way of genuinely engaging with students as consumers.

Personalisation and Demand Orientation

I believe that it is only a matter of time before various universities *do* transform and disrupt the dynamics of the higher education sector. The mechanism for this transformation is effective digital distance education, DDE, which reflects a demand orientation that goes beyond the supply orientation required by formal compliance.

Let's consider what a demand orientation might resemble. If we place ourselves in the shoes of 21st-century clients of other institutions and transfer our expectations on to universities, we can imagine what demand-driven, personalised service might resemble (acknowledging that some of these features are already in play). For my part, here is what I would expect.

- As a personalised learner, I am paying more than ever for the privilege of our education. It's not just the higher fees; I also see those around me currently earning the sort of money I might be earning were it not for my decision to study. There's an opportunity cost to me studying, and so my sensitivities are high! I'm also working to support myself. I view the university as a service organisation that must centre its activities on my busy and often unpredictable lifestyle. I'm not afraid of the commitment study requires, it's just that it's not always easy for me to regularly make that commitment.
- As a personalised learner, I expect to be able to begin my study when it is convenient for *me* to do so and for deadlines to flex around the reality of my broader life demands. I don't mind a schedule, but I do mind having to wait months (or even weeks) before being able to start! I would also expect to be able to access all notes and study materials digitally, even if I still required textbooks as part of my learning – and if I did require an additional textbook, I would question why course notes would not be enough for my learning.
- As a personalised learner, paying a considerable amount for my study, I don't choose to enrol on a whim. I may not know what I'm getting myself into, but that doesn't mean I'm casual about it. I may not be entirely ready, but that doesn't mean I'll benefit from a 'sink or swim' experience. As I start, I expect to be gently immersed in what study demands. I'll still work hard and rise to the occasion but, at first, I'm not sure just what the occasion is.
- As a personalised learner, I expect the service I receive to be seamless and consistent. I would be surprised to find departmental boundaries interfering with or changing my points of contact, and I would be alarmed if anyone I interacted with did not have access to my record of previous queries and outcomes. I also expect my educators to know me by name, and to prioritise my learning over their other responsibilities.

- As a personalised learner, I expect a seamless digital experience that works across my multiple devices, synchronises for offline access and doesn't require proprietary plugins. I expect to be personally notified about and reminded of due dates and anything else expected of me. As part of this experience I don't want to have to find my way to where I last left off. Why would I need to, when Kindle books, Spotify tracks and Netflix series are remembered from one device to the next?
- As a personalised learner, I expect to be able to relate my life experience and perspectives to what is being studied. My experience may well be tangential, and my perspectives uninformed, but for me they are a helpful starting point. I have opinions I'd like to test and half-formed ideas I'd like to get feedback on. I begin study out of an awareness that I don't know it all so I'm not afraid for my ignorance to be exposed, provided I get useful and encouraging feedback. I want to grow and receive advice about what I need to do to further develop as a thinker and practitioner in my chosen area of study.
- As a personalised learner, I anticipate learning alongside a group of people involved in the same course as me. They don't need to be exactly like me. There need to be enough of them that dialogue is possible, yet not so many that my voice is drowned out; I anticipate the intimacy of a coffee shop, not the squeeze of a crowded market. I don't want to learn *from* these people; I want to learn *with* them. There's a critical difference there, in that I expect to have an active subject expert as part of the community. I also expect to have that expert's ear from time to time when I need it, and for them to provide me with the feedback I need to achieve my goal of being educated.
- I know that education is demanding. I would not expect learning to be anything less than hard work. But as a personalised learner, I would expect the hard work to be cognitive rather than administrative. I would expect the university to do all in its power to assist me to succeed, and to consider my failure its own failure.

So, where is the evidence for this fictitious personalised learner's set of expectations? It's in the echoes of every student survey I have seen across various higher education institutions. More importantly, it's in the DNA of many organisations outside of the university sector, which are making themselves beloved by their personalised consumers. The personalised learner clearly expects a demand-orientated approach to education, one that is not apparent across most universities as I write.

I'm not advocating a decline in standards or a shift away from the engagement, enlightenment and empowerment that education must provide. I'm not advocating abdication to student whims. I'm promoting better, reasonable and personalised levels of service. I'm not trying to change the ends; I'm challenging the *means*. Technically, pedagogically and systematically the service levels described above are entirely possible, and it is only a matter of time before universities find that such a personalised experience is an expected means of remaining competitive.

14 Introduction

The Last Bastion

It is only a matter of time before serving the 21st-century university client through personalisation becomes an *expected* element of university education. It's also only a matter of time before the factors providing so much comfort to the incumbent sector – limited availability of specialised gatekeepers, no demand crisis, economic benefit, challenges of systematic change, supply-centric services and high barriers to entry for competitors – become much harder to justify in the context of out-of-control costs. Demand for accessibility, scalability and personalisation that reflects 21st-century customer service will eventually erode many of the generic, big university campuses in Drucker's sights at the start of the chapter. It's difficult to change how universities work, but it is inevitable that most will need to adapt their operating models to remain competitive as digital education continues to unfold.

Importantly, accessibility, scalability and personalisation can all be enhanced without universities losing their identity and without education losing its edge. The sort of digital distance education described in this book can engage, enlighten and empower students within current compliance requirements.

Let's see how it might be done.

Activities

1. Education is defined as a 'wicked problem' in this chapter. What are the current problems as you perceive them? What do you think is needed to fix education?

   a. Are the problems you perceive represented in this introduction?
   b. Does the solution you're considering require systematic change, or could universities adopt your solution without much having to change?

2. With the benefit of hindsight, I would opt to study again on a part-time basis, at a distance – assuming it is done well. This may or may not be true for you. What are your reasons for agreement or disagreement?

3. Consider your own university setting, programme or course.

   a. How open is your university, programme or course to being described as an economic entity?
   b. How aligned are academic, administrative and student expectations?
   c. If your university, programme or course suddenly had to cope with double the enrolments, what additional resources would you immediately require and how would you cope?

4. This book is based on the assertion that university education ought to be more accessible, scalable and personalised. What is your immediate reaction to these objectives?

5. Consider the approach to quality applied by your own university setting, pro-gramme or course. What evidence is there that student needs beyond academic compliance are measured and valued?

6. Consider the 21st-century client personalised learner list.
    a. Which points are particularly important for you as a contemporary learner?
    b. Which might be important to school-leavers entering university for the first time?
    c. Which seem to be unrealistic or beyond the realities of a university education?

Notes

1. Data drawn from www.hesa.ac.uk/data-and-analysis/students/whos-in-he and www.hesa.ac.uk/data-and-analysis/finances/income. Note that the income figures used exclude research grants and contracts, other income, investment income, and donations and endowments.
2. There are exceptions. Those universities with significant reserves and reputation, able to justify higher fees or draw on endowments, which are less exposed to changes in public funding, have an entirely different context of practice. What I write here is certainly the case in those nations where tertiary education is heavily publicly subsidised, in the form of allocated fees and loans underwritten from the public purse.

References

Archibald, R. B., & Feldman, D. H. (2011). *Why does college cost so much?* New York, NY: Oxford University Press.

Bekhradnia, B., & Beech, D. (2018). *Demand for higher education to 2030.* Oxford, England: Oxuniprint. Retrieved 29 January 2020 from www.hepi.ac.uk/wp-content/uploads/2018/03/HEPI-Demand-for-Higher-Education-to-2030-Report-105-FINAL.pdf.

Department for Business Innovation & Skills. (2013). *Benefits of participating in higher education: Key findings and reports quadrants.* Retrieved 29 January 2020 from www.gov.uk/government/uploads/system/uploads/attachment_data/file/254101/bis-13-1268-benefits-of-higher-education-participation-the-quadrants.pdf.

Evans, P., & Wurster, T. S. (2000). *Blown to bits: How the new economics of information transforms strategy.* Boston, MA: Harvard Business School Press.

HEFCE. (2015). *Higher education in England 2015: Key facts.* Retrieved 29 January 2020 from https://webarchive.nationalarchives.gov.uk/20160106190423 www.hefce.ac.uk/media/HEFCE,2014/Content/Analysis/HE,in,England/HE_in_England_2015.pdf.

Laurillard, D. (2008). Digital technologies and their role in achieving our ambitions for education. *Analysis*, 1–40. Retrieved 29 January 2020 from http://discovery.ucl.ac.uk/10000628/1/Laurillard2008Digital_technologies.pdf.

Lezner, R., & Johnson, S. S. (1997). Seeing things as they really are. Retrieved 29 January 2020 from www.forbes.com/forbes/1997/0310/5905122a.html.

OECD. (2019). *Education at a glance: OECD indicators.* Paris: OECD. https://doi.org/10.1787/f8d7880d-en.

Siegel, H. (2009). *The Oxford handbook of philosophy of education.* New York, NY: Oxford University Press.

Chapter 2

On Learning and Formal Education

It is not that universities are now institutions that are distributed in virtual space (with the onward march of electronic communications), even though that is part of the picture. The dissolution in question that the universities are facing is conceptual. Universities no longer stand, it appears, for anything in particular. Nothing of substance attaches to their formerly core concepts. Their key practices run into those of the surrounding world.

(Barnett, 2003, p. 567)

At the heart of this chapter is a simple theme: in universities, and in digital education, *education* is more important than *learning*. At first glance this might seem pedantic, but by the end of the chapter it will be apparent that the issue is entirely substantial and foundational to both digital education and the identity of the university. If digital education is going to be meaningful, its ultimate objective must be understood and transparent. Broadly, the difference between education and learning is between being shaped as a thinker, and knowing more things. It is possible to know more things without being shaped as a thinker (that is, to learn without being educated), but it is not possible to be shaped as a thinker without knowing more things (you cannot be educated without learning). The difference is fundamental to implementing digital education and the meaningful transformation of universities.

I began thinking along these lines about a decade ago, and in a keynote I prepared around that time I asked a question relevant to this chapter: what do you see yourself contributing to, as an educator? Even if you are not a lecturer, academic, tutor or teacher, I invite you to take a few moments now and note down some ideas. What does it mean to educate?

Your response will reveal a lot about your views of teaching and learning, and what a university stands for. My own response to that question required two sentences. The first is somewhat jargonistic: 'To help students further develop a complex mental schema by means of the concentrated study of a discipline, resulting in perspective transformation.' What I mean by this will (hopefully!) become clearer by the end of this chapter. The second is one that has remained with me for many years: 'To enable students to think and do what a (plumber, manager, nurse,

On Learning and Formal Education 17

theologian, psychiatrist) thinks and does, rather than just know and recall what a (plumber, manager, nurse, theologian, psychiatrist) knows and recalls.' The worth of the latter sentence lies in its applicability to education for any subject at any level.

The value I place on education is not universally shared. Many people's views of education are woefully impoverished. Consider some of these quotations, which are frequently echoed among education's critics (these quotes are widely available online and are followed here by their most popularly known attributions):

- 'I prefer the company of peasants because they have not been educated sufficiently to reason incorrectly' (Michel de Montaigne).
- 'An inventor is simply a fellow who doesn't take his education too seriously' (Charles Kettering).
- 'Education is a method whereby one acquires a higher grade of prejudices' (Laurence Peter).

And a personal favourite:

- 'Bachelor's degrees make pretty good placemats if you get 'em laminated' (Jeph Jacques).

It is all too easy to be cynical about the pursuit of education. Education can be considered an irrelevant, stifling, dangerous and limiting hindrance to real learning. However, consider these alternative views:

- 'It is the mark of an educated mind to be able to entertain a thought without accepting it' (Aristotle).
- 'Education is what survives when what has been learned has been forgotten' (B. F. Skinner).
- 'Education's purpose is to replace an empty mind with an open one' (Malcolm Forbes).

My favourites are a tie between two classicists:

- 'Only the educated are free' (Epictetus).
- 'It is only the ignorant who despise education' (Publilius Syrus).

Education is often scoffed at (particularly by those who do not have a formal qualification) as irrelevant to real life, forming blinkered thinkers who have developed an immunity to creativity and innovation. Looked at another way, education can unlock new ways of knowing that lead to constructive criticism, comfort with ambiguity and the valuable ability to synergise conflicting views. Education is much needed in our contemporary world.

The purpose of education is not to provide answers, nor to merely pass on information. Education is much more ambitious. The goal of education is to *change* people. It is to *engage* them, *enlighten* them and *empower* them. Graduates of formal education are different people. They think in different ways – ideally ways that are more open, yet also more discerning. Well-educated graduates can entertain a thought without accepting it. They have benefitted beyond what they have learned. They embrace new ideas and are actively discerning in their assessment of them. They are also able to benefit from the experiences of others as they approach the challenges of professional life. They pursue learning not just to gain new knowledge, but as the means of using knowledge to further improve their interaction with the world.

If we are to transform universities such that they benefit from the prospects of digital education, it is vital that we first explore what universities are and what they are designed to do. Unfortunately, educational writings are quite correctly described as a babel (Phillips & Siegel, 2013), and it is far from easy to navigate through them. It is important, therefore, that I begin with a transparent set of assumptions and a carefully explained set of terminology. Before seeking to transform universities, let's begin with what they are and the parts learning and education play in them. In doing so I also hope to lay to rest any concern that this book has more to do with technocentric or techno-determinist promotion than it does with a sincere appreciation of – I'm not afraid to even say love for – education.

What is the Role of a University?

Many important questions can be asked about education: how it is best practiced, what constitutes effective teaching, how learning can be measured. More contemporary debates relate to the extent education should advance creativity over facts and transferable skills over discipline-based knowledge. The most fundamental issue regarding education is what it ought to be concerned with. Is it for the benefit of the individual student, for employers, or society as a whole? Is it enough to simply make students more informed, or should we seek to liberate students into independent thought? How do we best educate? These questions are not easy to answer, and debate around them dates to earliest recorded philosophy. Of course, there is no reason why education cannot benefit individuals, employers *and* society, and provide more informed students who are *also* developed as independent thinkers. Matters of power over education then come to the fore: who sets the agenda? Who has the control? Who decides?

Such questions are always debated in the background within a functioning university. Universities are complex institutions, dynamically balancing the expectations of accrediting and funding agencies, academic and administrative staff, and students. Each of these groups is important, and so none has a uniquely privileged position. The interests of each group are magnified by the substantial investment of money and time, and the high stakes of personal opportunity and benefit – so it is only natural that the questions of why universities exist and how they should be run are subject to tension. Adding still further to the intensity of debate is that those involved are highly intelligent people!

The Oxford Dictionary defines a university as 'A high-level educational institution in which students study for degrees and academic research is done' (University, n.d.). As a general definition this is a good start; in practice, how this definition is embodied is rather complex. The concept of a 'university' changes over time, though many of the trappings still familiar to us today can be traced back to the Humboldt University of Berlin in the early 1800s where teaching and research were initially fused. Change as to what constitutes a university is readily apparent across history. For example, the first universities were ecclesial. In their early configuration, when theology was known as the queen of the sciences, universities were typically organised around a programme of theological study. In modern universities, theology as a subject area is barely found. Public funding for universities has only been a significant portion of income for the past 200 years or so.

There is no universal consensus as to how a university must function. Anyone with an idealistic or nostalgic dogma as to the form of a university is, intentionally or not, guilty of presupposition. Universities are best considered social constructs, subject to ongoing development in response to the demands of broader society in consideration of all stakeholders. Far from being a fixed ideal, a university is an always contemporary construct whose identity is, particularly since the introduction of public funding, subject to those who legally define them. Of course, this doesn't mean that the term 'university' cannot be defined in a general sense, but it does give some background to the fairly pessimistic view of Barnett in the opening quotation of this chapter! What constitutes a university, and the role it plays, will continuously evolve. However, beneath this evolution there is something very definite that will forever be relevant and purposeful and which, in contradiction to Barnett, will always stand a university's practices apart from 'those of the surrounding world'.

In his book *What Are Universities For?*, Stefan Collini writes that universities serve intellectual, educational, scientific and cultural objectives. He further notes that a university has, at absolute minimum (and most enduring), four characteristics (2012, p. 7):

1. That it provides some form of post-secondary-school education, where 'education' signals something more than professional training.
2. That it furthers some form of advanced scholarship or research whose character is not wholly dictated by the need to solve immediate practical problems.
3. That these activities are pursued in more than just one single discipline or very tightly defined cluster of disciplines.
4. That it enjoys some form of institutional autonomy as far as its intellectual activities are concerned.

What is missing from Collini's list is that universities in the United Kingdom, Australia, New Zealand and many other countries must also be compliant with formal criteria around how they are organised and how they operate. In the United Kingdom, for example, the title of university is open for application to any organisation with degree awarding power (DAP) able to meet various academic quality criteria. At the time of writing, in order to secure DAP (the first step towards securing university title) a higher education institution must have first been effective in teaching up to degree level for at least 4 years. DAP can be awarded for taught and

20 On Learning and Formal Education

research degrees separately. For an institution to achieve DAP, the granting body must be assured that the institution can demonstrate requirements related to governance and academic management, academic standards and quality assurance, the scholarship and pedagogical effectiveness of academic staff, and an environment supporting the delivery of taught higher degree programmes. To extend into research degrees, an institution must meet further stringent criteria related to policies and practices around research and advanced scholarship, have academic staff actively engaged in original research and provide evidence of a robust research culture. The purpose of my writing this policy-rich paragraph is to underscore an important point: to be a university is to be *regulated*.

So, while a university can be simply described in terms of teaching, study, scholarship, research and qualifications, it is more accurately understood when the dimensions of governance, management and administration – with their added activities associated with policy, quality assurance and infrastructure – are added. A university is not solely made up of academics and their teaching and research activity. To maintain its identity and status, a university must integrate the teaching and research work of its academics with a well-tuned and standards-compliant administrative engine. To be a university, it is not enough for an institution to simply employ top scholars. It must also align the activity of those scholars across robust institutional policies and practices, and appropriate teaching environments. A university must be understood as a complex system from which teaching and research cannot be neatly isolated or idolised.

A university, then, is most properly a system of interrelated academic and administrative activity with the main objective of providing quality education, supported by or alongside research, in compliance with the standards of regulating agencies. As this definition implies, universities are marvellously multifaceted and have great potential for internal conflict. It is not uncommon for academic and administrative[1] staff to perceive their opposite's objectives as being counter to what makes a university a university. Crudely, academics often perceive administrators as being too process and budget-driven, hindering effective teaching, research and innovation, and so losing sight of the student. Conversely, academics can be perceived as demanding prima donnas ignorant of the hard choices administrators are forced to make in the name of compliance, efficiency or long-term viability. Critically, both academics and administrators ultimately want the same thing: a university streamlined towards providing *an effective education*. Administrative staff and managers do not exist merely to support the work of academic staff; rather, administration and managerial staff exist to support the concept of the university itself.[2] Academics who understand a university's sole function to be teaching and research are as misguided as administrators thinking solely in terms of compliance and efficiency. The best universities operate as aligned systems based on mutual respect and teamwork.

Compliance in the form of mandated quality standards is a fixed reality for universities. Regulation is the baseline of identity on which further improvement can be built.

Beyond Regulation Towards a Demand Orientation

Regulation sets the standards by which a university becomes and maintains its status as a university. As mentioned previously, regulations do not set the parameters of competitiveness. There is no necessity for a compliant university to be a demand-oriented one.

For any university seeking to improve access, scalability and personalisation, a systems approach is a requisite step. A systems approach as defined by Moore and Kearsley 'consists of all the component processes ... including learning, teaching, communication, design, and management' (1996, p. 5). The sorts of shift associated with the personalised student experience proposed in the introduction require such an all-of-institution response; digital transformation of a university cannot take place without thinking in big-picture, systematic terms. A common mistake for universities seeking to improve access, scalability and personalisation to their education offering is to try to simply bolt digital approaches on to existing ways of working and overall infrastructure. Adding a VLE (virtual learning environment), TEL (technology enhanced learning) support staff and professional development options simply does not go far enough. In reality, operating factors such as resource allocation, quality assurance, support systems and – more controversially – the teaching role all require purposeful alignment if education is to become more accessible, scalable and personalised through digital means. Not taking a systems view simply results in increased cost through fragmented effort.

Taking a systems approach to digital education requires an understanding of just what a university is, and how it is configured. A systems approach requires thinking about a university in terms of overall design; that is, considering a university's operation in terms of the activities and flows that require coordination. These themes of systems and design will be picked up in Chapter 8. For now, it is sufficient to note that the benefits of accessibility, scalability and personalisation through digital education *can* be achieved such that the current social construct or compliant criteria defining what a university is are satisfied, and academic freedom is maintained. A demand-oriented university can still be a regulated and compliant one.

The model for digital education proposed in this book does not challenge the current social construct of a university, even though the model requires change to elements of practice. Intellectual freedom, another key feature of universities, is also maintained by the model – although changes to teaching are assumed. Critically, academic freedom is not a licence for academic staff to teach in any way they choose. Intellectual freedom is defined by Academics For Academic Freedom (n.d.) in the United Kingdom as affirming:

(1) that academics, both inside and outside the classroom, have unrestricted liberty to question and test received wisdom and to put forward controversial and unpopular opinions, whether or not these are deemed offensive, and

(2) that academic institutions have no right to curb the exercise of this freedom by members of their staff, or to use it as grounds for disciplinary action or dismissal.

So, a university is a social construct concerned with education and research (both reflective of the quality of academic activity) in the context of formal regulation (the quality of administrative activity). As such, a university is a complex system of activity regulated by various standards to do with teaching and learning, student outcomes, qualification quality, financial responsibility and funding eligibility. Critically for my purposes, there is (at the time of writing!) nothing in the current social and legal definition of a university that challenges the viability of a digital university as described in this book. The digital university I advocate is a true and robust university in every way, otherwise it would not be legally entitled to call itself a university; it just chooses to educate through digital means. It is perfectly possible for a digital university to implement an accessible, scalable and personalised approach to education with no compromise to its quality compliance and academic standing. Digital education does not somehow dumb down or compromise the activity of a university unless issues of compliance are neglected. A digital university can educate just as well as a traditional one, and is expected to meet the same overall standards of quality; indeed, part of my goal in this book is to demonstrate how a digital university can *better serve* its student (client) constituency, including students with disabilities and in secure environments.

Importantly, the compliance activities required to gain and maintain university status are there, for the main, to ensure that effective education takes place. Education is the primary activity of a university. Defining just what constitutes education is an important measure for evaluating the merits of a *digital* education.

Education as Engagement, Enlightenment and Empowerment

If the main activity of a university is providing education supported by or alongside research, how are we to define education? Principles of teaching fall short; they address the *how* and not the *why* of education. Our interest is what education aims to achieve, not how teaching works. My approach here will be to begin with a brief exploration of learning theory, which will lead to key themes.

If we are to properly engage with learning theory, we must start with what it means to learn.

What it Means to Learn

Let's turn again to the Oxford English dictionary. To learn, it tells us, is to 'gain or acquire knowledge of or skill in (something) by study, experience, or being taught' (Learn, n.d.). Once more, the dictionary provides us with a good start – but does not travel far enough. Learning in the context of education goes much, much further. My favourite definition of learning is 'a smudge between a self that knows to a self that knows more' (Ellsworth, as cited in Kamler & Thomson, 2006, p. 18). To learn, then, is to be personally smudged from one state of knowing into another. The definition describes learning as a somewhat imprecise event, where the start and end points are qualitatively different but hard to position. The definition recognises that learning is about the self. There is more to learning than simply increasing what we know; rather, learning subtly *changes* us. Neither does learning start with a blank slate. Instead, anything learned is an extension of what has already been learned. There is no blank canvas to be added to, only the reshaping and extension of pre-existing ideas that might be helpful, wrong or simply irrelevant to what is being learned. The definition also nicely incorporates the notion that, as knowers, we are forever incomplete: there is always more to know, more to be smudged. Even what we think we know is always subject to revision and nuance through further encounters with knowledge. Learning is a never-ending relationship of *knowing* more and, as a result, *becoming* more.

So, a university programme of study might be thought of as an intentional, extended smudge. Education is based on purposeful learning, taking the student passenger on a voyage to the destination of graduation. A student is a knower who, by progressing through a programme of study, becomes a self who knows more. Completing the intentional study journey results in a self who knows more, with a qualification to prove it. To achieve this great goal, education applies the dynamics of teaching and learning.

Importantly, universities do not view themselves as storehouses of knowledge; this was at one stage a common misconception for those who thought that the internet would replace universities. Knowledge is available to anyone with an internet browser (or a library for that matter). Providing access to knowledge is not the main activity of universities. Instead, universities use knowledge as a raw material applied to their real task of education. Knowledge is like the substance of the smudge characteristic of learning. Education directs the smudging, requiring students to memorise, process, apply, critique and otherwise wrestle with knowledge to create personal understanding, which the university assesses against qualification standards. Put crudely, the student as self is smudged through the education process, and the university checks for evidence of that smudging against its own pre-prepared patterns and objectives.

So, universities might be considered cognitive smudging factories, transforming willing and hard-working students into graduates through a series of purposeful teaching activities. Extending this into an admittedly yet clumsier production metaphor, the centre of the university as an educating institution is not the library (raw materials store), lecture theatre (factory) or administration (office). Rather, the central focus of the university's activity is the development that takes place *within the student*, a development fuelled by encounters with knowledge. At the heart of the university is the mechanism by which a self that knows is smudged into a self that knows more. The open-endedness of such smudging applies to both learning and education; Peters remarks that '[t]o be educated is not to have arrived at a destination; it is to travel with a different view' (2007, p. 67).

Learning theory helps to further this view of what it means to learn and be educated.

Linking Learning to Education

There are many learning theories and luminaries of educational thought, and choosing a favourite is always grounds for contention. Palmer (2001) proposes 50 modern

24 On Learning and Formal Education

thinkers on education. Bates (2016) identifies some 103 learning theories of note, while Illeris (2018b) presents a more refined 18. The sheer multiplicity of perspectives and techniques that exist in terms of what constitutes effective learning (and therefore teaching) generates a complex landscape. Some theories are much better evidenced than others; indeed, some listed by Bates (such as Fleming's VARK model of learning styles) are utterly discredited. That there are various views reflects both the imprecise nature of learning and the multiplicity of contexts and subject areas it is practised in. It is likely that we will never be able to provide a comprehensive theory of learning without straying into the territory of existential speculation. So, my objective in trying to link learning to education in what follows is merely to provide insight into several perspectives and provide a vocabulary useful for understanding universities. Along the way I hope to demonstrate universities' specific contribution to the overall learning landscape through education.

Peters (as cited in Phillips & Siegel, 2013, sec. 2.2, para. 2) suggests that a person who is educated is:

(i) changed for the better;
(ii) this change has involved the acquisition of knowledge and intellectual skills, and the development of understanding; and
(iii) the person has come to care for, or be committed to, the domains of knowledge and skill into which he or she has been initiated.

The reverse order of these points, perhaps unintentionally, reveals something important about what it means to educate: the domains of knowledge and skill (iii) are the means by which students acquire knowledge, intellectual skills and the development of understanding (ii), which results ultimately in their being changed for the better (i). Education is designed such that graduates of geography, engineering and business studies are, in one important way, similar: each student has been changed for the better (first characteristic) and has been provided with new knowledge, intellectual skills and understanding (second characteristic). The main difference across graduates is the academic accent gained from the disciplines they have studied (third characteristic).

Ultimately a university qualification recognises a graduate having experienced a change for the better through the acquisition of knowledge, intellectual skills and understanding. The domain of knowledge and skill the graduate is initiated into represents the practical skills and concepts the graduate can immediately draw from. This is not to imply that how a graduate thinks is more important than what they know; in reality, there is a symbiosis across these two things. A graduate cannot learn to think differently without having concepts to think about, but simply knowing concepts does not encourage someone to think differently. There is a close relationship between a student being changed for the better, acquiring knowledge and intellectual skills, and the development of understanding.

Various learning theories help to further explain how the dynamic between Peters' three elements – commitment to a domain of knowledge, acquiring knowledge, intellectual skills and understanding, and a change for the better – works in practice. Mezirow, for example, would likely claim that a 'change for the better' is the equivalent of perspective transformation, as defined in his theory:

> Transformative learning is defined as the process by which we transform problematic frames of reference (mindsets, habits of mind, meaning perspectives) – sets of assumption and expectation – to make them more inclusive, discriminating, open, reflective and emotionally able to change.
>
> (2018, p. 116)

Someone changed for the better through education has developed a richer frame of reference, one that engages with ideas, knowledge and circumstances in constructive and discerning ways. The extent to which this occurs is naturally difficult to isolate; it is likely not by accident that Peters and Mezirow refer to 'change' and 'more inclusive …', both using relative rather than absolute terms. Related to Mezirow's work, Kegan (2018) contrasts *in*formative learning with *trans*formative learning, the difference being between changing *what* we know and changing *how* we know. Transformative learning, which we might claim as the ultimate role of the university, is concerned with changing someone's point of reference rather than merely filling their mind with knowledge. Kegan's point is not that we ought to pursue one and not the other, but that we should look to inform (improving what is known) in order to transform (changing the approach towards what is known). Kegan describes it in this way:

> If one is bound by concrete thinking in the study of, say, history, then, yes, further learning of the informative sort might involve the mastery of more historical facts, events, characters, and outcomes. But further learning of a transformative sort might also involve the development of a capacity for abstract thinking so that one can ask more general, thematic questions *about* the facts, or consider the perspectives and biases of those who wrote the historical account *creating* the facts. Both kinds of learning are expansive and valuable, one within a pre-existing frame of mind and the other reconstructing the very frame.
>
> (2018, p. 35)

An educated university graduate, then, doesn't simply *know* more – important and necessary though this is. Instead, a graduate is able to *navigate knowledge* such that they are better able to dialogue with it, critique it, extend it, consider it from different perspectives and confidently use it as the basis for a complete rethink or reinterpretation of everything. Education, then, might be thought of as deepening rather than filling the mind, as Kegan goes on to illustrate in Figure 2.1.

University education, then, can be confidently defined as being concerned with transformative learning rather than solely informative learning. However, this isn't always obvious from how students are expected to learn as they progress towards their qualification. At first glance many individual courses or modules[3] seem more geared to inform rather than transform students; indeed, it is all too common to hear digital education advocates talk about courses and modules in terms of 'content'! Yet, as will

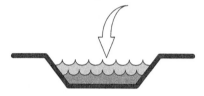

Informative: Changes in *what* we know

Transformative: Changes in *how* we know

Figure 2.1 Informative and Transformative Learning.

Source: Kegan, 2018, p. 36. Copyright 2018 from *Contemporary theories of learning: Learning theorists ... in their own words* (2nd ed.) by Knud Illeris (Ed.). Reproduced by permission of Taylor and Francis, a division of Informa plc.

be reinforced later in this book, this ought not be the case. Helpfully, Illeris (2018a) suggests a fourfold escalation of learning types that climax in learning as transformative.

1. *Cumulative*, or mechanical learning. A new fact is learned, potentially in isolation from things already known. Illeris gives the examples of learning a PIN, and the experience of young children encountering specific stimuli for the very first time.
2. *Assimilative*, or additional learning. New things are learned in relation to existing knowledge, as an expansion upon what is already known. This is the sort of learning that takes place in schooling through purposeful subject study and through experience.
3. *Accommodative*, or transcendent learning. New perspectives are added to what is known, which might be alien or contrary to what is already known. Illeris notes that 'this can be experienced as demanding or even painful, because it is something that requires a strong supply of mental energy' (2018a, p. 7).
4. Significant, expansive or *transformative* learning. New knowledge and perspectives challenge the self, in that one's view of the world and position within it shifts to accommodate new ways of knowing (and a new relationship to knowledge).

An education will typically adopt cumulative and assimilative techniques as the means of securing accommodative and significant (transformative) outcomes.

On Learning and Formal Education 27

We will return to this list, and relate the four types to general, high-level learning paradigms as they apply to learning activity design, in Chapter 7. For now, suffice to say that learning in education involves far more than simply learning new things. Rather, the objective is to change a student's relationship to knowledge; in other words, to transform them in ways appropriate for a graduate.

The term 'relationship to knowledge' is helpful for describing the dynamics of education. Education is characterised by a particular form of learning that culminates in a graduate being *related* to the subject they have studied. A graduate becomes conversant with their subject of study, in that she or he can use the vocabulary, understand and converse with the ideas (both mentally and externally with those sharing the same vocabulary), and talk and think with their subject's own accent. A degree might be considered a certificate of adoption into a way of thinking or practice. Thought of in this way, education consists of a deliberately structured learning journey designed for a learner to know (and even sense they are known by) a series of subjects or a discipline. The learner develops the ability to think more discerningly and develops a self-awareness about their own standing with those subjects or that discipline as a relational partner. A qualification is the university's endorsement that the graduate has achieved a certain relationship with knowledge and, in more vocational areas, is also able to demonstrate the various practical competencies viewed as important for entering the workforce (being adopted into the practitioner family, as it were). This view of learning is, of course, simplistic and incomplete. But in the current social construct that is a university, promoting, assessing and evidencing transformative learning is the requirement of a university education. There is a new form of *being* that learning can lead to, and it is this form of learning that universities and, ultimately, digital education must make possible.

To be clear, I am not claiming the only way to achieve this sort of learning is through a university education. My position is that universities are specifically charged with deliberately providing the sort of learning that develops a graduate. So, from a learning theory perspective, education can be broadly considered to be the development of an interdependent thinker, trained through the intensive study of various subjects to have a discerning relationship with knowledge. Jarvis (2006) further endorses learning as an all-of-person endeavour that goes well beyond 'book learning' and cognition. Education, regardless of subject matter, is intended to be life-changing and transformative. As should be abundantly clear by now, the education activity of a university draws on but transcends the actual subject content a student encounters and applies student learning as the means, not the end, to educating.

Theory into Practice: A Model of University Education

Let us now integrate the learning theory covered thus far with the social construct of the university considered previously. In doing so, I will make clear some terminology that will be useful for subsequent chapters.

Almost a decade ago I found myself in the position of having to write a teaching and learning strategy for New Zealand's Open Polytechnic. I freely admit that I

28　On Learning and Formal Education

struggled with this task. How was I to adequately and succinctly describe the central themes of education? What words could I possibly employ to describe teaching and learning that were not contrived, pandering or sycophantic? How could I make the definition simple, yet not simplistic? How could I avoid simply listing buzzwords in order to satisfy all stakeholders that all of their preferences were covered? Further, how could I articulate the ambition of teaching and learning in ways that would communicate to staff that what they did was both understood and highly valued?

Fortunately for me, I encountered thoughtful answers to these questions a few months later. In 2011 I gave an invited address at another polytechnic's staff conference. I found exactly what I was looking for in the presentation of the keynote given by Professor Emeritus Sir Mason Durie, of Massey University, New Zealand. Sir Mason talked of education as consisting of three main elements. He presented these elements in *te reo* (Māori language) terms, with English translations:

- *Whakapiri*: engagement.
- *Whakamārama*: enlightenment.
- *Whakamana*: empowerment.

These three terms captured perfectly the characteristics of education that I knew but was unable to articulate: education captures and activates a student's mind, reshapes it through new ideas and intellectual challenge and provides graduates with evidence testifying to the changes that have taken place in their cognitive ability. Education is intimate, nuanced and purposeful. Engagement, enlightenment and empowerment neatly describe the immediate, intermediate and ultimate concerns of education and are important markers for how effective education is practised. The concepts of transformation over information and learning as an all-of-person experience can be discerned across these three key terms. Whakapiri, whakamārama and whakamana – engagement, enlightenment and empowerment – provide a neat shorthand of the university's education role and a useful framework for summarising the learning theory discussion thus far. Table 2.1 brings together Peters' view of someone educated, Durie's three elements of education and the educational mechanisms employed by universities in their teaching and learning activity.

The dividing lines are purely illustrative, because there is substantial interrelationship across all three layers. However, this simple model is adequate to show how learning theory can be brought into educational practice.

From a student perspective, a university education begins with the selection of a subject area of interest. Students are pedagogically engaged with the concepts, theories, practices and ideas (the knowledge base) related to that subject area as they are initiated into the domains of knowledge and skill, progressing from module to module. Students encounter the subject through a series of learning activities. From time to time students are asked to prepare an assessment, which will typically challenge them to consider or apply the knowledge base in a new, deeper way and

On Learning and Formal Education   29

Table 2.1 A Model of Education Outcomes, Elements and Mechanisms

Education Outcomes (Peters)	Education Elements (Durie)	Education Mechanisms in Practice
iii. Initiation into domains of knowledge and skill	Engagement	Learning activity design[a]
ii. Acquiring knowledge and intellectual skills, and development of understanding	Enlightenment	Module learning outcomes and assessment
i. Change for the better	Empowerment	Qualification level, credits and graduate outcomes

require them to become more intimate with the subject (deepening their relationship with it and encouraging smudging). As students successfully achieve each module's outcomes, they find themselves enlightened in their thinking: they are learning new things, making new connections in their thinking and understanding discipline knowledge in deeper ways. Ultimately, once all modules are successfully completed, they are empowered graduates. Their qualification is the university's declaration that the student has met the graduate outcomes required for their course of study, and that their university education has changed them (naturally for the better!).

The student is likely to commence their studies not so much from the perspective of 'Who will I become?', but rather, 'What will I learn?'. The university begins its own qualification journey from the opposite end to the student. Qualification decisions – the level of award, the volume of study and graduate outcomes – come first, because explicit, properly calibrated and appropriate graduate outcomes are an administrative requirement for a degree to become formally substantiated (and, where appropriate, recognised by professional bodies; there will be more about this in Chapter 7). So, for the university, the concept of an empowered graduate is central: what would a change for the better for a student look like, in the form of a graduate? What form of empowerment will this degree offer? Assuming a single, named qualification (that is, ignoring possible majors and subject variants), a university will next plan a specific course of study made up of modules that might be studied in order or concurrently. These modules will have their own intended learning outcomes, which must demonstrate a contribution to the overall graduate outcomes and reveal the enlightenment (in the form of outcomes) that the module is designed to provide. Each module requires students to attain and demonstrate particular knowledge, intellectual skill and understanding. Within each module various elements of knowledge and skill are included; learning activity design is applied in order to engage students with these elements. The term 'curriculum' is often used to describe how all of these components fit together. The university's beginning point, then, is not so much 'What will we teach?', but 'What will our student become?'.

So, there is something unique about a university education that it goes well beyond what might be expected of short courses, professional development or

30　On Learning and Formal Education

work-based learning (so-called non-formal learning) and completely self-directed (informal) learning. The sheer scale of a programme such as a university degree – the equivalent of 3 full-time study years, roughly some 3,600 hours of study time – provides significant and substantial opportunity for engagement, enlightenment and empowerment across a domain of knowledge and skill. Further, a university education is designed to be cumulative based upon a course of study towards a higher set of graduate outcomes than might be possible for non-formal learning options.

The difference across the three forms of education – formal, non-formal and informal – is expressed in the role of the curriculum. Universities have a formal curriculum, providing an overall structure to the education experience leading towards an empowered graduate, changed for the better. Non-formal education may well have a series of module or unit outcomes, however, these are typically discrete, aligned with performance or the development of specific knowledge or skills. Seldom will non-formal education be concerned with transformation over information. Informal education simply does not have a requirement that enlightenment or intellectual skills be developed.

None of this commentary is intended to disparage the benefits or importance of non-formal or informal education, rather my point is that these are quite different from a formal, university education. Valuable ideas are certainly encountered through non-formal and informal education, but it is only in formal education that students are, *as a matter of requirement, purposefully transformed* through encountering these ideas.

At the beginning of this chapter I gave my definition of education as 'To help students further develop a complex mental schema by means of the concentrated study of a discipline, resulting in perspective transformation'. In the terminology of this chapter, I might reframe my response to read:

> To change a student for the better (*perspective transformation*), by helping them to develop new ways of thinking (*further develop a complex mental schema*) as they are initiated into various domains of knowledge (*by means of the concentrated study of a discipline*).

I might just as easily say 'to empower a student, enlightening them through their engagement with the knowledge associated with a discipline'. How a digital university might best achieve this objective is the focus of the remainder of this book.

Educating Digitally

We are now ready to reflect on what I consider an important assumption digital education professionals and advocates must bring to any conversation about digitally transforming universities: *the practice of digital education is different from that of digital learning*, in the same way that formal education is different from non-formal and informal education. In other words, digital education is specifically designed to facilitate the sort of education characteristic of a university.

The term often used to describe the use of digital technologies in universities is TEL (technology enhanced learning). This is unfortunate for two reasons. First, the order of terms: 'learning' is at the tail end and 'technology' comes first (sadly the implementation of TEL reflects this from time to time). Second, learning is not the primary activity of universities; education is. By definition, it seems TEL has limited itself to a secondary pursuit! Ultimately the difference between digital education and digital learning is a matter of objectives and contribution. Digital *learning* might seek primarily to engage the learner, perhaps to enlighten them. Digital *education*, on the other hand, seeks to go the whole way: to engage the learner as the means of contributing towards the enlightenment and empowerment of the graduate. The pedagogies applied to formal digital education will be subtly, but importantly, different from those that might be applied in non-formal and informal situations.

A university is very different from a provider of non-formal or informal education, though naturally universities might also include short courses and professional development as part of their education offering. As is clear from the discussion thus far, formal education is concerned with outcomes quite dissimilar to those of professional development and short courses, and so the sorts of pedagogical approaches so effectively used for digital training and just-in-time learning will not entirely transfer into digital education. One reason MOOCs (Massive Open Online Courses) are yet to redefine formal education is that, despite their low (once free) cost, their graduate outcomes are much less ambitious than those of formal education programmes and their digital approach to education is generally too limited to a particular form of engagement, making it difficult to bring about the level of enlightenment and, ultimately, empowerment that a formal education requires.

The context set in this chapter for digital education serves as a valuable foundation for practice. Rather than attempting to redefine education itself, as many early advocates of digital education sought to do (see Gourlay & Oliver, 2018 for critique of this tendency), digital educators have the opportunity to *reframe the practice* of education in ways that are more accessible, scalable and personalised while also at least maintaining the quality of graduate outcomes that make formal education so valuable. Digital education need not challenge the identity of the university. Rather, digital education is best applied in ways that improve how universities serve their students. Indeed, if a university is to be transformed such that it offers effective digital education, it has no option but to do so in ways that reflect the current social construct of a university – otherwise it ceases to be a university.

Formal education doesn't need to be challenged, and neither does the concept of the university. What needs transformation is *how* universities operate in their provision of formal education.

The sort of transformation I am advocating can be unpacked with reference to the SAMR model (Table 2.2), which proposes that digital technology can be applied by teachers at different levels:

While SAMR is usually considered with reference to teacher practice, it can be extended and applied to how *entire universities* frame the role of digital technology. Universities invest substantial funds each year in developing and maintaining a digital infrastructure. Administratively, this investment often results in streamlined and automated ways of working as well as providing new ways to attract, register and otherwise process students and their results. With reference to SAMR, evidence of

32 On Learning and Formal Education

Table 2.2 The SAMR Model, Based on Puentedura (2006)

Enhancement	*Substitution*	Technology acts as a direct tool substitute, with no functional change
	Augmentation	Technology acts as a direct tool substitute, with functional improvement
Transformation	*Modification*	Technology allows for significant task redesign
	Replacement	Technology allows for the creation of new tasks, previously inconceivable

the Modification and Replacement of administrative workflows is easy to find. However, as far as education *practice* is concerned, Transformation examples are somewhat more difficult to locate. A lecture capture system, for example, might Substitute for lecture attendance but not substantially change lecture practice – and lecture capture systems certainly do not replace the lecture as a means of education. PowerPoint might be an Augmentation alternative to overhead slides. An ePortfolio system might lead to an Augmentation of a traditional paper-based journal, though it also has the potential to Modify and replace what a student portfolio might traditionally contain. Despite this potential, an ePortfolio system will usually be applied alongside an otherwise unchanged educational model based on lectures.

What tends to restrict the educational use of technology to Puentedura's Enhancement options of Substitution and Augmentation is the scope of institutional change required for digital technology to truly transform the provision of education. The operating model of most universities tends to reinforce Enhancement behaviour. What I am advocating in this book is that universities ought to configure their education practice – the *how*, rather than the *what* – such that elements of traditional teaching are Transformed in the SAMR sense: Modified and Replaced. Put simply, for many universities, digital technologies do not improve the accessibility, scalability or personalisation of education practice because digital teams are not given the operational scope to do so. The scale of this change will be the specific focus of Chapter 8. The chapters in between will provide a series of principles that digital education might aspire to, along with some detail as to how these principles might be applied. Effective digital education requires change to how universities operate, such that demand-oriented university service becomes embedded within the sacrosanct endeavour of formal education.

It is perfectly possible for digital education universities to provide accessible, scalable and personalised education within established quality and compliance regimes. The digital university, just like any other, is concerned with engaging, enlightening and empowering students. However, if a university seeks to achieve a digitally driven demand orientation, it must reconsider its current operating model. As we will see, it is helpful to consider a Transformation (Modification, Replacement) model of education based on what a digital *distance* university might resemble.

Activities

1. At the opening of this chapter, I challenged you to answer the question 'What does it mean to educate?' Now, at the conclusion of the chapter, has your answer changed in any way?
2. In this chapter, a university is defined in terms of compliance. How controversial is this, in your thinking? Should universities be thought of solely in academic terms, or is the addition of administrative activity and compliance appropriate?
3. I have highlighted some of the tension across academics and administrators.
   a. What is your (honest!) perspective of those not in your own camp?
   b. Is there evidence of this tension across your own university?
4. This book proposes that universities become more demand-driven. To what extent does this notion concern you? Are your connotations of the term 'demand-driven' positive?
5. In this chapter, learning is described as a smudge. How do you think you have been smudged as a result of reading this chapter? What new ideas or concepts do you think you've picked up?
6. This chapter introduces the SAMR model. Which of the four options proposed by the model – Substitution, Augmentation, Modification and Replacement – best describes how digital education is expressed at your university?

Notes

1. I include managerial and academic-related (professional) staff as administrative in this book, out of convention rather than preference.
2. As a (PhD qualified) senior manager I was once respectfully yet clearly told by an academic that I was simply overhead, that it was his work that defined the university. I remain grateful to that academic for motivating me to consider the essential nature of my contribution, and for adding such clarity to the thinking in this chapter.
3. The terms 'course' and 'module' can be used differently across universities. For clarity's sake, I will apply terms as follows: a module is a specific, enrollable unit of learning, also called a paper or a course, towards the achievement of a qualification; a course, or course of study, is a selection of modules chosen by a student towards the achievement of a qualification.

References

Academics For Academic Freedom. (n.d.). *AFAF statement*. Retrieved 29 January 2020 from www.afaf.org.uk/afaf-statement/.

Barnett, R. (2003). Universities in a fluid age. In R. R. Curren (Ed.), *A companion to the philosophy of education* (pp. 561–568). Oxford, England: Blackwell.

Bates, B. (2016). *Learning theories simplified … and how to apply them to teaching.* Los Angeles: SAGE.

Collini, S. (2012). *What are universities for?* Great Britain: Penguin.

Gourlay, L., & Oliver, M. (2018). *Student engagement in the digital university: Sociomaterial assemblages.* New York, NY: Routledge.

Illeris, K. (2018a). A comprehensive understanding of human learning. In K. Illeris (Ed.), *Contemporary theories of learning: Learning theorists … in their own words* (2nd ed., pp. 1–14). New York, NY: Routledge.

Illeris, K. (Ed.). (2018b). *Contemporary theories of learning: Learning theorists … in their own words* (2nd ed.). New York, NY: Routledge.

Jarvis, P. (2006). *Towards a comprehensive theory of human learning.* New York, NY: Routledge.

Kamler, B., & Thomson, P. (2006). *Helping doctoral students write: Pedagogies for supervision.* New York, NY: Routledge.

Kegan, R. (2018). What 'form' transforms? In K. Illeris (Ed.), *Contemporary theories of learning: Learning theorists … in their own words* (2nd ed., pp. 29–45). New York, NY: Routledge.

Learn. (n.d.). In *Oxford English dictionary.* Retrieved 11 June 2019 from https://en.oxford dictionaries.com/definition/learn.

Mezirow, J. (2018). Transformative learning theory. In K. Illeris (Ed.), *Contemporary theories of learning: Learning theorists … in their own words* (2nd ed., pp. 114–128). New York, NY: Routledge.

Moore, M. G., & Kearsley, G. (1996). *Distance education: A systems view.* Belmont, CA: Wadsworth Pub. Co.

Palmer, J. (Ed.). (2001). *Fifty modern thinkers on education: From Piaget to the present day.* London: Routledge.

Peters, R. S. (2007). Education as initiation. In R. R. Curren (Ed.), *Philosophy of education* (pp. 55–67). Oxford, England: Blackwell Publishing.

Phillips, D. C., & Siegel, H. (2013). *Stanford encyclopedia of philosophy.* Stanford University. Retrieved 29 January 2020 from https://plato.stanford.edu/entries/education-philosophy/.

University. (n.d.). In *Oxford English dictionary.* Retrieved 11 June 2019 from https://en.oxforddictionaries.com/definition/university.

Chapter 3

Models of University Education

> The traditional form of higher education may have remained dominant to date but vast change is in prospect. Entrepreneurs are actively exploring new ways of breaking old moulds in education, many of them backed by significant funding or powerful institutions. Within the university there are both institutional and academic professional futures at stake. However the future develops, the potential offered by new forms of education should encourage more attention to be given to how universities can add value, and may present a much needed opportunity to reduce the cost of higher education without compromising quality.
>
> (Coaldrake & Stedman, 2016, p. 158)

A university shapes itself in response to its mission, regulatory obligations, operational results and assumptions about how education is best provided. We noted in Chapter 2 that universities are social constructs that bring together academic and administrative expertise. Education, we saw, is based on teaching and learning yet goes beyond these activities to change a student for the better; the terms 'engagement', 'enlightenment' and 'empowerment' were introduced as shorthand for the actual elements of education.

We begin this chapter with consideration of four fundamental elements of a university's very identity: student segmentation; cost and access; levels, curriculum and outcomes; and academics and their roles. Significantly, each of these four elements is the result of conscious choices, reflecting deliberate strategies put in place when the university was first established. The dynamics across these four elements define each university's identity and contribute to an operating model (that is, a description of the university's internal workings) that determines the extent digital technologies will influence how things are done. The elements also determine the basic assumptions of how education takes place, which I term the *core*.

In this chapter we will move beyond the concept of digital education and apply it more specifically to distance education. We will also explore the defining facets of the digital distance education (DDE) model the remainder of this book is concerned with, and the importance of systematic thought on how universities work.

36 Models of University Education

Four Critical Questions

How a university operates reflects its response to four critical questions:

1. Who are you going to educate?
2. What qualifications, subjects and disciplines will you offer?
3. What model(s) of education will you employ?
4. What roles will be involved in the education endeavour, and what will they do?

To some extent these four are listed in a descending order, though they are tightly intertwined. Very seldom will any university find itself in the enviable position of being able to answer these questions from a blank slate. For universities already engaged in education, the answers to these questions were made many decades previous; asking them here is an opportunity for you to reflect on your own university's identity and prospects for digital distance education. Answers to these questions determine the opportunities and limitations digital education presents to a given institution.

Who Are You Going to Educate?

The first question can be addressed in multiple ways. Rather than attempt an exploration of the various market niches a university may seek to attract, for the purposes of this work it is useful to think in terms of two major categories: students fresh out of the compulsory schooling sector seeking a full-time study experience, usually around the age of 18, and adults seeking a part-time study experience that can flex around their life circumstances or responsibilities.

Since the 1970s, open universities have provided opportunity for those lacking traditional entry criteria or full-time capability to study towards degrees. However, serving such students is no longer unique. Most universities seeking adult enrolments are now catering specifically for second-chance learners, and all universities now make specific provision for disabled and minority (priority) students. Being an open university no longer provides a competitive benefit (see Tait, 2018), as most university sectors are now far from the elitist, inflexible norm of over 50 years ago.

Ultimately, then, the decision facing a university is really one of priority: whether the young, full-time student or the older, part-time one is considered the most important. Of course, prioritising one does not automatically mean the exclusion of the other. Instead, the placement of one over the other influences how the campus experience and facilities are designed, what residential facilities might be available, and the forms of student support put in place. The student group selected will most influence the operating model of the university.

Having residential facilities does, to some extent, reflect a deliberate choice to cater for school-leavers studying full-time and certainly means the educational model employed will be an on-campus one.

What Qualifications, Subjects and Disciplines Will You Offer?

The decision of qualifications, subjects and disciplines is also fundamental to a university operating model. Qualification decisions might be at undergraduate, graduate and post-graduate levels, each of which have compliance requirements that further shape how the university actually works. The breadth of actual subject areas will further determine how the university is structured, which in turn will have important implications for how education is practised.

Generally, the more diverse the subjects and disciplines on offer the more faculty units will be in place; subsequently, the more variable teaching practice is likely to be, and the more complex back office systems will have to be. Unless a university is highly specialised, it is usually possible to add additional qualifications, subjects and disciplines to the curriculum simply through investment in academic staff and the resources and infrastructure required for teaching the subject.

The level of qualifications on offer is one of the main determinants of a university's education practice. By level, I mean the formal standard of learning outcomes the qualification is expected to reflect. Many countries have their own frameworks, designed to ensure equivalence of education across institutions. There are similarities across them, however, no universal equivalence; the New Zealand system summarised in Table 3.1 is provided for the purposes of illustration.

Qualifications frameworks are invaluable for ensuring outcome and activity equivalence across the educational system. For example, a New Zealand student graduating with a bachelor's degree will have studied across 3 full-time equivalent years (roughly 3,600 hours of study) beginning at Level 5 (Year 1) and completing at Level 7 (Year 3). Frameworks such as this provide assurance to all stakeholders about educational standards and form the basis of measuring quality and equivalence. The levels are based on a logical progression of knowledge and give important clues about the appropriateness of learning activity design (as we will see in more detail in Chapter 7) as a student progresses from one level to the next.

What Model(s) of Education Will You Employ?

Of the four critical questions posed at the beginning of this chapter, the question of which model(s) of education will be employed is the most pertinent for determining the operating model of the university.

There are three standard models of education: on-campus, blended and distance. For reasons that I will explain shortly, I differentiate between blended *on-campus* and blended *distance*, making four categories. All four of these models might make use of digital education, and so I will later add the term *digital distance education* to distinguish a fifth form of digital practice. Table 3.2 provides an overview of our initial four options as typically practised.

As noted, I have proposed two forms of blended learning. One extends on-campus education, the other is an extension of distance education. The reason for this distinction is that on-campus and distance education are very different models, and blended is not some form of middle ground between them. Instead, the way a

38 Models of University Education

Table 3.1 National Qualifications Framework Levels of the New Zealand Qualifications Authority, Showing Knowledge Dimension (The New Zealand Qualifications Authority, 2016, pp. 29–30, drawn from Tables 1 and 2)

Level	Qualifications	Expected Knowledge Outcomes
1	Certificate	Basic general and/or foundational knowledge
2	Certificate	Basic factual and/or operational knowledge of a field of work or study
3	Certificate	Some operational and theoretical knowledge in a field of work or study
4	Certificate	Broad operational and theoretical knowledge in a field of work or study
5	Certificate/Diploma	Broad operational or technical and theoretical knowledge within a specific field of work or study
6	Certificate/Diploma	Specialised technical or theoretical knowledge with depth in a field of work or study
7	Dip./Grad. Cert./Grad. Dip./B. Deg.	Specialised technical or theoretical knowledge with depth in one or more fields of work or study
8	PG Cert./PG Dip./B. Hons. Deg.	Advanced technical and/or theoretical knowledge in a discipline or practice, involving a critical understanding of the underpinning key principles
9	Master's Degree	Highly specialised knowledge, some of which is at the forefront of knowledge, and a critical awareness of issues in a field of study or practice
10	Doctoral Degree	Knowledge at the most advanced frontier of a field of study or professional practice

blended model works reflects the starting point of the university as either a lecture-based (on-campus) or resource-based (distance) institution.

- A **lecture-based** university places the lecture at the heart of a student's educational experience. A lecturer makes all pedagogical decisions about the overall structure and format their class takes and is responsible for all elements of learning design and assessment. A module is very much an expression of the lecturer responsible for it. Central to the lecturer's identity and function is the lecture, and so a blended on-campus model of education will likely be based on recorded lectures or video presentations hosted by the lecturer. The blend might also include online discussion forums and use of online materials including articles, videos, animations, simulations and extended communities; critically, each of these is choreographed by the lecturer, who remains central to the educational experience. As indicated in Table 3.2, this approach can improve accessibility but not scalability, as interpersonal dynamics begin to fail once a class becomes too large. There are limits to how much peer-to-peer engagement can take place without online moderation or tutorial provision, and how

Models of University Education   39

Table 3.2 Four Different Models of University Education

Model	Description	Typical Student Group	Observations from Typical Practice
On-campus (lecture-based)	Classic campus-based university; lectures are the main means of teaching	• Young school-leavers • Predominantly full-time • Can be residential	• Semesterised • Adult, part-time students can feel isolated or alienated from the designed student experience • Little flexibility for part-time learners (class attendance assumed) • Difficult to scale • High variable costs
Blended, on-campus	Campus-based university extending into more flexibility, perhaps involving flipped approaches	• Young school-leavers • Adults • Full-time and part-time	• As above, though more suitable for part-time and non-attending students • Higher variable costs, hopefully off-set by more accessibility and therefore higher enrolments
Blended, distance	Distance course materials provided to students, with some face-to-face contact	• Adults • Full-time and part-time	• Semesterised • Sometimes required for qualifications with specific learning outcomes • Limited scalability and increased variable cost
Distance (traditional, resource-based)	Distance course materials (print) with tutorial support (telephone or email)	• Adults • Part-time	• Semesterised • Most potential for flexibility • Highly scalable • Systems approach required • Variable quality of practice

much individual attention a single lecturer can provide to each student. An on-campus blended model has some additional concerning elements, particularly variability of the student experience (lecturers might adopt different blends based on personal preference or a different evidence base). Universities also face the expense of revising a course when an incumbent lecturer moves on (a new lecturer will legitimately need to place their own stamp on the courses they teach). In terms of the SAMR framework introduced in the previous chapter, blended on-campus models tend to Substitute or Augment the traditional lecture-based approach to education. Despite the inclusion of peer-engagement and use of additional resources, which might serve to further Modify the lecture-based approach, MOOCs also tend to reflect a blended on-campus model, though students do not have any compulsion – or in most cases even permission – to attend related on-campus classes.

40 Models of University Education

- The **resource-based** model used by traditional distance universities places module materials at the heart of student education, usually (and significantly) supported by a dedicated tutorial role and additional services in the form of administrative contacts and counsellors. A blended expression of the distance model normally includes options for face-to-face small group interaction with a tutor and student peers (which may also feature some lecture-type activity from tutors). In some blended distance education face-to-face activity is optional, however, a blended distance model is also used when qualification or module learning outcomes require the development of specific interpersonal or practical skills, skills that cannot be reliably developed using solely distance methods. In my definition of blended distance in Table 3.2 I have specifically mentioned face-to-face tutorial contact. There are, of course, many means of offering distance education. Some means often described as correspondence may not have a tutorial role at all, and instead require students to work independently with module materials. For the purposes of this book I have decided to define distance education such that *it assumes a tutorial role*. If the tutorial role includes a face-to-face tutorial it is blended, whereas if the tutorial role is virtual (be it synchronous or asynchronous) it is a pure distance approach. So, it is not tutorials being offered that differentiates blended distance and pure distance models. Instead, the differentiating factor is the *availability of a face-to-face option*.

I differentiate between blended on-campus and blended distance for good reason: there are critical operating model, pedagogical and academic role characteristics that differ across the two, with important implications for access, scalability and personalisation. These will become obvious as we further explore the digital distance education (DDE) model later.

You may have noticed my bias towards distance education in the 'Observations' column of Table 3.2. This is based on my professional context since 2001, when I graduated with a Master of Arts in Open and Distance Education with The Open University, United Kingdom. Distance education is immensely scalable, and it is the model with the most potential for flexibility. The international adoption of the open university format to assist in making degrees more broadly available, each university frequently having hundreds of thousands of enrolments, is ample evidence of the system's success. However, I need to elaborate on my final observation in the table: 'Variable quality of practice'. I mentioned in Chapter 1 that digital distance education is easily done, *poorly*. Universities sometimes consider distance education to be simply making readings, PowerPoint slideshows, lecture recordings or podcasts available to students, without any serious consideration of learning activity design or support mechanisms that dedicated distance universities bring to bear. As already observed, Moore and Kearsley (1996) note that distance education requires a systems approach whereby the entire institution caters for the distance student. There are subtleties of perspective a distance education specialist brings to practice that help shape and optimise how distance education might operate. Distance education can be done exceptionally well; that it is often not is my reason for highlighting variability.

Models of University Education   41

A personal frustration is the oft-cited belief that distance education courses have a 20-percentage-point deficit retention rate when compared with on-campus and blended on-campus courses. This supposed 20-point deficit needs critique. It is perfectly possible to practise distance education such that there is *no difference* across student outcomes compared with on-campus education. How the distance experience is designed and supported is really the key, as I demonstrated in a comparison study published a decade ago (Nichols, 2010). Online digital education is readily proven to achieve effective outcomes; see, for example, the initial experiences of HBx described by Anand (2016). With a 'spot the leaks' lens and a willingness to adjust practice, it is perfectly possible to bring distance education on par with on-campus and blended on-campus student outcomes. A well-designed digital distance education model that includes a systematic application of data analytics might even give distance education an edge. Poor retention rates are often the result of presage factors such as open entry (Gibbs, 2010), rather than anything to do specifically with the model of education.

The choice of which model(s) of education will be employed is the most fundamental in terms of a university's operating model. However, with reference to the reasonable expectations of the personalised learner proposed in the introduction, none of those presented in Table 3.2 can go far enough in their flexibility.

What Roles Will Be Involved in the Education Endeavour, and What Will They Do?

The fourth decision universities make relates to which roles will be involved in the educational endeavour, and what they will do. The answers to these questions are shaped by the educational model the university employs.

A university's student-facing personnel will generally cover the following functions.

- Academic support for students (both general: for example, referencing and study skills, library access and item loans, and tutorial: subject-related, including marking).
- Administrative support (enrolment, registration).
- Helpdesk support (IT).
- Personal support (counselling, disability support, employment assistance, students in supervised environments).
- Tuition (lecture, tutorial).

The list is indicative because practice varies considerably. Academic and personal support, for example, might be the responsibility of the same role. Tuition might be provided by both a lecturer (academic) and tutor directly, by a lecturer alone, by a lecturer with marking done through tutorial academic support, or by a tutor providing academic support to students studying learning materials designed by a lecturer.

Blended and distance models of education frequently include an important additional function:

- Design and development (editors, learning designers, media developers).

42   Models of University Education

The mediated nature of blended and distance (including online) models of education relies on well-developed module materials; that is, those resources that underpin distance education as being resource-based. Design and development staff will usually assist academic staff and subject-matter experts in crafting materials suitable for mediated learning.

The lecturer or academic role is typically the one that all others are designed around. The relationship of the academic role with those of tutor and learning designer is often difficult to firmly situate. Where does one begin, and the other end? How should overlap be managed? The roles that are in place, and how they interact, will both reflect and determine the educational model and how the underlying operating model supports it.

The Potential for Digital Distance Education

Consideration of the four positioning questions – who will be educated; the qualifications, subjects and disciplines that will be offered; the model(s) of education that will be used; and the roles involved in education – sets the scene for introducing the digital distance education (DDE) model foundational to this book. The next chapter will demonstrate how the DDE model is very different from the four other education models in Table 3.2 and requires a reconsideration of how a university operates. Here we will explore why the DDE is a different model to those we have already considered.

The Digital Distance Education (DDE) Model and Transformation

Deliberately missing from Table 3.2 is consideration of the DDE model. I left it out because I did not want it to be seen as simply an extension of traditional distance education. Even though traditional distance education *can* be digitised, it is not what I have in mind for the DDE university. Instead, I see DDE as a model of education that, despite a similar operating model to more traditional forms, has important differences in practice that make it unique. These important differences mean that even a *traditional* distance education university would need to be operationally and organisationally transformed to become a *digital* distance education university.

In Chapter 1 universities were introduced as economic entities, and at the start of this chapter I cited Coaldrake's imperative that universities must demonstrate how they can give more attention to adding value, while reducing cost and maintaining levels of quality. If you are sensitive to my describing universities and their further development in these ways, it is my hope that you can acknowledge my doing so in the context of the university's educational role I described in Chapter 2. I understand the university as an economic entity, but with a fully appreciative understanding of its primary task. At the very least, for what follows I trust that you can consider a university functioning as an organisation, even if not as a business.

As organisations, every university has an operating model representing how it functions to add value to its clients, and an operational flow that can be demonstrated on an Operating Model Canvas (Campbell, Gutierrez & Lancelott, 2018). This will be explored in more detail in Chapter 8. For now, it is enough to note that choices

Models of University Education   43

related to education models and roles are deeply embedded in how the university operates and is structured. That each educational model in Table 3.2 requires a different operating model, with implications to student-facing functions and roles, illustrates the difficulty of implementing more than one means of education in the same institution. Implementing multiple education models means maintaining a more complex operating model (or even multiple operating models), with associated increased costs, dual systems and multiple (sometimes conflicting) roles for those who teach and support students. The form of DDE university I advocate in this book is sufficiently different from a traditional distance education one to require its own consideration. Critically, the DDE university requires a different operating model and a specific mix of educational role to the four other models already described.

Let me complement Table 3.2 with the DDE model I am proposing in this book.

In the DDE model (as demonstrated in Table 3.3) all learning activities are digital, all tutoring is online and data analytics are integrated across all functions. Where face-to-face tuition is required in pursuit of various graduate and module learning outcomes, it is provided by exception. Any blended tuition is an extension, rather than a necessary feature, of DDE.

The term 'specific proposal' in the Observations column simply means that I have a specific form of digital distance education in mind. Recall that just as distance education can be done *poorly*, so DDE can be done differently to what I am proposing here. I must add that, while elements of this model are already in use across various institutions (for example, at the Open Polytechnic of New Zealand), I am not aware of the model's implementation *in its entirety* at the time of writing.

Multiple immediate caveats to Table 3.3 are necessary.

*   The first is that *learning activities (digital)* replaces the 'course materials' listed in the distance education (traditional) entry in Table 3.2. This is entirely deliberate. Rather than conceptualising and designing modules in terms of materials to be studied (read, watched or listened to) the digital distance education model starts with those *activities* students are directed to perform so as to meet learning outcomes – even though learning activities may include reading, watching and listening. In other words, modules are prepared differently with *activities* rather than *content* shaping the learning design. While this does reflect much contemporary distance education practice, it is far from universal.

Table 3.3 The Digital Distance Model of University Education

Model	Description	Typical Student Group	Observations from Hypothetical Practice
Digital distance (proposed)	Distance course learning activities (digital) integrated with online tutoring and analytics	Usually adults and part-time, can also be for young school-leavers and full-time	• Non-semesterised, though structured • Most flexible model • Highly scalable • Specific proposal (see description)

44 Models of University Education

- The second caveat is related to the first. For any reader concerned at the apparent loss of print, I here state clearly that digital learning activities do not automatically rule out any provision of print material. Some of my own earlier work synthesising print and on-screen study (Nichols, 2016, 2018) readily acknowledges that *extended narrative* in the shape of articles, chapters and books is best provided to students in print form alongside digital versions. However, in the DDE approach, extended narrative ought to not serve as the foundation of learning activity. The digital distance model proposed in this book assumes digital as a central feature, though this does not rule out additional print where extended narrative is applied in support of a learning activity. One critical difference between how I portray traditional and digital distance education is that I assume the former to be typically based on printed learning materials and physical distribution, the latter on digital learning activities (which may include some printable extended narrative). This point will be picked up again in Chapter 7, when we consider pedagogies and learning design in more depth.
- The third caveat relates to the online tutoring role, which is highly structured and complementary to the overall education model. The various roles in the digital distance education model will be described in the next chapter, and in more detail in Chapter 6.
- Another feature of the DDE model is its suitability for all part-time learners, not necessarily only adult learners. The improved flexibility of the model lends itself to young school-leavers seeking a part-time learning option alongside a first job. The model is also attractive to those younger learners who have the option to stay at home for full-time study.

So far, we have considered the role and purpose of a university and the four decisions determining how it operates. Importantly, these four decisions influence what I term the *core* approach to education, which defines the dynamics of actual education provision.

Determining a Consistent (Core) Approach

Who is going to be educated; the qualifications, subjects and disciplines involved; the model of education employed; and the roles involved in education all combine to determine how education occurs – in other words, the response to the four questions influence the university's core approach to education. Often the shape of the core is simply assumed, though it is always shaped by the model of education selected. DDE makes some very specific assumptions about the core, which is one reason why transformation of universities is necessary if DDE is to be properly implemented.

By the core, I mean the basic assumptions that shape the teaching endeavour. It is everything meant in the phrase, 'how we teach this subject'. In a typical university the core consists of lectures assisted by tutorials. In some subjects, lab or workshop sessions are also part of the core. A core is made up of macro- (institution-wide), meso- (qualification-specific) and micro- (module-specific) layers.

There are many different core possibilities and they are seldom explicitly stated by a university; Table 3.4 suggests how these layers might be expressed across

Models of University Education 45

Table 3.4 Examples of Core Approaches at the Macro-, Meso- and Micro-Levels

	Layer	Examples
Macro	University-wide	• All courses will have two 50-minute lectures per week. • All digital artefacts will be WC3 compliant. • All lectures will be recorded and made available online through the VLE. • The lecturer will use their lecture time at their discretion. • All distance modules will be created by a development team. • All modules will provide lecturer contact details. • All modules will have a VLE presence. • All online modules will include a social asynchronous discussion forum that will be monitored. • The university VLE is [insert here]. • All module VLE sites will include a PDF copy of the course outline. • Tutors will generally have a 1:20 student ratio. • Any student enrolling can choose any module to begin with. • All modules will be available across at least one semester each year. • All modules will be available for enrolment at any time.
Meso	Qualification-specific	• The distance education social work qualification will have regional lecturers. • All courses in this qualification will consist of 30 credits. • All courses will refer to and make use of the ePortfolio. • All first-year courses will require at least one vlog assessment. • All distance courses will be provided in print. • All assessments in this qualification must be submitted online. • This specialist qualification requires a 1:12 tutor to student ratio. • First-time students must start with Module 101, which will benefit from additional support. • All students must be part of a study cohort group.
Micro	Module-specific	• All module units will conclude with a multiple-choice quiz. • The lecturer of this course will use a problem-based learning approach. • This course will require students to upload a video clip in support of their second assessment. • This course includes four optional 1 hour tutorials, across the regions. • This mentoring course requires a 1:4 tutor to student ratio.

46 Models of University Education

different universities, qualifications and modules. I recommend you give some thought as to how you see these levels at play across your own university, and across a qualification and module you may be particularly familiar with.

- Macro-layer elements of the core include those features that are university-wide, which may or may not be enshrined in policy. These shape the overall context for how education at the university takes place.
- Meso-layer elements of the core are those educational features specific to a particular qualification, which will both add more detail to the macro-layer and define any exceptions to it.
- Micro-layer elements are those educational features specific to an individual module. As with the meso-layer, the micro-layer will contain more detail and specify any exceptions the module requires to the overall university and qualification core.

A core is typically unstated; however, a clear description of the core at each level is fundamental to aligning the processes, people, technology and systems making up a university to provide accessible, scalable and personalised education. Defining a core approach is a first, fundamental step to making effective use of technology in any university. As we will see, defining a core is also central to DDE.

Many on-campus universities tend to have fairly loose macro-contexts, to the extent that the same university may intentionally be host to multiple VLE systems and variable module sizes. Some may simply provide broad guidelines as to how many contact hours might be required of students. At least one university requires all courses to make use of a problem-based learning approach. Some distance education universities make extensive use of regional lecturers or tutors and have optional face-to-face tutorials. Others require all modules to be designed such that students can complete them independently of other students. Each of these decisions influences the extent to which education will be accessible, scalable and personalised.

The remainder of the book picks up on developing a core for the proposed digital distance education model, beginning with a full description of DDE's characteristics (next chapter) and some narrative illustrations of its application (Chapter 5). Later, further detail related to the teaching roles it assumes (Chapter 6) and learning activity design (Chapter 7) are provided. The final chapter demonstrates the operating model characteristics of the model. Each of these chapters will assist you in considering your own university's core approaches, particularly for the university (macro-) and qualification (meso-) layers.

Activities

1. Consider the four fundamental questions and how they apply to your university:

    a. Who does your university educate?
    b. What qualifications, subjects and disciplines does your university offer?
    c. What model(s) of education does your university employ?
    d. What roles are involved in the education endeavour, and what do they do?

2. Does your university offer modules by distance? If so, which of the two models (blended or traditional) is used? Is your impression that the university provides effective distance education?
3. What student-facing personnel are employed at your university? What roles are academic staff responsible for, with reference to the six bullets listing personnel roles?
4. Consider the core of how your university teaches, choosing a particular module you are most familiar with.

    a. What are the some of the macro, university-wide elements of the core?
    b. What are the meso-level elements?
    c. What is specific to that module at the micro-level?

5. How easy would it be for your university to adopt DDE alongside its existing ways of operating? What barriers, if any, do you foresee?

References

Anand, B. N. (2016). *The content trap: A strategist's guide to digital change*. New York, NY: Random House.

Campbell, A., Gutierrez, M. & Lancelott, M. (2018). *Operating model canvas: Aligning operations and organization with strategy*. Zaltbommel, Netherlands: Van Haren.

Coaldrake, O. P., & Stedman, L. (2016). *Raising the stakes: Gambling with the future of universities* (2nd ed.). St Lucia, Queensland: University of Queensland Press.

Gibbs, G. (2010). *Dimensions of quality*. York, England: The Higher Education Academy. Retrieved 29 January 2020 from www.advance-he.ac.uk/knowledge-hub/dimensions-quality.

Moore, M. G., & Kearsley, G. (1996). *Distance education: A systems view*. Belmont, CA: Wadsworth Pub. Co.

Nichols, M. (2010). Student perceptions of support services and the influence of targeted interventions on retention in distance education. *Distance Education, 31*(1), 93–113. https://doi.org/10.1080/01587911003725048.

Nichols, M. (2016). Reading and studying on the screen: An overview of literature towards good learning design practice. *Journal of Open, Flexible and Distance Learning, 20*(1), 33–43.

Nichols, M. (2018). Addendum: Reading and studying on the screen. *Journal of Open, Flexible and Distance Learning, 22*(2), 49–60. Retrieved 29 January 2020 from www.jofdl.nz/index.php/JOFDL/article/view/347.

Tait, A. (2018). Open Universities: The next phase. *Asian Association of Open Universities Journal*. https://doi.org/10.1108/AAOUJ-12-2017-0040.

The New Zealand Qualifications Authority. (2016). *The New Zealand Qualifications Framework*. New Zealand. Retrieved 29 January 2020 from www.nzqa.govt.nz/assets/Studying-in-NZ/New-Zealand-Qualification-Framework/requirements-nzqf.pdf.

Chapter 4

The Digital Distance Education (DDE) Model

> Online learning is the most evolved form of distance education and offers unprecedented opportunities for innovation in teaching and learning, especially in how our institutions are structured and managed.
>
> (Moore, cited in Miller et al., 2014, Foreword, para. 2)

The proposed digital distance education (DDE) model I will now explore in more detail is designed to be much more accessible and scalable than the on-campus, blended (on-campus), blended (distance) and distance (traditional) models described in the previous chapter. Critically, the DDE model is also designed to provide a more personalised learning experience. Note that the quality of the education provided by DDE is assumed, as the DDE university is regulated like any other. As mentioned in Chapter 2, a university must demonstrate a baseline of academic quality if it is to be considered a university.

In the introduction I mentioned various personalisation features that a 21st-century learner might reasonably expect from a university. The DDE university proposed in this book is designed to cater for students seeking a life- and learning-centred, flexible, administratively simple, cohort- and expert-assisted, supported and consistent, high-quality student experience. That the model is digital also means all the potential of technology can be brought to bear. The model can be applied to most qualifications, subjects and disciplines directly, though may require some augmentation for highly specialised and vocational learning outcomes.

What I am offering in this chapter is a description of DDE at its purest. In practice, customisation is desirable and often necessary. This chapter indicates how the opportunities mentioned in Moore's quotation above might translate into practice.

The DDE model I have in mind is characterised as being:

- **Consistent**: based on a common core, and customisable to requirement and opportunity.
- **Data-analytics-driven**: objectively and continuously improved by data.
- **Digitally agile**: driven by the user experience, and extensible.
- **Evidence-based**: reflecting proven practice, with feedback loops.
- **Expert-taught**: combining the work of specialists as a complementary team.

The Digital Distance Education (DDE) Model   49

- **Flexible**: open and responsive, available to all.
- **Learning-activity-oriented**: pedagogically sound, with education at the centre.
- **Part-automated**: AI-assisted.
- **Relational**: tutor-supported and peer-assisted.
- **Success-driven**: outcome-oriented, in the sense of student achievement.
- **Systematic**: deliberately accessible, scalable and personalised.

I will explain each of these principles (which frequently overlap) in more detail in the remainder of this chapter. Though DDE will always feature these 11 elements some variations to the core at macro-, meso- and micro-levels are possible. A core based on DDE can be adapted for most disciplines, though as with all education there will likely be exceptions as macro-contexts ('our courses will be online-only') encounter meso-requirements ('this qualification requires at least 60 hours of contact laboratory time') and micro-possibilities ('this module is entirely project-based').

Even though the overall DDE model is conceptual, I will use definite (it *will* and *does*) rather than probable (*can* or *may*) statements in describing how it operates.

Consistent: Core and Custom

The DDE model rests on consistency of practice, based on a set core approach to education. I am proposing a *single* model of education as the universal panacea for universities, but within that model I am also assuming flexibility of practice; imagine, if you will, a panacea that can be provided in different colours, flavours and configurations. In some way this reflects the consistency students will typically experience on a university campus: lectures (regardless of the discipline), regular weekly schedules and semesterisation. There are always foundational elements of consistency across the provision of formal education, usually expressed as the university's macro-layer.

Consistency is a major determinant of student success in distance education and especially so for DDE. Meta-analysis at the Open University in the United Kingdom has demonstrated the importance of consistent workload and coherent learning activity design from one module to another (see, for example, Toetenel & Rienties, 2016 and Weller, van Ameijde & Cross, 2018). This also makes intuitive sense as it is easier for students to engage with the learning task from one module to another if the rules of engagement are already familiar, and if each module they study is based on proven good practice (Gibbs, 2010). From an operating model perspective, consistency also helps with the development of streamlined and efficient processes.

When I use the word 'consistency', understand that I mean it not so much in terms of *sameness*, but of *less inconsistency*. Consistency can lead to monotony; it is helpful to think instead of consistency as having core and custom elements.

We encountered the term *core* towards the end of the previous chapter. The various layers of the core (macro-, meso-, micro-) set the framework for consistency, as they serve as the basis for critical operating model decisions about what educational roles will be, which technologies will be applied, the activities of support services and administrative functions and what consistencies a student might expect

50 The Digital Distance Education (DDE) Model

as they progress from one module to the next. These core elements become baked into the operating model of the organisational function, be it a large faculty unit or entire university. A core is often merely assumed by a university ('it's how we do things around here'), though a core is best thoughtfully and intentionally designed.

I use the term *custom* to describe the learning activities, roles and technologies appropriate to a qualification, individual module or learning opportunity that are in addition to or exceptional from the core. It is the custom element of the model that permits and encourages innovation, which, if successful and transferable, might further serve to further enrich the core (for example, a successful use of VR in a module might be extended across the core as an option for the entire qualification).

- **Consistency** – the elements of the student experience that are the same or similar from qualification to qualification and module to module, which ensure students are not always having to orientate themselves unnecessarily to different study intensities, technologies, roles or learning activities. Consistency is intended to convey *not inconsistent* rather than *conforming*.
- **Core** – the pedagogical decisions that provide consistency to qualification and module design, and which in turn shape the overall roles, technologies and support functions of the digital distance model. A well-designed core will reflect transferable, evidence-based good practice.
- **Custom** – innovative approaches to pedagogy that might require roles, technologies and support functions additional to or different from the core. Custom opportunities reflect specific, creative approaches to learning outcomes. They may be required if specific learning outcomes cannot be met by the standard core approach.

Key to an optimal relationship across consistency, core and custom is recognising their granularity across macro- (university-wide), meso- (qualification-wide) and micro- (module-wide) layers. For example, New Zealand's Open Polytechnic has a standard core consisting of an online-only approach to tuition with face-to-face meetings only by accreditation requirement (macro). Exceptionally, the social work and early childhood education degrees (qualifications, meso) both require placements and the development of specific interpersonal skills, so at the level of qualification a slightly different core approach is used. At the level of the polytechnic (macro-level) these degrees are examples of a custom approach, because they make use of face-to-face sessions in addition to the standard core. The availability of face-to-face sessions represents a different core at the meso-layer (qualification), which is then applied consistently across all modules (the micro-layer).

Further examples:

- All digital artefacts will be WC3 compliant (macro-layer).
- A faculty or school involved with teaching science qualifications might require the same core elements across all modules, and add custom activities within various modules requiring students to make use of scientific equipment (macro-layer).

The Digital Distance Education (DDE) Model   51

- A theological education seminary might, across its entire curriculum, base the learning experience on students' church membership (macro-layer).
- An apprenticeship qualification might have a series of custom learning experiences designed to have the student interface with their work experience (meso-layer).
- A teaching degree might make use of an ePortfolio solution unique to that qualification (meso-layer).
- A business qualification requiring the development of interpersonal skills in a communications module might have a custom solution related to student group work, unique to that module (micro-layer) but compatible with the university's standard approach to group work requirements (macro-layer).

In each of these examples there is an identifiable core approach, which is further shaped as requirement and opportunity dictate. In the interests of consistency, custom elements require careful management. The most desirable approach involves custom aspects being added to a substantial core; inconsistency can easily result if too much custom development is built on an ill-defined core. Custom elements require management-by-exception and so add complexity to an operating model and, usually, additional cost as well as additional cognitive overhead for students.

As a further example, adopting a dedicated ePortfolio platform (such as Mahara) may make sense as a core requirement across a qualification (meso-layer), even if it is not used universally across the entire university (macro-layer). The customisation of an ePortfolio platform would not make sense at the micro-layer (that is, within a single module), because adding an ePortfolio at the level of a single module would require students to learn the entire application in addition to their normal study workload. In addition, exceptional management will need to be in place for adding students to the ePortfolio platform and tutors would require additional training (and likely adjusted reimbursement).

Consistency is a meta-theme of good practice for both pedagogical and operational purposes. The DDE model in this book assumes a core model for consistency across the entire university (or each academic unit, depending on the autonomy across these), which sets the overall approach used in all qualifications. DDE also assumes a macro-approach with deliberate and ambitious strategies across the other 10 elements of the DDE model, such that there is a standard range of analytics-informed data capture and practice, learning activity options, similar tutorial roles and tutorial availability, support services, technologies and workload modelling.

Consistency means there is a deliberate core approach to the model, which can be further shaped to accommodate innovation and additional requirements – which in turn might reshape the core. Consistency enhances student outcomes and streamlines operations, adding to the accessibility and scalability of education. The objective of consistency is not sameness but the avoidance of inconsistency.

Data-Analytics-Driven: Continuous, Objective Improvement

Few innovations in online higher education have generated as much anticipation as learning analytics based on big data (Daniel, 2015). One advantage of digital

52   The Digital Distance Education (DDE) Model

education is the generation of masses of data related to user activity, which can be used to further enhance the learning experience by adding validation to learning activity design, indicating which students might benefit from proactive support and providing students with direct feedback as to their performance and progress. 'Data analytics' here means both learning analytics (related to learners and their contexts) and data mining (analysis of large data sets) for the purposes of 'modeling student behaviour, predicting performance, increasing reflection and awareness, predicting dropout, improving assessment and feedback, enhancing social interactions in learning environments, understanding students' affects, and recommending resources' (Vieira, Parsons & Byrd, 2018, p. 120).

The application of analytics relies on the capture, storage, processing and analysis of useful data. The DDE model is digital by definition, so significant data can be applied to improving all aspects of education. Unlike the on-campus, blended and traditional distance models, the DDE model generates a much more detailed picture of actual student and tutorial behaviour and so helps better inform predictive models, all in the name of improving student success. Ethically it is both possible and desirable to gather and apply data in the interests of improving student success, provided data is used solely for this purpose, is appropriately interpreted in the context of a sound and transparent ethical framework (Slade & Tait, 2019) and the appropriate consent is obtained.

Because of its well-designed, integrated analytics function, those educating with the DDE model will:

- Contact students at the best possible moments for intervention.
- Improve learning activity design based on actual user data.
- Inform all elements of education provision, contributing to an objective evidence base for improved design and facilitation.
- Prioritise valuable tutorial support time by identifying those students who, through performance, behaviour or prior educational success, might benefit from additional support.
- Provide students with objective data related to their own behaviours.

Rather than being punitive, analytics are used to drive proactivity and enrich the student experience. Data dashboards provided to academic leads, learning activity designers, tutors, pastoral support staff and students provide up-to-date, objective views of activity that improve decision-making during a module. Analysis of big data also provides broad views of performance and yields still more information related to how well different elements of the model are working.

Confirming the right data sources, performing useful analysis and making the right data available to the right audience are important elements of designing an analytics system. Data sources include previous study experience, access behaviours (logins into the virtual learning environment, library and associated online systems), study behaviours (including discussion forum activity, tutorial attendance, note highlighting, activity engagement, grades and library access) and support contacts (logs of support requests and responses included in a constantly updated customer

The Digital Distance Education (DDE) Model 53

relations management or CRM system). Academic leads will be provided with dashboards showing overall tutorial activity and attendance. Learning activity designers will be interested in how students engage with each learning activity, including whether each task was completed and how much time students spent on it.

Big data analysis will be used to inform core elements of learning activity design, based on user evidence. Tutors will be interested in which of their students might require proactive contact, or a gentle nudge. Pastoral support staff will be able to get an immediate, data-driven context for each student they have contact with. Library access data will determine whether any student needs to be automatically reminded of library services a few weeks into their study; a few weeks later, if still no access has been made, a pastoral support member of staff will become involved. Students will also be able to see their progress in a module compared with their class average, and where they should be according to the study schedule. They will also be better informed as to the time a study session might take, and how much time they might need to put aside to catch up! Above a certain catch-up threshold their tutor will be informed and will make contact. Students will also be sent reminders about the support available to them.

Over time, data analytics will provide impressive information related to a student's study pattern that can be further used to assist in support. For example, a student with a regular study pattern of 7–9 pm Monday and Tuesday evenings and 2–6 pm Saturdays has provided the institution with the best possible time for initiating a support contact. A student with a small or erratic study footprint will be proactively contacted to check whether they might want assistance with study skills or personal timetabling.

It is the fact that engagement is digital that provides the analytics function with its powerful potential. Because students will not necessarily be able to always conveniently study online, it is important that the offline study function also captures learning analytics that can be synchronised with the main online system.

Data analytics add to the accessibility, scalability and personalisation of the student experience. The gathering and analysis of objective, performance-derived data in a DDE system generates extremely valuable evidence for improving student performance during a module and improving the core elements of the model overall.

Digitally Agile: Built for the User and Reusable

One tremendous benefit of digital materials is that they are easy to create, edit, distribute and redistribute. Digital agility is founded upon a digitally rich experience that benefits the university as well as the student. For example digital study encourages digital literacy, which is made up of 'those capabilities which fit an individual for living, learning and working in a digital society' (JISC, 2014, para. 1). DDE embeds digital literacies across its entirety, providing students with a valuable suite of skills immediately transferable to 21st-century life.

It is not unusual for students to have multiple devices including a desktop/laptop, tablet and smartphone. For those without an effective higher education experience is

54 The Digital Distance Education (DDE) Model

already compromised – and the costs of purchase and ownership are a very small fraction compared with the price of tertiary fees. DDE is designed to not only be usable across all devices a student might make use of, but to also synchronise across them and enable offline access. You may be familiar with Amazon Whispersync and Microsoft 365 applications, all of which are cross-platform and offer a powerful offline experience that synchronises across devices automatically. Following an initial module download, potentially requiring gigabytes of materials including offline video, only relatively small bandwidth is required to synchronise analytics, progress and response data with a university system and the student's other devices. A part-time adult student could study early morning at her desktop computer before switching to her mobile device on a train as she commutes to work. She will have a seamless experience even as the train goes through a long tunnel. Participation in forums and quizzes can also take place offline for later synchronisation.

DDE boasts a strong UX (user experience), based on interface testing that begins with W3C compliance and mobile device optimisation. Updates are automatically downloaded, and appropriate notification provided as necessary (including notification of when a synchronisation has not taken place for a few days).

The user interface facilitates logical interaction with the module, and the interface options available to the student are unobtrusive. The home screen provides a customised collection of analytics, update alerts, progress indication and ready access to the most needed options (including immediate access to where the student last left off). Individual media assets are accessible through both the main university digital interface and through native applications; for example, an audio clip might be opened from its place within course notes and from the student's mobile phone podcast app (where clips already listened to are marked as played, regardless of which app was used for listening). All video includes closed captions and all audio-visual media include full transcripts and playback speed options.

DDE also seeks to directly complement the applications students already use – or would benefit from using – to manage themselves and their workflows. Recommended module timetables will, at the student's request, populate personal online calendars and task lists. Reading lists of books and journal articles are provided in formats suitable for export into bibliographic software such as Mendeley and Zotero, and articles are automatically added to these applications already attached to their citations (appropriately licenced). Students can easily highlight and annotate their notes digitally, perform powerful searches and choose to take notes on paper if they prefer.

The university benefits from rich analytics data, described previously, and the reusability of materials prepared in digital form. Materials might be prepared in ways suitable for repurposing across different modules or learning opportunities; the same video clip used in a full module might also be the basis for a bite-sized piece of independent learning in a different context. Any materials that are updated might also be provided to students, perhaps as an ongoing post-graduation benefit.

Depending on the university's preference, all fully authored materials might be made available under a Creative Commons licence (from https://creativecommons.org/licenses, ranging from the open CC-BY to the less open C-BY-SA-NC-ND options), and be digital rights management-free (DRM-free). As should be clear by now, developing materials is not a core part of the value add of universities and so there is little to be lost by sharing. Openness of resource materials also encourages students to interact with them using other devices or applications they might prefer.

Digital agility adds to the accessibility, scalability and personalisation of the student experience. Integrating the study experience such that it is available across devices is based on sound UX design. Because modules can be offline and study assets are compatible with everyday applications, study is user-friendly, reuse is promoted and analytics data is generated, which is useful for further enhancement and support.

Evidence-Based: Driven by Data

The principles of Data-analytics-driven and Digitally agile provide substantial data that will be used to evidence good practice. Additionally, the DDE model encourages ongoing engagement with scholarship and subjective student feedback, promoting regular, intentional application of evidence across all modules and the core.

There are some caveats around the use of evidence in education. First, education practice is a wicked problem that cannot be finally solved. Practice does, and should, continuously evolve into different forms and education practice can never claim to have arrived at a perfect state. Improvements are always both desirable and necessary. Second, what constitutes effective evidence is difficult to establish, particularly if an idea is innovative (and so might have only circumstantial evidence supporting it). A requirement for absolute evidence immediately stifles innovation. Third, an incumbent practice always has the advantage over a new idea; the burden of proof is often on a proposal for change to demonstrate its benefits over an incumbent, rather than the other way around. Fourth, evidence, like data, is always subject to interpretation. As such, evidence always needs to be critiqued for interpretive errors (for example, where causality might be assumed across correlated variables). Finally, evidence is always related to a unique system of practice; what suits University A based on their findings may not suit University B for all kinds of reasons. Evidence from one source will seldom be perfectly suited to the specific situations faced by others.

These caveats to evidence make it clear that the DDE model presented in this book is, at best, a systematic starting point; it aims for a general way of operating that can be further shaped by evidence. There will be specific nuances related to university policy, constituency, subjects, level of practice and pedagogical and technological advances that will require all elements of activity, even the consistent core, to be reshaped by evidence over time. An accessible, scalable and personalised approach to education must always be subject to evidence-driven improvement.

Sources of evidence for the purposes of continuous improvement include the data sources indicated earlier, drop-out and would-be student research (preferably from one's own university) and student feedback in the form of evaluation. Module evaluation data is frequently overdone. I have championed a simple, 5-star rating for modules (similar to the format used in online shopping) with opportunity for students to add additional comment (and answer additional questions) should they want

56 The Digital Distance Education (DDE) Model

to. This approach, accompanied by analytics data, should be sufficient to determine which modules might need specific attention and in what way. At the other extreme are module surveys asking about the student's experience of enrolment and library services (which seldom change regularly) each time a student finishes a module! There is evidence that good use of the Course Experience Questionnaire (CEQ) gives insight into student behaviours and so provides useful feedback on teaching quality (Gibbs, 2010).

The evidence strategy promoted in the DDE model makes use of data before, during and after a module across learning activity design, support services and student engagement and performance. The strategy also assumes a single evidence function with responsibility for data gathering, analysis, reporting and implementation.

- Before a module, student prior performance data can be analysed to provide clues as to who might need specific assistance. A pre-first enrolment survey gathering information about a student's motivation, time available for study, computer confidence and self-appraisal of readiness (for independent study, reading and writing, note-taking and so on) provides further data useful for improving service to students (Nichols, 2010). Such data is provided to tutors in summary form and is continuously available to pastoral support staff for prioritisation of support.
- During a module, academic leads and learning activity designers make use of data to confirm learning activities and assessments are performing as intended. Changes outside of university norms to student engagement (such as learning activity engagement, forum participation, tutorial attendance and library access), withdrawal or assessment performance are immediately identified and analysed to see whether intervention is necessary and, if so, when it might be best activated.
- After a module, data related to student performance (retention and success), module feedback, re-enrolment (the proportion of students advancing to the next module) and summary data related to what is studied during the module is analysed. Lead academics and learning activity designers are tasked with improving those elements requiring adjustment.

The overall data set is further used to assist in continuous improvement across *all* elements of service, both generally and for specific points of high interest. Large data patterns are analysed to determine the effectiveness of such elements as the pre-first enrolment survey, variance of student success across tutors, student time spent on specific learning activity types, and the relationship of learning activity types to student outcomes. Data is also used to determine whether, for example, contacting students about library use is best timed for 4 or 5 weeks of non-library access, if altering a specific phrase in a forum introduction affects the length of student contributions, or if changing the button linking to library support results in more students clicking it. Evidence provides insight for micro-, meso- and macro-improvements.

Student support data from student requests and subsequent resolutions also add to the overall evidence base. All student support interaction, captured in a CRM system, is frequently mined for key student requests and exemplar interventions. Vast

The Digital Distance Education (DDE) Model   57

quantities of text information, usefully summarised through artificial intelligence, provide a further rich lens for determining how the overall service to students might be improved.

Of course, not every aspect of what students encounter during their study is possible (or even desirable) to capture as data. The objective is to capture as much data as is readily beneficial to service improvement. Evidence will eventually determine which pieces of evidence are most useful! Further, any specific issues identifiable from analytics, surveys, CRM data or student feedback where more specific data is not already gathered mean a more purposeful investigation is justified – which would include gathering further evidence to assist in making informed choices for improvement.

Evidence-based practice enhances the accessibility, scalability and personalisation of the student experience. The application of various forms of data to continuous improvement means performance levels are systematically improved before, during and after a module and across all elements of the student experience. Data gathering, analysis, recommendation and betterment are constant activities.

Expert-Taught: Involving Specialists

Teaching in the DDE model is a shared responsibility across various roles. In the distance education universities I have worked with, students rate the contribution that learning activities make to their understanding at least as highly as they do tutorial support; this indicates that the concept of who is involved in teaching must be broader than simply the combination of academic and tutoring staff. Learning activity designers, who help craft the learning journey, are valid teachers in the sense that they assist students to acquire knowledge and understanding. In DDE, all elements of teaching are the role of trained specialists who collaborate in providing an expert learning experience.

I have long subscribed to Palmer's description of subject-oriented teaching, 'the teacher's central task is to give the great thing [the subject] an independent voice – a capacity to speak its truth quite apart from the teacher's voice in terms that students can hear and understand' (2007, p. 120). In this sense, the role of the academic lead in DDE is to provide the voice of the subject, to speak on its behalf. It is the role of the learning activity designer to assist students in learning to converse with that voice, and the role of the tutor to respond to each individual student with feedback related to improving their accent, grammar and vocabulary. Pastoral support staff are there to ensure that students stay engaged with the conversation. All are responsible for ensuring that the voice of the subject, represented by the lead academic, is heard by students and that students become increasingly fluent in dialogue with it.

The DDE model recognises four teaching roles.

- The **lead academic** is qualified to represent the subject, providing and/or interpreting the appropriate learning outcomes for a module. The role provides the interface to the body of knowledge and ways of thinking students require to successfully complete the module and attain its learning outcomes as they

58 The Digital Distance Education (DDE) Model

contribute to those of the qualification. The lead academic is ultimately responsible for the performance of the module and its academic integrity.

- The **learning activity designer** is an expert in the application and design of learning activities. Their role is to identify key concepts and perspectives, and link them to teaching techniques that promote student engagement and understanding. The learning activity designer is responsible for the overall design of the module, including its alignment with the requirements of the consistent core and its contribution to overall qualification objectives.
- The **tutor** is the immediate academic representative available to students. Their role is to assist students in their understanding (remedial in the sense of basing everything on the learning activities and module resources), moderate online forums, mark all work and provide personalised feedback to each student. Tutors also provide feedback and advice on improving module design.
- The **pastoral support team** provides proactive and reactive student assistance in generic, non-module specific areas. They are responsible for assisting students in relation to IT support, library use, staying motivated and any other matters not directly related to tuition. The team consists of both general, triage roles and specialist advisers who may be in other university units.

We will explore these roles and their complementarity in more detail in Chapter 6.

A complementary team of specialists adds to the accessibility, scalability and personalisation of the learning process. Specialists are involved in the design, development and delivery of the education experience. Academics, learning activity designers, tutors and pastoral support staff all contribute to the teaching aspect of DDE.

Flexible: Universally Open

The terms *flexible* and *open* are always relative. The DDE model is not absolutely flexible nor is it entirely open, but it aims to extend the availability of higher education to the broadest student audience as possible. The extreme of flexibility would let students enrol in whatever they wanted to and start whenever they want to; pause, recommence and finish when convenient; and work fully to their own preferred pace and means of learning. Extreme openness provides all course resources freely to everyone, makes all elements of the learning experience fully available and lets anyone enrol in any qualification without prerequisite. Unfortunately, many of these extreme elements work against student success and the forms of engagement, enlightenment and empowerment that education is obligated to provide. Tempering the enthusiasm for comprehensive flexibility and openness are the more important concerns of student outcomes and institutional viability.

The sweet spot for flexibility and openness lies where students are challenged to extend themselves with the highest possible opportunity to succeed, and where openness serves an explicit institutional objective aligned with public service. These options are all the sweeter when *designed into* an education model rather than added to it as an afterthought. The DDE model offers flexibility and openness in the following ways:

The Digital Distance Education (DDE) Model   59

- Students can start their studies at any time convenient for them, though they work to a study timetable that places them alongside other students and within a learning cohort sharing the same tutor. The motivation provided by deadlines and the collaboration and peer engagement afforded by an identifiable class are crucial elements of student success. Cohorts, which might start on a regular basis (monthly or every 2 months) depending on the minimum number of viable students (20–25), can be transferred into if a student requires a temporary break from study (what constitutes a requirement being determined by university policy). For example, a student suffering a family bereavement might defer their study for 2 months, then pick up where they left off as they join a following cohort.
- Students can reach their study goal aspirations, but they may not be able to immediately start on their chosen module. One of the roles of a pre-enrolment survey is to determine which students might be counselled or, depending on university policy, *required* to undertake a bridging course or qualification to provide them with the best opportunity for ultimate success. If a student with no entry qualification aspires to a degree, their best first step might be to complete a module designed to introduce them to their subject area in a way that also builds the study skills they will need. From a social justice perspective, this does not mean that certain students are denied entry; rather, they are accepted subject to an additional activity designed to enhance their experience and likelihood of success. Such bridging or entry qualifications use the same educational approach as do regular modules, to provide an authentic introduction to study. Depending on university policy, such bridging modules might be offered free of charge or, in the case of requiring a student to undergo a prerequisite qualification at a lower level, initial study at their desired level might be discounted once they are ready to start it. Because students can start modules at any time, there is no great time penalty for beginning with bridging study.
- All learning activities are designed for accessibility in the sense of universality. Alternative text for images, closed captions for video, colour contrast and good layout design, compatibility with voice recognition, Text-To-Speech and text sizing features provide benefits for all digital learners. Each of these features are standard elements of digital learning activity design and the entire DDE experience.
- The creation of free and independent taster units is built into the module design process, enabling a suite of open-access and free courses to be provided to the wider community. Such tasters are self-contained, self-study pieces of up to a few hours of study, which are also made available as open education resources (potentially under a less stringent Creative Commons licence). Taster units do not provide tuition or certification but may do so for a fee; their primary purpose is to serve a social service, with the added benefit of promoting full qualification modules.

These flexible and open features have major implications for all other elements of a university's operating model. The flexible start times and cohort membership affect

60 The Digital Distance Education (DDE) Model

processes related to registration, student tracking, results, tutor workload and module availability. Bridging courses or qualifications mean considering curriculum from an additional, vertical perspective (in level terms) and tracking student discounts for when the desired qualification is started. Universal design and taster unit development require specific mechanisms to be in place for module design and for advocates of these products to be well-positioned in the development process. Building flexibility and openness into the DDE model provides benefit for all.

Flexibility and openness enhance the accessibility and personalisation of education – and, with the right underlying systems and student volume, they are also scalable. Providing students with choice as to when they start, recognising the diversity of student circumstances and anticipating accessibility needs are important elements of enabling education to fit in with their daily lives. Rather than providing everything in an entirely open format, DDE recognises the importance of structure in the form of deadlines and tutor groups.

Learning-Activity-Oriented: Designed to Educate

The term 'learning activity design' is used in the DDE model. The addition of the word 'activity' within learning design challenges any assumption that *content* is key. Reading, watching and listening, the activities encouraged by 'content', are certainly activities. But so are sharing ideas, thinking about implications, researching things for oneself and constructing audio clips to summarise what is learned. The Open University applies a seven-fold list of learning activities to its module design, shown in Table 4.1.

Table 4.1 Learning Design (LD) Activities (from Rienties, Nguyen, Holmes & Reedy, 2017, p. 136)

LD Activity	Details	Example
Assimilative	Attending to information	Read, watch, listen, think about, access
Finding & handling information	Searching for and processing information	List, analyse, collate, plot, find, discover, access, use, gather
Communication	Discussing module-related content with at least one other person (student or tutor)	Communicate, debate, discuss, argue, share, report, collaborate, present, describe
Productive	Actively constructing an artefact	Create, build, make, design, construct, contribute, complete
Experiential	Applying learning in a real-world setting	Practice, apply, mimic, experience, explore, investigate
Interactive/ adaptive	Applying learning in a simulated setting	Explore, experiment, trial, improve, model, simulate
Assessment	All forms of assessment (summative, formative and self-assessment)	Write, present, report, demonstrate, critique

Traditional distance education is based very much on the written word, supplemented with audio-visual content, reflective activities and various learning tasks. Digital tools vastly extend the learning activity designer's palette. Online library services provide students with rich, independent access to scholarship, in addition to standard online searches for information; online communication tools including asynchronous forums and synchronous video chat present broad options for peer exchange and conversation, and help to link activities and assessment to the student's life and work contexts; powerful authoring tools for virtual and augmented reality, and additional forms of immersive media (including remote access to physical equipment) add to the experiential and interactive options that might be provided to students. Learning activity design is also optimised for student retention and success, based on the ICEBERG principles identified by The Open University (Weller et al., 2018) whereby design is intentionally:

- **Integrated:** aligning learning outcomes, learning activities and assessment.
- **Collaborative:** encouraging participation and the establishment of an academic community.
- **Engaging:** keeping students challenged and interested by including contemporary ideas, promoting achievement, relevant case studies, and enthusiastic teaching.
- **Balanced:** encouraging a regular pace of study behaviour.
- **Economical:** in the sense of not providing too much extraneous or additional activity not required for success in the module.
- **Reflective:** encouraging deep learning through self-assessment, revision and self-directed activity.
- **Gradual:** intentionally guiding the student into more and more complex ideas and tasks as a means of enlightenment.

As mentioned earlier, DDE informs learning activity practice through the analytics data it generates. Over time, learning activity designers can improve their mix of learning activities in module design drawing on evidence of student engagement and retention (Holmes, Nguyen, Zhang, Mavrikis & Rienties, 2019; Mangaroska & Giannakos, 2018).

There is a very rich scholarship about learning activity design and various models for practice, which we will pick up in Chapter 7.

Learning activity contributes towards personalising education. Rather than being about making content, learning activity design encourages students to be active participants in building knowledge for themselves. This certainly involves assimilation of information, but intentionally aims to go well beyond merely attending to information. DDE vastly extends the possibilities for learning activity.

Part-Automated: Applying AI

As I write, artificial intelligence is challenging how we imagine our everyday future. Self-driving cars are on the verge of commoditisation, and predictions of AI disruption

62 The Digital Distance Education (DDE) Model

to some standard tasks performed by professional accountants and lawyers are becoming realistic. AI development consists of two independent streams of research and practice (Franklin, 2014), both with very different implications for education. Symbolic (or weak) AI involves the manipulation of data according to set rules, whereas neural networking (strong AI) aims to represent thinking in the sense of replicating actual intelligence. How the neural networking potential of AI will eventually reshape education is unclear and very contentious. The DDE model assumes that symbolic or weak AI already has a part to play; it is already proving its worth in education (Holmes, Bialik & Fadel, 2019).

There can be no doubt that, as strong AI becomes established, the shape and dynamics of education will change dramatically. It is also likely that some form of regulation will become necessary to ensure educational standards remain in place, and that data and algorithms are ethically applied. Because of the uncertainty surrounding the impact of strong AI on education, it is not useful to consider how it might be applied in the context of the model proposed in this book. However, weak AI informed and improved by machine learning has significant potential.

Weak AI, or intelligent analysis of data for the purpose of simple tasks, will be used in the DDE model in the following ways:

- Analysing vast amounts of qualitative data (such as through student feedback) to identify key themes. Discussion forums will also benefit; chat bots will respond to frequently asked questions and provide regular summaries of key themes emerging from discussion threads.
- Assisting students with study-related tasks such as forming library searches, constructing essays and correctly referencing data sources.
- Automatically marking short-answer questions, expanding the potential for students to gain feedback on their understanding.
- Chatting with students, either via text or voice, to answer simple administrative or study queries as an immediate 24/7 service.
- Diagnosing student misconceptions related to structured knowledge, for example in mathematics, and tailoring learning opportunities to reinforce correct understanding.
- Giving feedback on study behaviours and recommending study activities and pathways.

Eventually it will be viable for AI to suggest and provide alternative study options and further complement (rather than replace) tutorial and pastoral support roles. For example, AI might be able to provide insight as to which students might be feeling frustrated, by conducting content analysis of student feedback or forum posts. DDE recognises this potential and applies AI where there is clear benefit to the education endeavour, where algorithms support fairness and equality and there is transparent opportunity for students to understand and challenge any decisions made. Important ethical considerations must underpin these uses of AI, including making it clear to students that they are in an AI environment and have the option to not participate.

The Digital Distance Education (DDE) Model   63

Artificial intelligence has multiple applications in DDE to make the experience more scalable and personalised. Automating certain tasks in education is already viable, and the reach of AI will only extend as technology matures. The DDE model recognises the potential of AI and seeks to appropriate it wherever it is complementary to accessible, scalable and personalised education in the context of engaging, enlightening and empowering students.

Relational: Interpersonal

Early forms of distance education consisted of correspondence materials distributed via post. Communication with a tutor was by letter, and peer interaction did not take place unless, by exception to the rule, local tutor groups met (either face-to-face or, later, by teleconference). Nipper (1989) suggested that online discussion forums defined a third generation of distance learning which could add a further, peer-to-peer dimension to distance education while also providing more convenient access to the tutor. This interpersonal element is a standard part of much contemporary distance education. MOOC platforms also seek to provide interpersonal components to their modules, primarily through the mass sharing of ideas and peer-marking of activities. The benefits of interpersonal education are well established and will not be rehearsed here, though interpersonal engagement must be well structured, manageable and meaningful if it is to be beneficial to students. Interpersonal activities in DDE can be synchronous (through videoconferencing or text chat) or asynchronous (as in discussion forums) and can assist with the following tasks:

- Achieving learning objectives requiring collaboration or demonstration, such as where students are required to develop teamwork skills, provide meaningful feedback, make something or present something to others.
- Creative learning activities such as role play, debate and collaborative problem-based learning.
- Developing peer relationships: an early-module introductory exercise or forum and VLE profiles can help students to get to know one another, which can enhance social engagement and promote mutual encouragement. Students might also be invited to share their personal LinkedIn, Twitter and WhatsApp accounts.
- Grounding theory in personal experience: taking a concept and having students share their own experience related to that concept adds a further dimension to learning, providing opportunity to either validate or further explore theory.
- Pacing: setting timeframes for interpersonal activities and synchronous events can help focus students on their studies and maintain a certain pace.
- Peer mentoring activities.

There are numerous possibilities for online discourse in DDE, which are considered again in Chapter 7 (the scope of structured online discourse is determined by the role of the tutor). The tutor relationship is a critical one for DDE; depending on intentional core decisions, synchronous tutorials and discussion forum activities (with summary posts) might be a regular tutor activity – though a core might also limit a

64 The Digital Distance Education (DDE) Model

tutorial role to assessment marking and rich student feedback. Ideally, tutors will intentionally contact individual students who might benefit from additional, one-on-one tuition via videoconference as part of their core role. In addition, or even alternatively, peer mentoring and engagement might be part of the consistent experience across the entire educational journey as part of a formal scheme.

Students are also encouraged to form their own social network groups and channels. These are optional, in that membership is considered ancillary to education, though universities may want to provide a scheme registering and promoting social network groups whose student moderators have agreed to adhere to set standards of engagement, perhaps also providing the moderators with special access to academics.

Interpersonal communications assist with accessibility and are a vital element of personalising education. An active tutorial role and structured peer engagement are core elements of DDE. Many creative possibilities for communications exist within and across modules, and students are also encouraged to form their own social networks.

Success-Driven: Focused on Student Achievement

The ultimate focus of the DDE model is student success, in the sense of students achieving the learning outcomes associated with each module and proceeding to graduate. A successful student is one transformed through the achievement of their qualification. Assisting a student to completion, particularly through their first module, is an explicit element of DDE.

Evidence from the distance providers I have worked for is clear that the best predictor of student success in a module is the successful completion of any previous module (this also makes intuitive sense). In other words, in distance education, previous success is the strongest indicator of subsequent success. The first module therefore becomes a critical one, providing a unique opportunity to set the student up for successful completion of the entire qualification they are pursuing. So, a success-driven model will provide a carefully crafted initial module experience. I have witnessed the potential of a simple, compulsory pre-first enrolment survey that indicates a student's need for support (Nichols, 2010), which shows which students might benefit from pre-enrolment counselling and additional support as they progress. It is here that the DDE model strays into the territory of qualification design, in that the model proposes a first, compulsory module with standard features for all students undertaking a qualification.

The initial module of a programme of study will:

- Give as much feedback to the student as possible. Self-assessment quizzes and personally reflective assessment aligned with core study techniques such as note-taking, reflection, finding information and referencing – all aligned with the subject being studied – help ease new students into the disciplines of education as they take their first steps.
- Introduce students to the qualification or profession their qualification is preparing them for. Initial modules provide a meta-view of the disciplines and subjects they may encounter, serving to reassure them of their chosen study path

The Digital Distance Education (DDE) Model   65

(or, alternately, to given them ample notice that they need to change) and whet their appetite for the learning to come.

- Prepare students for digital distance study. While most students enrolling in a university qualification will be familiar with computers, tablets and smartphones, the actual applications involved may take some getting used to. The digital features might be deliberately introduced in the initial module, and online communication activities will provide additional time before videoconferences to give students opportunity to configure their microphones, webcams and speaker settings.
- Provide students with insight as to any remedial work they need to do. As part of the first module meta-view, students might discover that they would benefit from a refresher in, for example, study skills or mathematics. The initial module is designed to help students diagnose their readiness for success in later modules and support them in deciding whether a refresher course (perhaps a MOOC, lower-level qualification or other bridging option) might be timely before continuing. Flexible starting dates mean that students choosing to complete refreshers do not have to wait before recommencing with their qualification studies.
- Scaffold first-time students with additional attention. For example, tutors will have additional responsibilities and smaller cohorts, and pastoral support staff will make additional efforts to contact students on their first module, particularly those whose pre-enrolment survey indicates they might benefit from it.
- Set a foundation for subsequent engagement with core approaches. By the completion of the initial module, students will have encountered all core pedagogical approaches and the technologies used to facilitate them.

One challenge for such initial modules is making sure that they are relevant to the qualification being studied. Imagine, for example, being excited about starting your management degree only to see that the first unit is about referencing sources! Initial modules will carefully and purposefully embed foundational study skills within engaging activities designed to inspire the student about the qualification they have chosen.

There is a social cost to student drop-out, such that many students who withdraw from study may decide that it is not for them and never return to it. Regrettably, students who drop out do not always appreciate that the university might have done more to support them. Providing a suitable pre-enrolment and initial module experience will go some way to ensuring first-time university students have the best possible chance of achieving their qualification objectives. These activities, and the additional characteristics already described, ensure that the DDE model is and remains student-centred in its application.

A success-driven approach enhances accessibility and personalisation. Directing first-time students into specially designed initial modules goes a great way towards building their confidence, and the core skills learned are directly relatable to subsequent modules.

66 The Digital Distance Education (DDE) Model

Systematic: Accessible, Scalable, Personalised

It will be clear by now that the components of the DDE model are highly interdependent, reinforcing the need for a systematic approach. They also transcend the activities technology-enhanced learning is usually associated with (such as VLE and learning technologies infrastructure and, in some cases, learning activity design). The DDE model necessarily strays into the territory of administrative systems, business information, IT infrastructure, teaching roles and curriculum design. Without acknowledging and purposefully building this additional reach, DDE practice is constrained to merely (in SAMR terms) Substitute and Augment educational practice, resulting only in small gains (or additional expense). DDE, then, is a model of education and a system of practice. To successfully adopt DDE requires more than the incremental progress made by digital education advocates. The scale of institutional shift required to achieve DDE in an established university takes senior-level commitment, major investment and a clear vision.

As a system the DDE model requires strong centralised coordination and so is difficult to adopt piecemeal. Different features reinforce one another such that removing one will have an adverse effect on another. For example, removing the concept of a core approach will immediately add variability to the student experience module by module, and so the initial module experience may not be viable; the function of the tutor role may also subsequently become ad hoc by module. Such changes will reduce the scalability of the model. Not having the analytics function removes major aspects of digital agility, lessens the effectiveness of the tutor and pastoral support roles, and vastly reduces the longer-term potential of learning activity design and success-driven focus, which in turn will reduce accessibility, scalability and personalisation benefits. Attempting to combine the lead academic and learning activity designer roles may compromise a solid core and hinder the development of a pan-university learning activity design evidence base. Some aspects, such as not using weak AI or aligning cohorts with work-based learning timetables, are easier to accommodate. In terms of SAMR, the DDE model is designed as a Replacement more than a Modification, and so those seeking to implement it in their own university must count on at least some level of transformational change.

As far as which specific technologies might support DDE, the model is agnostic. Any virtual learning environment that can accommodate the analytics-rich, offline, UX-based features of the model – or else be customised to provide them – would be a logical candidate. Importantly, multiple solutions knitted together through a single sign-on (SSO) might provide the solution though care must be taken to ensure a consistent experience. Even multiple solutions should be based on a solid core and integrated UX.

Conclusion

In the previous chapter we considered how each university can be broadly described in terms of the student body it aims to serve (young school leavers or part-time adults), the qualifications it seeks to offer in terms of levels and disciplines, the model

The Digital Distance Education (DDE) Model   67

of education that are employed and the different roles involved in providing education. Each of the four models apparent in modern education – on-campus, on-campus blended, distance-blended and traditional distance – seek to apply digital technologies in complementary ways that do not transform universities to provide more accessible, scalable or personalised education. The DDE model is a clear departure from the four main models employed by universities and is an ambitious extension even from the distance education model it most closely resembles.

The DDE model is possible, coherent and desirable, representing a logical way of achieving accessible, scalable and personalised education aligned with the modern conceptualisation of a university and the imperative to engage, enlighten and empower students.

The digital distance model is based on the following principles:

- A consistent (core and custom) student experience.
- Data analytics to provide a continuously improved experience and evidence for practice.
- UX-based interfaces and user-friendly technologies.
- Evidence drawn from a broad range of sources.
- The teaching contributions of experts, specialists in the academic, learning activity design, tutorial and support facets of education.
- Flexibility and user accessibility.
- Learning activities, which extend the education experience well beyond reading, watching and listening into more active domains.
- Weak AI to automate time-consuming tasks and maximise feedback opportunities to students.
- Interpersonal communication, with a tutor and peers.
- Student achievement, with an emphasis on the first-time student experience and meta-level system improvement.
- A system of practice, linking all the above features into a coherent and aligned way of operating.

The ways in which each of these factors is applied will reflect the levels of study and discipline areas being taught.

In the next chapter we will consider how the model might be experienced from the student perspective, to help illustrate the ideas presented in this chapter. In Chapter 6 we will turn to the teaching roles the DDE model relies on, before addressing learning activity design at different levels of study in Chapter 7. Finally, we will consider operating models and organisational change in Chapter 8.

Activities

1. Consistency is listed as the first of the 11 elements of DDE.

    a. What do you understand by the term, and what risks or opportunities do you see from applying it in universities?

68 The Digital Distance Education (DDE) Model

b. Consider the layer (macro-, meso-, micro-) you are most familiar with. What are some specific custom approaches you think would be desirable to adopt?

2. Which of the 11 elements do you think your university would most immediately benefit from?
3. This chapter is written in the present tense, as if already in action. Which descriptions of DDE in action most resonated with you? Which seemed the most unrealistic?
4. I've suggested that 'the DDE model presented in this book is, at best, a systematic starting point'. How close do you think your university is to the proposed starting point? Which of the 11 areas is it most, and least, adjacent to?
5. Consider a module you teach or have taught. Which of the 11 elements of DDE would most enhance the experience of your students?

References

Daniel, B. (2015). Big Data and analytics in higher education: Opportunities and challenges. *British Journal of Educational Technology*, *46*(5), 904–920. https://doi.org/10.1111/bjet.12230.

Franklin, S. (2014). History, motivations, and core themes. In K. Frankish & W. M. Ramsey (Eds.), *The Cambridge handbook of artificial intelligence* (pp. 15–33). Cambridge, England: Cambridge University Press.

Gibbs, G. (2010). *Dimensions of quality*. York, England: The Higher Education Academy. Retrieved 29 January 2020 from www.advance-he.ac.uk/knowledge-hub/dimensions-quality.

Holmes, W., Bialik, M. & Fadel, C. (2019). *Artificial intelligence in education: Promises and implications for teaching and learning*. Boston, MA: Center for Curriculum Redesign.

Holmes, W., Nguyen, Q., Zhang, J., Mavrikis, M. & Rienties, B. (2019). Learning analytics for learning design in online distance learning. *Distance Education*. https://doi.org/10.1080/01587919.2019.1637716.

JISC. (2014). Developing digital literacies. Retrieved 29 January 2020, from http://web.archive.org/web/20141011143516/www.jiscinfonet.ac.uk/infokits/digital-literacies/.

Mangaroska, K., & Giannakos, M. N. (2018). Learning analytics for learning design: A systematic literature review of analytics-driven design to enhance learning. *IEEE Transactions on Learning Technologies*. https://doi.org/10.1109/TLT.2018.2868673.

Miller, G. E., Benke, M., Chaloux, B., Ragan, L. C., Shroeder, R., Smutz, W. & Swan, K. (2014). *Leading the e-learning transformation of higher education: Meeting the challenges of technology and distance education*. Sterling, VA: Stylus Publishing.

Nichols, M. (2010). Student perceptions of support services and the influence of targeted interventions on retention in distance education. *Distance Education*, *31*(1), 93–113. https://doi.org/10.1080/01587911003725048.

Nipper, S. (1989). Third generation distance learning and computer conferencing. In R. Mason & R. Goodfellow (Eds.), *Mindweave* (pp. 63–73). Oxford, England: Pergamon Press.

Palmer, P. J. (2007). *The courage to teach: Exploring the inner landscape of a teacher's life* (10th anniv). USA: Jossey-Bass.

Rienties, B., Nguyen, Q., Holmes, W. & Reedy, K. (2017). A review of ten years of implementation and research in aligning learning design with learning analytics at the Open

University UK. *Interaction Design and Architecture(s) Journal, 33*(Ld), 134–154. Retrieved 29 January 2020 from www.mifav.uniroma2.it/inevent/events/idea2010/doc/33_7.pdf.

Slade, S., & Tait, A. (2019). Global guidelines: Ethics in learning analytics, (March). Retrieved 29 January 2020 from https://gallery.mailchimp.com/2c137fb8d5b2c00e44c649471/files/ fe776a62-826b-4234-9b53-1c1098161e4a/Global_guidelines_for_Ethics_in_Learning_ Analytics_Web_ready_March_2019.pdf.

Toetenel, L., & Rienties, B. (2016). Learning design – creative design to visualise learning activities. *Open Learning: The Journal of Open, Distance and e-Learning, 31*(3), 233–244. https://doi.org/10.1080/02680513.2016.1213626.

Vieira, C., Parsons, P. & Byrd, V. (2018). Visual learning analytics of educational data: A systematic literature review and research agenda. *Computers and Education, 122*(March), 119–135. https://doi.org/10.1016/j.compedu.2018.03.018.

Weller, M., van Ameijde, J. & Cross, S. (2018). Learning design for student retention. *Journal of Perspectives in Applied Academic Practice, 6*(2). Retrieved 29 January 2020 from http://oro. open.ac.uk/57277/1/JPAAP%20weller.pdf.

Chapter 5

Module Narratives

> Student satisfaction is student acceptance of learning outcomes, enjoyment for the technology-based learning environment, the levels of interaction with faculty and students, and that expectations are met or exceeded.
>
> (Miller et al., 2014, p. 10)

The previous chapter described the DDE model as being consistent, data-analytics-driven, digitally agile, evidence-based, expert-taught, flexible, learning-activity-oriented, part-automated, relational, success-driven and systematic. What I presented in abstract terms in Chapter 4 I will now describe using narratives, to illustrate what this distinctive educational mix resembles from a student and educator perspective. In this chapter you will meet two different fictitious students, each studying in a different discipline and for different reasons, and two educators – one a tutor, the other a lead academic.

Unfortunately, any narrative is at best a crude indication of reality. There is no such thing as a typical student or typical subject, and so no collection of four narratives can give a reliable or comprehensive illustration of how an educational system might be experienced by all. I have also had to assume a particular context and core approach, whereas the DDE model permits much more in practice. So, what I am providing here is more indicative than exhaustive.

For two of my narratives I have drawn from The Open University's set of eight student personas, a conglomerate of student characteristics developed from quantitative and qualitative research with actual students.[1] The students have an average age of around 30. I have kept the qualifications associated with the two students from their original profiles but have removed country identifiers to help make the cases more generic. My fictitious tutor and lead academic reflect the sorts of values I am certain most would portray in their respective roles, noting that the tutor is based on someone I once trained as a tutor and the lead academic is based on discussion with an actual professor.[2] The subject areas I have selected are those I am broadly familiar with. The scenarios are as follows:

1. Yasmin – studying a degree in social work.
2. Chantelle – studying a qualification in management.

Module Narratives 71

3. Malcolm – tutor in a degree of Christian ministry.
4. Ellen – lead academic in a degree in science module.

Before embarking on the narratives, I will describe the basic core approach underlying all four scenarios. I've opted to apply the same core to each scenario to demonstrate it as a means of consistency rather than conformity. This core is one I consider broadly optimal; others are certainly possible.

The Generic Core and Back Office Systems

The Consistency principle suggests a core approach characteristic to all modules. A core helps a student to know what to expect as they progress from module to module, and assists tutors and lead academics in providing consistent, high-quality engagement with students. Articulating the core also includes description of those back office systems that assist in effective student support.

I'll begin with the back office systems.

- A customer relations management (CRM) database, with access restricted to the pastoral support team and the active tutor. The database includes the student's pre-enrolment survey information, registration details, transcript, study history and notes from previous interactions with the university.
- A real-time data warehouse combining student demographic, access and activity (analytics) data, providing summary data to tutorial staff via an online dashboard.
- An AI system assessing student risk of withdrawal drawing on data warehouse information. The AI continuously adjusts its parameters based on live results; in other words, grades, withdrawals and completions are continuously monitored to help fine-tune the system. Students will occasionally receive automated messages from the AI system.
- A virtual learning environment (VLE) capable of providing full offline access for learning activities, including offline forum reading and message drafting, analytics-informed dashboard, student and tutor messaging system, access to all module-associated media, and links to library and registration systems.[3] A dashboard includes the date and time at which the offline experience last synchronised. A synchronous online videoconferencing system, useful for one-to-many and one-to-one interaction across multiple platforms and devices, is also assumed.

A core approach to education should normally be disclosed in much more detail than I will here. Here are some of the features assumed for these narratives.

- All students are required to complete a pre-enrolment survey as part of initial registration, asking about their motivation, study behaviours and personal circumstances as they relate to study outcomes (see the example used by Laidlaw College's Centre for Teaching and Learning in the Appendix).

72 Module Narratives

- Each module consists of 30 credits, designed to have a weekly workload of approximately 25 hours (making a 12-week study period based on 10 hours of study per credit). Students can opt to complete in 24 weeks if it better suits them, and can transfer across cohorts should they need to defer study for a period.
- Part-time students are limited to studying one module at a time in series, rather than multiple ones in parallel. This simplifies student engagement and removes any need to align module activities (such as assessment due dates) across modules students might otherwise do side by side. Full-time students can do two modules in parallel and are flagged as full-time in the system so that tutors are aware of the specific challenges they may face.
- A new cohort starts every month across all modules, providing maximum flexibility to students and enabling them to fluidly defer or progress in their studies.
- On engaging with the digital learning system, students are given a view of their progress compared with expected progress and various alerts. Alerts include AI-based messages recommending they seek support, links to feedback from recently returned work, tutor messages, direct responses to their forum posts and any upcoming events (including pending due dates).
- All modules have compulsory fortnightly discussion opportunities associated, keyed to the learning activities planned for that 2-week period (though with some exceptions, such as when an assessment is due). Some discussions are in the form of quick check-ins, though others are case studies or structured exchanges of ideas and perspectives. These are designed to help pace students and reinforce the cohort as a learning community.
- Each fortnight a summary message for the class forum is prepared, and an optional online class tutorial is held.
- Tutors are expected to personally contact students considered at risk at least once a fortnight, until the AI model indicates that the individual is no longer at risk.
- The first module is especially designed to provide an orientation to study and the qualification the student has enrolled in and provide insight into the sort of work done by a graduating professional.

Yasmin: Degree in Social Work

Yasmin lives with her husband and 2-year-old daughter. She works part-time as a sales assistant and her husband works full-time. Yasmin is the primary carer for their daughter, but her husband is supportive and helps with the child-care.

Yasmin is an independent learner who is very focused and driven. She likes to study alone and doesn't feel she needs to be around others to study effectively. Her mantra is that her 'study must be done' so she has made it a non-negotiable part of her daily routine. She always studies at home and has set aside 2 hours early each morning before leaving for work while her husband gets their daughter ready for nursery. Occasionally, if she has an assignment or assessment to prepare for, her husband will arrange time off work to take over the childcare. She wants to obtain her degree as quickly as possible and generally finishes assignments well ahead of deadlines.

Yasmin is studying for a degree in social work to improve her prospects and take up a career in the field, as she didn't have the opportunity to go to university after leaving school. She uses her laptop for all her online research and to produce her work. She likes working with a mix of online and offline resources and so uses several printed books for reference. She finds the process of writing things down with pen and paper a substantial aid to her learning.

Yasmin enrolled in her degree in social work programme having successfully completed her highest secondary school qualification and she is largely an independent learner. However, she values one-to-one and face-to-face tutor feedback on her work to give her reassurance that she is progressing as she should. Yasmin likes studying away from the 'distractions' of other students, preferring to only engage with her tutor. She doesn't like other students commenting on her work and doesn't feel qualified to comment on theirs. Despite being happy to study alone, she is concerned that she might be missing out on the pastoral support she would get from studying at a conventional, campus-based university.

Yasmin enrolled in a DDE degree because of the flexibility it provides. If given the opportunity she would prefer to attend a campus-based university but, in her words,

> I really want to achieve this, and I think the time is right. Chloe is 2, and we've got a good pattern going. The nearest university is about an hour away and I just can't take the time to attend classes. I get about 2 hours early each morning free for study plus a solid block on Sunday afternoons. Otherwise I'm either working, looking after Chloe or spending time with my husband.
>
> I decided to begin study about 2 months before I enrolled with X University. I'm the type who likes to make informed decisions, so I spent ages looking for a degree that is recognised by the profession and that I can do part-time. I realised straight away that my chances of studying on-campus were zero unless I left my job and was prepared to travel. I knew that X University would be more flexible than other distance options, but it was more its reputation than anything else that made me enrol. It was slightly cheaper, too, but my husband and I agreed that I should commit to the university that would provide the best experience.
>
> My secondary school results meant that I could enrol straight away. I also needed formal background checks done, but I was permitted to enrol provisionally without having to wait for those to come through. It was very easy to enrol, probably because I had no unusual things to worry about. My pre-entry test gave me some positive reinforcement about my readiness. I was quite surprised when, just after confirming some personal details and my payment options, I received a link to my first module materials and a welcome email from my tutor. It was late-night Friday!

The degree in social work at X University is a 360 credit, 3-year full-time equivalent qualification recognised by the country's professional body. Most of the 12 modules making up the qualification can be completed digitally, but some require

74 Module Narratives

verified practice learning in an authentic social work environment and practice-skills workshops. In the first year these requirements are relatively light, but later they become more demanding.

- Year 1: five 4-day workshops (interpersonal skills, cultural awareness, practice skills).
- Year 2: one 5-day workshop (practice skills) and one 60-day placement.
- Year 3: two 5-day workshops (practice skills) and one 100-day placement.

To cater for these requirements, X University has employed multiple regional tutors who work from home. These tutors support and coordinate student activities in their region and network collegially online (with the exception of get-togethers every 6 months). No regional premises are owned; instead, X University rents locations as required. Each module has a formal cohort of students start every 2 months.

> At first I was worried about the time for workshops and placement. We live about 2 hours away from the nearest regional location! It was helpful having the workshop schedules available in advance. There were quite a few options across the year, and so I was able to plan which ones I might go to for the first year with my employer. It meant taking a few holidays and swapping some shifts, but I wanted to make sure I had this organised before enrolling.

The first module, Social Work in Y Country, required attendance at two 4-day workshops. The first workshop was designed as an opportunity to get to know others in the cohort and introduce the qualification, along with some interpersonal and cultural awareness skills. These workshops were available locally at 2-month intervals, timed to start with each new cohort. Yasmin was unable to attend the initial workshop for her cohort and so instead joined the one for the following cohort, but she was able to join her cohort's second workshop.

> I was disappointed to not be able to attend my cohort's first workshop. I was looking forward to meeting my fellow students. But I'm getting ahead of myself. On the Friday night I enrolled I downloaded my entire module and began looking into the different things I was going to study. I was clearly guided to a 'Start here' page, which welcomed me to the module and qualification with a video clip. I was welcomed into the X University social work community, which felt kind of special. I was assured that though there was a lot to get started with I would be gently guided into the various services and options available to me. There was a required book called *Caring for Others: Social Work in Y Country* provided as an eBook, which I could also request a free printed copy of. I ordered that straight away. The 'Start here' page gave me a very simple view of the support available and the library service. Video clips introducing the Social Work team at X University were a nice touch, too. The last clip I watched that evening was the one introducing my tutor, Mohi. He was actually just at the start of 2 weeks' leave, so my initial email was an automated

one that also introduced me to his colleague from the next region who was covering for him.

That weekend I spent another few hours looking at the study activities of the module. The next time I accessed the digital system, I was given an automated orientation to some of the features I would need to use. It wasn't that difficult really, but it gave me confidence. The first thing introduced was the internal email and calendar systems, which I could connect to my normal email account, Skype, Messenger and WhatsApp. I use WhatsApp all the time, so I chose the receive notifications, session reminders, full messages and response options along with the regular email and calendar ones. It was there that I saw the email from the covering tutor, Alice. It looked like an automated message, inviting me to a videoconference with her. There was a link to her online calendar showing her free times. I chose one on Tuesday and received a one-click link to the event, accompanied by another one inviting me to test my device settings. I was surprised that even my 4-year-old laptop worked easily first time, and to see that the event was immediately added to my personal calendar.

I decided to leave it there until the videoconference with Alice because one of the very first things X University wanted me to do was establish my online profile, which would be made available to the entire X University social work community. I'd never done this before and wasn't sure about it, and there were quite a few privacy options I didn't understand. I was also unable to join the full online community until my pre-checks were completed and my enrolment formalised. My copy of *Caring for Others* arrived in the Tuesday post.

My initial conversation with Alice was a huge relief. She was able to answer all my questions and we discussed what I might add to my personal profile. I had looked at the sample student profiles, so I knew to make mine about general stuff about family and motivations for study. Once I was formally enrolled, I could see all the other actual student profiles. Some were very transparent, down to where they lived, their hobbies, family photos and links to Twitter and Facebook accounts. I wasn't prepared to offer all of that. Alice advised that I should just start by sharing what I was most comfortable with, so I provided my name, a photo and a brief comment about my family. As the first module unfolded, I added reflections on what motivated me to study social work and gradually got more confident opening up.

Alice said that my enrolment took place 3 weeks before the formal cohort start, so I could afford to take things slowly. One thing she encouraged me to do was to set up an agreed study pattern with my husband. Alice shared that she was not an experienced social worker but that Mohi was. It was wonderful talking with her. She said that I could contact her at any stage and that Mohi would be keeping an eye on my progress. He would contact me on his return.

By the time the cohort officially started I had already completed many of the first module activities. It was interesting seeing the other student profiles appear as they enrolled. One lived quite close to me, so I messaged her introducing myself and updated my own profile to indicate the town where I live. We got together for a coffee and connected really well. My first video session with

76   Module Narratives

Mohi went well, too. He said he was very confident in my ability to study and achieve, but if I ever felt the need, he would be happy to talk with me. It was clear that I was going to be well looked after.

I mentioned that I missed my cohort's first workshop. This meant that I hadn't been able to meet my cohort peers face to face yet. But even though we weren't studying together in person, it was clear that we were a definite class group. Mohi worked hard to make sure we were all included and was careful to remind us that we were on this journey together, as peers. I'm certain he was doing a lot behind the scenes. I attended the following cohort's first workshop, which gave me opportunity to meet Mohi and the new cohort of 23 students. By this time all my checks were completed, and I was formally enrolled in the programme. They sent me an exclusive, student-only X University T-shirt, pen, lapel pin and planner in the post!

My regular study pattern meant that I was able to stay on top of things. The first assignment, due Week 6, was a reflective one based on a series of video clips of actual social workers talking about what they did and how they felt about it. The assignment took quite a bit of time, mainly because I was new to referencing and essay writing. I followed the initial instructions on how to use Zotero, set up an account and imported all the module readings, but I decided to keep taking notes on paper for now. The feedback I received was really brilliant. It looked as though Mohi had spent as much time marking it as I had writing it! By this stage the cohort had gotten into a pattern. We had fortnightly online discussions about the role of social workers, each based on a video case study. The case studies featured actors re-enacting some actual social work encounters. At the end of each fortnight Mohi would summarise the online conversation by drawing together our key points, linking to key messages (he would link to them using the names of those who posted them) and suggesting some further things for us to think about. The forums helped us to keep pace, though I was often working ahead.

When you log in to the online system the first thing you see is your own home page. It shows you your progress, links you back to where you last were, and alerts you to any messages or upcoming events. My progress indicator was always green. If it was even close to amber I would put in some more effort. I was regularly 2 weeks ahead, which is how I like to do things. I would draft my forum posts in advance and re-write them before posting them when they were due. I think Mohi knew about my study patterns because at one stage he asked if I would like to finish the first module 2 weeks early! The final assignment was a fairly big one, looking at Y Country's social work infrastructure and services. It meant a lot of library work and website research. To be honest I was counting on the additional 2 weeks I had and so I declined. Mohi then asked if I'd be prepared to act as a mentor for another first-time student. I was really surprised that he thought I'd be up to this, so I promised to think about it for the next module. I knew that senior peer mentors were available from the third-year students but hadn't signed up for one. As a mentor I would receive an additional endorsement with my qualification and a future discount on tuition, so it was an attractive offer.

Module Narratives 77

I got an A for the first module, and things from there went very well. I enjoyed the pattern of study and the different ways we learned about new things. One stand-out thing for me was my first 60-day placement, which I had to do in three parts. It was with a local agency working with teenagers, but it was a 1 hour commute each way. Chloe got sick and then the person I was shadowing got a promotion, so it took some time to sort it out. I was grateful that I received a provisional pass for that module so that I didn't need to wait for the placement to be completed before continuing to the next module.

I was also impressed with how we were taught the code of practice and legislative framework. Both were clearly illustrated using video case studies demonstrating good practice, and required us to prepare some reflections in an ePortfolio that we would maintain throughout our professional career. We were gradually immersed into how the ePortfolio system worked. It drew from our online profile and became our personal space throughout our studies for reflection, personal disclosure and evidence-gathering. Our tutors would provide feedback on our ePortfolios that we could choose to make public.

Video case studies were often used. Some of them were very in-depth, and they covered a range of scenarios including mental health, domestic troubles, children, bullying and young parenting. One module had a vast library of encounters of social workers with clients, showing interview skills and interpersonal communication. Most of them were quite similar, and after a while I developed a sense of what I might expect in real life. In one module we did a useful assignment where we reflected on and critiqued the standard pattern from across any 10 of these encounters. For another assignment we had to formally write up one of these interviews as a real social worker would be expected to and outline what intervention we would propose. Post-assignment we were able to consider the interventions others had suggested. It was interesting seeing the variety of possibilities.

Of course, it was the workshops and placements that really got me thinking and acting like a social worker. At all times we had the constant support of a tutor – I worked with five across my studies – and our class cohort. By the time I completed my second module I had gotten in the habit of completing early, so the cohorts of each module were mostly new faces. But we were informed at the very start that we were to consider ourselves like a full community. Tutors always reinforced this community identity and by this stage I knew of several other students living in my general locality. I only took a few months off, so studying back-to-back I was able to complete my full degree in a little under 4 years, studying part-time.

Chantelle: Degree in Management

Chantelle is a returning student. She previously completed a BA in history and ended up working as a client manager for a marketing agency. Now, 10 years after her on-campus university experience, she wants to upskill in order to advance her career.

78   Module Narratives

I've been with the agency now for 5 years, and I'm keen to take on some wider management responsibilities. My experience looks good on my CV, but I know that without a management qualification I won't be taken that seriously.

Chantelle lives with her partner, who studies full-time. They have a very active social life and so she was wary of how she would find time to focus.

In the end I decided to start early and stay late after work, 2 hours on Mondays and Wednesdays and 3 hours on Tuesdays and Thursdays. I also head in to the local library on Saturdays for a few hours. I've left Friday and Saturday nights free, and much of Saturday afternoon with all day Sunday. I study for up to 20 hours a week, but I often do the full weekend when an assignment's due. It works for us.

Chantelle has a reliable laptop but prefers to print her notes out.

It's confusing having multiple windows and things open, and if I want to go back to something I've already read it's much easier to find it on paper. So, I like to print notes and attack them with highlighters. I found this difficult because the modules weren't designed to be printed. After a while I got into the habit of only printing things I would refer back to later, but I would have preferred fully printed materials. The first module contained orientation advice, and they said I would learn to work with the screen more. I think I'm getting there and perhaps I might work on my next qualification differently, without printing anything. We'll see! I did end up purchasing a tablet, which has helped me be a bit more mobile with my study.

When I was young, I took my study very seriously. I was worried that I wouldn't be able to do that again, and until I got into my routine of evenings and Saturday mornings I really struggled. I would rather have gone to an on-campus university, but it would have meant more time than I wanted to commit – plus it would be more expensive than X University. It turned out that X University was designed for people like me in mind, too, though I wasn't aware of how good they were until I needed to defer study for a month. My mother passed away on the other side of the world, and because it was around Christmas, I extended my time away to catch up with family after the funeral. I was able to do this easily, whereas with the on-campus university I was looking at I might have needed to fail the module and wait to start it again or defer and lose my momentum.

The first module in Chantelle's graduate diploma was a general introduction to management, which included embedded study skills.

Some people don't know how to study. I did, I have my BA, but it's been 10 years! The first module was a surprise. I felt like I was being eased into it, while also being challenged to think about myself as a manager. There were clear instructions, and the tutor was extremely approachable and helpful. I would have liked real face-to-face tutorials, like those I enjoyed while on-campus for my BA, but the online ones were enough for what I needed.

The qualification Chantelle opted for involved modules in management, leadership, finance, strategy, marketing and project management.

The first module, in management, was the one that got us thinking about what it meant to be a manager in a real organisation. We were encouraged to relate everything to the place we already worked in. Some people weren't in work, so they were asked to volunteer, or to select a place they were already involved in, be it a fortnightly quiz event, mosque, social agency or sports club. The importance of context was made clear right from the start and was a theme across the entire programme.

We would continuously be challenged to relate what we'd just learned to this organisation. Our first assignment required us to write up the organisation as a case study. We didn't need to include as much detail as the case studies we were looking at in the course, but we had to suggest a management issue our organisation was or might be facing. It challenged us to consider what it meant to think managerially about the organisation, which was a new way of thinking for me. Later we had to build on and extend the case study into different situations. That was tricky. I thought I'd chosen something easy with my partner's tramping group, but having to take that same organisation into a profit-making international setting really stretched things! There were plenty of case studies featuring a variety of organisations, but we were often asked to apply things to our own one, too.

It was interesting learning about others' organisations, and it led to some in-depth forum work in small groups. I think some people really struggled with that part, particularly those not already working and those whose organisations changed as they studied. I suspect the tutors were working hard with these people. One person in my group had to use a case study organisation instead.

The first module was a challenge but looking back I can see that it was designed differently from the others. We had much more time for the assignment, and a lot of peer interaction. By the time the second module came around I was ready for it. I had my study routine sorted and I learned to use the progress indicators to get a handle on where I was up to.

Most of the modules had a similar design. We would base our learning around different case studies, usually fortnightly. We would discuss these in forums, first with our initial impressions and then in a second round we'd provide our analysis with a bit more detail, drawing from the theory. Sometimes we would work on these cases in groups. When we did group work, we were encouraged to videoconference early in the activity, which helped us to get to know one another and allocate tasks. Case studies were built around the different modules: finance ones put us in situations where we had to interpret what was going on by looking at the financial statements of real organisations,

80 Module Narratives

released that year; marketing case studies required us to think in terms of market opportunities and activities, again drawing on recent and public examples.

The tutor would always be in the forums, challenging our thinking and reminding us of key parts of each case. I think the tutors were always at work behind the scenes. I got a phone call during my normal evening study session a few times, just as a general catch-up. These were always welcome, because they were often when I needed a bit of encouragement. One took place a fortnight after my mother got sick, which had distracted me from everything. When I deferred study the tutor already knew why.

There were two modules that had a different design. These were the leadership and project management modules. The leadership module required much more self-disclosure. We also had to interview three leaders, one of whom had to have a public profile (we were told the criteria for this). In the leadership module we worked more closely one-on-one with the tutor. There were various leadership tests and exercises that I found interesting and useful. It made me think about my leadership style and I learned a lot about myself. One of the excellent parts of the leadership module was the coaching sessions we all had with an actor, giving us feedback on our interpersonal style. It was done by videoconference. I'm really grateful for the feedback I received. The project management module made use of an in-depth simulation. It was artificial, but it did get us thinking about the different parts of project management and gave us an end-to-end view of a project and showed how complex it can be!

Students were given a study home page with access to data analytics related to their progress and anticipated study commitment.

There was an indicator showing me where I was up to compared with where the cohort should be up to. There was also a 'this week study time commitment' figure, which suggested the number of hours I would likely need to spend that week to properly cover everything. I learned from group members that this number would be different for different people. I don't think it helped me a lot, but other people talked about how useful it was to know that they might need to put some more time aside for the week. I used it to get a general sense of what I should do. Towards the end of my studies I disabled it, because most of the time my normal study calendar was enough.

It was always helpful that I could go back to my studies where I had left off and see the latest forum posts ready for viewing. A lot of my learning took place through the forums. At the end of each case study forum the tutor would prepare a summary post and host a videoconference. Apparently, the videoconferences were timed for when most students could make it. It was hard for me because most of them were on Friday evenings. I only attended a few of them, because I was mostly out at the movies! They were recorded for the cohort to review at any time though.

Malcolm: Tutor in Bachelor of Christian Ministry

I graduated with my Master of Divinity degree about 15 years ago. I enjoyed it and have since worked as a lay leader in my local church. Pastoring wasn't for me, but my previous engineering degree has kept me busy 3 days a week in a small manufacturing plant. I tutor part-time because it interests and stimulates me, and I believe in investing in others' education. Tutoring takes me between 15 and 30 hours a week, looking after a single student cohort. Some of the other tutors work full-time for the university, but I enjoy looking after a single cohort alongside another stimulating part-time job.

It works out like this. We're paid a generous hourly rate, with time allocated for up to 20 students across the 12 weeks the module goes for, plus an additional 2 weeks either side of the cohort starting. We're reimbursed for 15 hours each cohort regardless of student numbers for familiarisation, tutorial preparation and hosting, and administration. We're also allocated a further 18 hours per student. We're expected to allocate almost half of this time solely to marking! A further 4 hours per student is for dedicated personal support, though in reality there are overs and unders across the students. The balance is allocated to forum monitoring and general contact. There's a formula for how hours are affected by students changing cohorts, though you gain more from new students transferring in than are taken back from any transferring or dropping out. It's a much fairer system than it used to be, because at one stage it was all variable by student number, and we were required to do much more than we were paid for.

In a typical fortnight I'll log in to the virtual learning environment and look at my cohort dashboard. There are usually four or five students the system throws up as needing some sort of assistance, and so these become my priority. The dashboard informs me of the automated messages they've already received, and links to their CRM data, VLE analytics and personal profiles. I'll do a bit of homework on each one by reading through their CRM and analytics history and decide on how I'll approach them; these are the students whose circumstances I become most familiar with. I'll also check my message inbox in case any of them have tried to contact me, but I don't start with my messages as I like to get my interventions list sorted first. It's handy seeing student study patterns as it allows me to suggest a time that suits both them and me to catch up. My intervention will vary from an email request, phone call, or proposal for a video tutorial, depending on what the issue seems to be and my previous experience with each student. It takes a lot of management, but the system structures it well and I'm focusing on the exceptions needing some additional help.

Once I've done the interventions, I look at my message inbox in more detail. Often there are a few messages in there asking for clarification on something, requesting an extension or wanting some advice. Most are quickly dealt with. Some I refer on to the student support team, particularly if it looks like someone's requesting an extension but they might be better instead to transfer cohorts. It's the difference between a few weeks extension and getting behind

82 Module Narratives

or transferring to a later cohort and taking more time. I always make it clear to the student if I ever decide to make this recommendation.

Depending on recent forum activity I'll also try to seed something related to that fortnight's planned conversation. In the first fortnight I'll be all over the forums, welcoming each individual as they introduce themselves and getting the module-related conversations going. Later, once students know how things work, I tend to be a bit more relaxed and keep a general eye on how things develop. I'll only directly intervene if things get stilted or controversial, or if it looks as though someone's confused. About halfway into the module I spend less time in forums and more time marking. The end-of-fortnight summaries take a few hours, but that's in a concentrated block of time and I always find that part interesting and rewarding.

Marking is my main activity. We were trained to focus on ideas, assumptions and perspectives as much as on what students actually submit. Students upload their work into the online system, and their documents are automatically sent on to us electronically. The marking system works well. Full rubrics are provided, which makes grading much easier. We mark the student work in Word, tracking changes and adding comments. We are required to rewrite passages where argumentation could be better, correct referencing and annotate any insight we have that would help student thinking. All of this can take a lot of time. We're given a target of 500 words of comments per student essay, from in-text and overall summary comments. Most of the time it's easy to meet and even exceed this target. Ironically, it's the really good students I find difficult to comment on! We're also required to provide class-wide feedback on each assignment. Many of the first-year students just aren't used to thinking more deeply, so I try to draw that out in my feedback to them.

I did have a student cheat once. When I started marking his essay something didn't feel right. His forum posts were typically late with the odd typo, and yet here's an assignment submitted 2 days early with fluent prose! I followed Z University's guidance and requested an appointment with him for a viva, in accordance with University policy. At the start of the videoconference I explained why I was calling following the university script and requested if I could record the conversation for evidence. He admitted cheating straight away. The university script was really good, in that it's careful to explore rather than accuse. We provide students with an opportunity to contact us about their assignments and feedback if they want to. Most don't, but those that do find it helpful and I enjoy connecting with them. You can see the growth.

Much of the role is administrative really, but the admin systems are designed to flow. Not anyone can tutor, because you need the subject knowledge for the forums, tutorials and marking. I enjoy keeping up with the subject, and seeing students understand things for the first time. I've tutored the Church History course four times now, so I know it inside out. I might see if I can switch to a different one next time to keep things fresh. Most of the modules follow a similar model, so they work the same way.

Module Narratives 83

I don't really have a typical student. They're all curious, experienced and motivated by the time they get to me (I'm tutoring the module most of them do third), but they differ in their actual needs and expectations. Most require very little personal attention outside of marking. Some are always on to you, wanting additional assurance and one-on-one video tutorials. That's fine, because eventually they become more confident and independent, and you see the fruit when you mark their assignments. My cohort dashboard is really useful in helping me know who to focus on. If there's too much to deal with the central support team helps with some of the less subject-intensive things.

After a few weeks you really get to know your students. They all have an online profile, and as a tutor I can get additional insight through the CRM and their study analytics. I'll talk with most of them one-on-one or in small groups for online tutorials. They're all individuals and I treat them that way. I know my students far better than any of my lecturers ever knew who I was, and these students get personalised treatment from all of us as they go from module to module. I've only actually met three of my students in settings outside of graduation ceremonies!

There are other benefits to tutoring. One is I can study with Z University for free. I also have discounted tuition for family, and full online library access. Because the module is constantly updated, I get ready access to the latest recommended articles and ideas. I also have direct access to the lead academic, who often sends out articles and book recommendations to her tutors. She also gives webinars from time to time that we're invited to, and there's an opportunity to attend events for tutors. We're even invited on stage for graduation ceremonies and can wear our academic garb!

I mainly tutor because I love helping others learn. Sure, assignment marking is a challenge. But we use rubrics and have some automated comments we can use. I like treating it as what Holmberg used to call preparing a 'guided didactic conversation'. That was in our training. We were taught to see marking as providing a personalised tutorial, and to write comments as if we were talking directly to the student. So, in a very real way I'm not simply marking; I'm actually teaching. I'm engaging with the student's thinking, in the most academically intimate way there is. It requires me to have a broad subject knowledge and a firm interest in the ongoing success and development of my students. It's both of these things that make me a professional tutor.

I won't deny that there are times it all gets a bit much. I've had cohort breaks of up to 4 months sometimes. It is good to know that I'm not alone; there is a community of us all tutoring the same course. We all have our own style, but the expectations on us are the same. We are all required to provide tuition in the hours I mentioned earlier, and to meet the same marking standards. It's not for everyone. We're not employed as lecturers, and those who spend tutorial time just talking or – as I saw once – presenting a lecture with slides are quickly, and I think rightly, told to get back to the task at hand. The learning activities teach the students and my role is to bring these to life as much as I can.

That's not to say I don't have opportunity to contribute to how the module works. I give feedback to the module team at the completion of each cohort,

84 Module Narratives

and my advice helped improve one of the online discussion briefs. I participated in the latest revision as well. I'm also not an automaton! Automated systems can't foresee every possibility, and neither can they respond to an individual quite the way a person can. The automated systems make it possible for me to engage more properly with those who need it. I've been able to have some very helpful conversations with students who've been struggling. But it's a team effort. For every individual I've helped, I've been able to update the CRM so others can see that supportive history. All of us tutors and the support team help one another in that way. The ultimate benefactors are the students. They're what this is all about.

Ellen: Lead Academic in a Degree in Science Module

I'm a full professor in organic chemistry. I've spent my entire career as an academic in this area, though lately I spend more time working with industry than I do writing academic papers. Seeing thousands of people use something I helped design is much more rewarding than writing academic papers for 20 readers! I also get real satisfaction from seeing things I made in a catalogue. I can draw on my industry experience in the construction of my module, and students really appreciate the connection between what they're learning and real-life application. I guess I'm well grounded and that's a real strength of my teaching.

I've taught students for long enough to know where they struggle. One main difficulty in teaching organic chemistry is getting students to work across three realms: the real, symbolic and conceptual. An important part of what organic chemists do is design molecules. That's the real stuff. But we design these molecules on the basis of symbols, which further rely on foundational concepts. Students need to confidently and seamlessly align all three – real, symbolic and conceptual – in their practice if they are going to be in any way useful as graduates.

What further complicates all of this is that our conceptual models are in three dimensions. On paper, and in my day in the lecture hall, these had to be explained in two dimensions. I had to learn how to represent three-dimensional models into two dimensions, and vice versa. For example, carbon has a tetrahedral structure. On paper we would draw this with the carbon atom at centre, with one bond up, one on the plane of the paper going to the left, and two bonds to the right – trying to show one in front of the plane of the paper, one behind. We use wedges to show a location towards the reader and dotted lines to indicate the bond stretches away from the reader. Eventually students need to learn to visualise this in their heads in three dimensions. Some of the transfers students will need to make across dimensions are highly complex, so the ability to think spatially is important.

Nowadays all of this can be done electronically. In fact, most of the tools used by organic chemists are now digital. I can draw my compounds in two dimensions in software and can get the three-dimensional version at the press of

Module Narratives   85

a button. So, we no longer need to teach the detail of how this is done. We can instead focus on the concepts and relationships. Students simply don't need to be able to draw these by hand anymore, which is also why I'm against the traditional exam for my subject. Handwritten molecular structures are no longer authentic, so why should we ask students to prepare them in an exam? Most of organic chemistry is about problem-solving, not recall. It's about knowing how to use the tools properly to get the job done.

Synthesising, that is, making a molecule, is like being an architect at the molecular level. It's similar to using Lego. What I might want is a complicated structure at the molecular level, made from basic building blocks. I need to know how I can make and break bonds to build the structure I want in a controlled way, such that I don't lose something as I go. You're using specific chemical tools and reactions to create your target molecule, and that's where you need to leap again into the real world. You get the stuff off the shelf and do the reactions. You've got to achieve all of this while optimising yield. A synthetic problem requires you to set the outcome, to solve it conceptually, drawing on the database of what's already known, and to create the solution without losing too much along the way.

So, the module we produced emphasises problem-solving and the use of the problem-solving method. We've developed multiple case studies that make use of the fortnightly online discussions and we encourage students to use the tools available to them in an informed way. Students don't physically do reactions, but then they don't need to – and they wouldn't need to in the real world, either. We give students online access to the sort of kit used in industry. We work with the manufacturers to help them develop online interfaces to the sorts of lab equipment actual organic chemists use for their daily work. It's no longer about assembling the equipment and having the physical dexterity to link test tubes. It's about designing the experiment properly and interpreting the results.

We provide students with authentic chemistry experiments, using the online interfaces. Students can run actual experiments in this way. One example is how titrations are done, where you work out the concentration of a particular analyte. It's boring to do. And no one does it by hand anymore. People use automatic titrators. You can do the experiment and get the data using a titrator, so we give students virtual access to one. It's a better reflection of how things are actually done, sort of like chemistry in the cloud!

So, my module has students learning the actual skills of organic chemistry. It's not about putting equipment together, it's about being able to assemble real molecules based on symbols, whose relationships are based on concepts. In my module there are no labs besides what students do themselves through the online experiment interface. They get to know what they really need to know; they apply the techniques they will actually apply, and they learn to think how they will need to think. This approach corresponds with the way the learning activity designers like to do things, so we were able to align the custom use of virtual kit seamlessly on top of the normal core approaches used across the qualification.

86 Module Narratives

Essentially the bread and butter of organic chemistry doesn't change much over time, so the module learning activities are reasonably robust and don't need constant revision. The case studies are regularly changed though, to reflect the latest trends of application and some of the things I encounter with my industry connections. From time to time I will give webinars, which are optional for students to attend. I talk about my work and how industry applies organic chemistry. It's especially useful for me to emphasise the importance of effective molecular development; yield is important to industry, but not so much to the chemist. If I lose 50% of a chemical through reaction to get the result I want, I'm inclined to accept that as a chemist. But in industry that might represent a great deal of money. In my webinars, I try to give students a broader perspective of the reality of the job and to get them to think about the elegance of efficiency.

Teaching digitally immediately forced me to think differently. For me, teaching has always been about the creativity of the teacher using the tools available to them to enhance student learning. With the help of the learning activity designers we put together a module that is digital, flexible and much better aligned with the sorts of skills and activities organic chemists actually require. We've refined the learning outcomes and have assembled a course that I believe is better than what is typically done on-campus. Our students may not have experience in physically mixing chemicals and putting glass components together, but they quickly get that on the job. Our students are better problem-solvers, and that's what it's really about.

I don't have a lot of involvement with students enrolled in the module. I've tutored a few classes myself, so I know how students tend to get on and this also gives me a window into how they're experiencing the learning activities. I meet virtually with the online tutors on a regular basis and they also give me feedback. One of them, an industrial chemist, even provided me with a very useful case study now included in the module. I give the odd webinar, do some marking confirmation, keep an eye on the analytics and generally make sure the module is doing what it should be doing as well as it can do. I still meet with the learning activity designers from time to time to discuss any enhancements we might want to make, sometimes in areas identified from the analytics data but also from the sorts of things I'm learning from the latest developments in the discipline and from my industry work.

We noticed from the data at one stage how students with no background in science were struggling with the issue of chemical bonds. Bonds are an essential part of our work, so students need to really understand these. My module is actually a second-year one, so students ought to have a better grasp on this by the time they get to me. Working with the learning activity designers we assembled some additional activities students could use to link into bonds from a novice's starting point. We're still looking into how effective this intervention is. If it's not as effective as we'd like, we may need to prepare some sort of introductory section as an additional prerequisite or, more likely, change the way it is taught in the first-year module. We'll see what the data says!

I've found that working with learning activity designers helps me to focus on my strengths. I know what's going on in industry and how organic chemists need to be prepared. I'm also working directly with equipment manufacturers to help them to develop and improve online interfaces to their kit. I don't have the same level of knowledge about how things such as online discussion might be used, or about some of the other learning activities that we now use. I also don't have the personal capacity to teach all of the 1,200 or so students who take this module annually. So, it requires teamwork. I think we've done this well. Our completion rates are constantly improving, and we're getting good feedback from our students.

Closing Comments

The purpose of this chapter was to describe one version of the DDE model, based on a specific core, in action across multiple disciplines from different perspectives. The narratives illustrate the model in action, albeit applying only a single core approach and solely across a small sample of undergraduate degrees. Though the narratives are fictitious they are not overly idealistic; I have met many Yasmins, Chantelles, Malcolms and Ellens across my own practice.

You'll have noticed a high degree of automation and systems in action. DDE requires a great deal of forethought, planning and alignment of activity. This is the value of having a strong core approach to design, as it assists in simplifying the systems required to provide complex services. The payoff is a clean student interface, both technologically clean (simple, clear options and choices) as well as interpersonally (logical, supported next steps). The first-time student experience of Yasmin was also very deliberate. Initial tutor contact and the initial module experience were designed to provide a first-time student with context, contact and reassurance. From the very beginning, students encountered a strong service and support culture that emphasised one-to-one contact and relationship with the university. There are clear benefits to student retention in taking this approach (Baxter, 2012; Brown, Hughes, Keppell, Hard & Smith, 2015).

Both Yasmin and Chantelle are described as using laptops. Some 80–90% of students studying on-screen make use of laptops (see Nichols, 2018). Unfortunately, laptops are not the most study-friendly devices. Their boot time, bulk and landscape screen orientation are not optimal for digital study. Much better would be a convertible tablet PC that can be configured as a desktop, laptop and tablet device. Reading on-screen is easier through the tablet functionality. Highlighting is improved using a stylus or the touchscreen interface, rather than the manipulation of a mouse (which requires a desk or other hard surface). Note-taking can be done with a keyboard attachment, and more intensive study can make use of a full-size external keyboard and additional screens. My own setup is, I think, ideal; a laptop-tablet hybrid with two external monitors, one in landscape orientation and the other portrait. I have full portability and flexibility through the one device. In internet connectivity there is the concept of 'the last mile'. The last mile is where the customer connects to the commercial service, and it is also where the connectivity

88 Module Narratives

speed is typically most constrained by local firewall, old home cabling, or Wi-Fi transmission at a lower rate than the modem input. Similarly, the student's own computer device makes up a last-mile constraint to study, in that it will either enable or reduce the potential of their digital experience. Assisting students to make wise choices about the technology they use will make a key difference in the success of DDE and the overall student experience.

Malcolm's (tutor) role was very structured, yet it was also flexible. His 15–30 hours per week indicate a variable workload, and the 18 hours per student per cohort (half of which should be spent marking) with overs and unders built in shows an approximation of activity that will not suit everyone. It is clear from Malcolm's account that a tutor must be a subject expert first, and that reliability and accountability are key requirements for the role. The tutorial task is also highly dependent on smooth working systems. In the narrative I showed how Malcolm is perceived as a member of the university's community through library access, study discount and peer access to the lead academic.

Finally, Ellen (organic chemist) talked mostly about the design of her module in terms of learning outcomes. For her, what students needed to learn provided the mechanisms for how it might best be learned. You'll have noticed the comment 'Teaching digitally immediately forced me to think differently', and the link from this to creativity. DDE need not be perceived as a constraint by academic staff, as it can unleash innovation and provide opportunities for tuition that would not otherwise be possible. Ironically, the move towards DDE brought the pedagogical activities of Ellen's module into a closer alignment with actual practice. Underpinning her account is a dedication to student outcomes and success, and a respect for the subject that translates well into the overall core. I intentionally made Ellen's account quite technical, because I don't think lead academics should shy away from their expertise in module design conversations.

In the next chapter we will further consider the roles played by teachers in DDE.

Activities

1. The choice of core makes a great deal of difference to the student perspective. Consider your own institution and its core. How would the various student accounts differ, had they studied at your university? Would they have succeeded?
2. What are the greatest examples of accessibility, scalability and personalisation that occur to you from the narratives?
3. The narratives are far from representative of all students. Imagine how the core might serve the following possible students, both studying the same qualification as Yasmin (degree in social work). How might they experience the support offered through the core?

   a. A student with no previous study experience and no relationship, with a full-time job.
   b. A young school-leaver with an emerging interest in social work wanting to study full-time through DDE.

4. It is common for readers of narratives to perceive them from their own point of view, either as student, academic, tutor or administrator. Consider one of the narratives from a different perspective of the one you represent. What benefits and challenges seem different from this new perspective?
5. The scenarios feature flexible support systems that add to the cost of education provision. To what extent do you think the additional costs enhance and detract from the education endeavour? To what extent might we consider such costs administrative, rather than educational?

Notes

1. I am grateful to Louise Olney, Davina Beegoo-Price and Tammy Alexander of the Online Student Experience team at the United Kingdom's Open University for permitting me to use the basic characteristics of two of their OU Student Personas, Yasmin and Chantelle. Note that a number of personas together form a composite, so Yasmin and Chantelle are illustrative of some and not all of the needs and behaviours of students who study there.
2. Professor Peter Taylor of the United Kingdom's Open University.
3. Note that not all these systems need be available from within the VLE. Analytics data, for example, can be captured from across all online solutions and exported to more powerful BI systems, where it is more easily analysed and reported on.

References

Baxter, J. (2012). Who am I and what keeps me going? Profiling the distance learning student in higher education. *International Review of Research in Open and Distance Learning*, *13*(4), 107–129. Retrieved 29 January 2020 from http://oro.open.ac.uk/35456/.

Brown, M., Hughes, H., Keppell, M., Hard, N. & Smith, L. (2015). Stories from students in their first semester of distance learning. *The International Review of Research in Open and Distributed Learning*, *16*(4). Retrieved 29 January 2020 from www.irrodl.org/index.php/irrodl/article/view/1647.

Miller, G. E., Benke, M., Chaloux, B., Ragan, L. C., Shroeder, R., Smutz, W. & Swan, K. (2014). *Leading the e-learning transformation of higher education: Meeting the challenges of technology and distance education*. Sterling, VA: Stylus Publishing.

Nichols, M. (2018). Addendum: Reading and studying on the screen. *Journal of Open, Flexible and Distance Learning*, *22*(2), 49–60. Retrieved 29 January 2020 from www.jofdl.nz/index.php/JOFDL/article/view/347.

Chapter 6

Teaching Roles

> Good teaching is getting most students to use the level of cognitive processes needed to achieve the intended outcomes that the more academic students use spontaneously.
>
> (Biggs & Tang, 2011, p. 7)

Teaching is a highly challenging, personal and rewarding endeavour for most academics. Traditionally, on-campus universities have afforded their academics tremendous freedom in teaching. In turn this has generated enormous volumes of scholarship and a great variety in teaching method.

Teaching, the relationship mediating the subject knowledge between academic and student in education, is typically approached through the lecture. Lectures give substantial opportunity for an academic to customise their approach, and the freedom granted in most universities enables lecturers to supplement their lecture activity with additional teaching methods inspired by personal interest. Many distance universities are broadly based on this same freedom, though innovation and individuality must be squeezed into the necessary production system required to make learning resources available to students at scale. The non-face-to-face mediation of distance education has traditionally led to an emphasis on the development of learning materials in print form, supplemented by additional media. Individualism is much more difficult to express because learning materials are typically designed by teams and must conform with production norms.

Part of the difficulty of navigating the literature concerned with *digital* teaching is that what constitutes teaching is typically taken for granted. Even though teaching in an on-campus model differs from teaching in a distance model, the term 'teaching' is seldom critiqued. Much recent literature explores the relatively new phenomenon of blended or hybrid teaching. Across these different contexts the role of the teacher can differ substantially, as can the relationship across those teams whose role it is to support the student.

When digital tools are made available to on-campus lecturers, various options become possible to further enhance lectures and add a richer palette of digital activities as the lecturer sees fit. In classic distance education contexts, academics might see new digital tools as providing the means to bypass traditional production norms

Teaching Roles 91

and deliver online lecturers to (at last!) claim their modules as their own, and so teach directly to distance students. Digital tools make online lectures possible from the desktop. Web pages might be authored and maintained directly by the academic. Students can be contacted directly and engaged with synchronously or asynchronously. With the advent of the internet, the role of the distance education academic can become educationally independent. Teaching in classic distance education universities is based on the teamwork required for developing traditional, print-based distance education materials. Should digital distance education, then, be harnessed to resemble the on-campus, lecture-based model of teaching?

This chapter further extends the Expert-taught principle introduced in Chapter 4. The key feature of this principle is that it is centred around complementary teamwork based on a distribution of responsibilities. In DDE teaching is not an individual pursuit.

One of the challenges for universities seeking to adopt any form of digital education is the effect it will have on the traditional teaching role of the academic. There are, I suggest, four schools of thought as to what digital education might mean for on-campus academic staff.

1. **No change**. The academic continues to lecture and teach as they always have. Technology is used to record and broadcast lectures and classroom sessions. This does not require much more from the academic. It reflects the on-campus model introduced in Chapter 3.
2. **Blended addition**. As above, with the added possibility of additional materials made available online and some asynchronous discourse. This places more demands on the academic as facilitator. It reflects the blended, on-campus model introduced in Chapter 3.
3. **Academic as designer**. As above, although with fewer lectures and more use of learning activity design, which is developed by the academic (with some practical assistance). This places more demands on the academic as designer and facilitator. It reflects the blended, distance model introduced in Chapter 3 (though it is sometimes also used in traditional distance education).
4. **Specialist-assisted**. The academic role is made complementary to that of other specialists. This places less demand on the academic but requires that they share teaching responsibility.

Of the four schools of thought listed above, the DDE model assumes the specialist-assisted possibility. This is more aligned with the classic distance education academic role in Chapter 3. In the specialist-assisted approach, the task of teaching is distributed across the four roles of lead academic, learning activity designer, tutor and pastoral support team. In most on-campus universities the academic is directly responsible for the first two of these roles, meaning academics can teach students in the ways that seem most appropriate to them, within the general bounds of the university's requirements.

On-campus academics will typically combine lead academic and learning activity designer responsibilities for their courses, a combination broadly considered

92 Teaching Roles

appropriate for those who have reached the pinnacle of their discipline. Academics have studied, trained and researched for many years to develop their expertise and have dedicated themselves to a profession that is typically more intrinsically than financially rewarded. Teaching is viewed as a solo academic pursuit.

However, the traditional role of the academic as sole teacher, designer and lecturer is incompatible with the DDE model. The major reason for this is the systematic nature of DDE itself, whereby the education model is deliberately designed to be accessible, scalable and personalised. Adjusting the academic role into areas of more discreet focus is known as unbundling (Sandeen, 2014; Seelig, Cadwallader & Standring, 2019), and it is not without contention (Kezar, Maxey & Holcombe, 2016).

A systems approach recognises that the pedagogical decisions made within each module influence how the entire system functions. Recall the Consistent principle; academics acting independently will invariably lead to a variety of teaching approaches and techniques being applied. While on the one hand such diversity can be enriching, it can also ultimately confuse the student experience, limit the alignment of effective student support processes and lead to complex back office systems. Students beginning a new module find it difficult to first learn new rules of engagement, and for administrators even slightly different arrangements specific to each module quickly turn back office systems into a quagmire. Accessibility, scalability and personalisation require a systems-based filter to be applied to the overall educational objective in ways that work across the university as a whole.

Leaving adoption of the DDE principles to the discretion of individual academics works against the very benefits that DDE is designed to provide and complicates the university operating model. Constraint is in fact always a feature of university teaching; while academics are largely able to teach the way they want to, they are never given complete freedom. Arguably the constraints of DDE focus and enhance the academic role rather than diminish it. As I hope to demonstrate, there are some very interesting possibilities that shifting from a traditional academic to a DDE lead academic can bring to those staff who are so fundamental to the identity and function of a university.

That education and teaching are fundamentally about relationship, or more accurately, *relationships*, cannot be overlooked. As we saw in Chapter 2, there is more to education than simply passing on information to students and having students learn that information. If education is truly going to engage, enlighten and empower it must do so on a foundation of multiple relationships, between student and university, student and academic, student and tutor, and student and student. There are two additional significant relationships: those between the student and the subject, and the student and her or himself. Such relationships are as important in DDE as they are in more traditional forms of education and must be effectively nurtured.

The four teaching roles of DDE are designed to complement one another to form an interdependent relationship mesh responsible for all student interfaces. In DDE, teaching is not considered the sole domain of the academic. Instead, DDE weaves together the expertise of multiple roles who together enhance the educational experience of the student.

Teaching in DDE

What constitutes teaching and therefore the responsibilities of teaching roles in any context depends on the university's overarching approach to consistency in education, made up of a core and allowing custom options. It is helpful to think about the teaching role across two dimensions, learning activity (assimilative or facilitative) and the immediacy of activity (synchronous or asynchronous). Table 6.1 suggests high-level teaching activities that might apply across these four characteristics.

The term 'assimilative', you may recall, is one of the learning design activities mentioned in Table 4.1; it refers to anything students must attend to for information. The term 'facilitative' here is used in contrast, to refer to anything students must otherwise do for learning purposes. Synchronous simply means same time, though not necessarily same place; for example, a telephone call is synchronous. The term 'asynchronous' literally means without same time, so refers to time independence. The first thing you will notice in Table 6.1 is that on the surface there is not a tremendous amount of difference as far as facilitative possibilities are concerned, with the exception that asynchronous conversations will always be technologically mediated.

Assimilation tends to be the learning activity students most encounter in formal education. It is also the one that they tend to expect! Consequently, the form of assimilative technique chosen becomes a major determinant of both how a university operates and how academics express their teaching function. Students enrolling on-campus expect synchronous lectures, either in a lecture theatre or online, with the option of later access to asynchronous recordings. They also expect access to synchronous teaching tutorials, again either on-campus or virtual. Traditional distance students are more likely to be satisfied with asynchronous assimilation approaches, including readings supplemented with additional media (such as additional video lectures, pre-recorded). Blended education stretches these extremes more towards one another. In blended models it is not unusual to find examples of on-campus students also having access to the asynchronous assimilative options that were once the domain of the distance students or of distance students learning from synchronous, streamed lectures.

Table 6.1 Teaching Possibilities Across Learning Activities and Immediacy of Activity

	Synchronous	Asynchronous
Assimilative	• Lectures (lecture theatre and/or streamed) • Teaching tutorials	• Readings • Supplemental video and audio materials • Recorded lectures
Facilitative	• Conversations (face-to-face and/or virtual) • Practica/placement/application	• Conversations (virtual) • Practica/placement/application

94 Teaching Roles

The Potential of Asynchronous Dialogue

While the assimilative mix is the one that students will most encounter, it is the mix of facilitative activities that will determine the tutorial role. In the narratives of Chapter 5, a highly collaborative set of fortnightly conversations was assumed as part of the core; clearly, facilitating these conversations becomes an important part of the tutor's function. A core needn't require fortnightly conversations. In fact, in DDE it is possible for online conversation to not be applied at all and for the tutor role to consist of marking and student support. However, the asynchronous nature of DDE links it naturally to the potential for online discussion forums to deepen education and broaden student support options.

The DDE model is decidedly asynchronous in nature, but it can also accommodate additional synchronous activities. A main difference between on-campus and DDE is that in the latter, synchronous events are not at the heart of the model. Asynchronous approaches lend themselves well to engagement, enlightenment and empowerment and are also compatible with accessibility, scalability and personalisation. Asynchronous techniques provide a very powerful means of facilitative activity. Wegerif (2013) introduces the notion of dialogic education, whereby learning takes place as perspectives are shared rather than solely as the result of information transmission. Part of the role of education, Wegerif proposes, is to expand students' ability to appropriately participate in dialogue and therefore expand their capacity for thinking; he claims that 'the aim of education is not only an educated person but also a better quality of conversation' (2013, p. 27). Asynchronous means of communication such as discussion forums are ideal for such interaction. Table 6.2 contrasts synchronous and asynchronous dialogue, with online discussion forums in mind.

Additionally, in asynchronous communication a message's author can be quickly identified and their profile checked; it is easy to read a message in the context of its

Table 6.2 Features of Synchronous and Asynchronous Communication

Synchronous	Asynchronous
• **Immediacy** – students are together at the same time, enabling conversational dialogue and exploration of ill-defined problems • **Spontaneity** – there is room for the unexpected • **Presence** – participants can see and respond easily to one another's emotional states, making it easier to enthuse others (especially in face-to-face sessions); communication is likely to better reflect student feelings • **Efficiency** – a matter can be settled in minutes, whereas with asynchronous communications it might take days	• **Flexibility** – independence of time and place • **Broad participation** – not restricted to linear discussion, nor requiring assertive interjection • **Time to reflect** – students can read and carefully consider the contributions of others • **Time to compose** – students can carefully prepare their contributions before communicating them • **Review** – communications are stored, and can therefore be reviewed by students (also true of recorded or archived synchronous sessions)

author. The features of Table 6.2 can be readily appreciated by a comparison of stylised synchronous and asynchronous dialogue flows in Figures 6.1 and 6.2 below.

Figure 6.1 illustrates the single flow of conversation in synchronous dialogue, initiated by the educator (E). The conversation progresses from one student to the other, with Students 1, 2 and 3 most dominant. Student 4 only participates once. The advantage of an asynchronous dialogue is clear from Figure 6.2.

In Figure 6.2 there is much more participation (including from Student 5, who couldn't get a word in edgeways in the synchronous comparison!). There is also much more for the educator to summarise at the conclusion of the conversation. Asynchronous dialogue is a recommended component of a core approach to DDE, which has obvious implications for the function of the tutor. Using asynchronous dialogue well in education requires a foundation of relevant subject knowledge, effective learning activity design and professional facilitation.

It seems that asynchronous online forums no longer get the press they once did, perhaps because in any model other than DDE they are simply not scalable; they are also technologically simple, so not as flashy as other approaches such as, say, game-based learning, VR and custom learning pathways. There are alternative means to forums for encouraging asynchronous interaction. Blogs, ePortfolios and social media interaction can also be applied. In on-campus and on-campus blended settings student still get to meet face-to-face, so such means are seldom considered necessary.

Student group size is also an important element for effective online dialogue, though the appropriate size of each student group will depend on the core selected

Figure 6.1 Dialogue Flow in Synchronous Discussion.

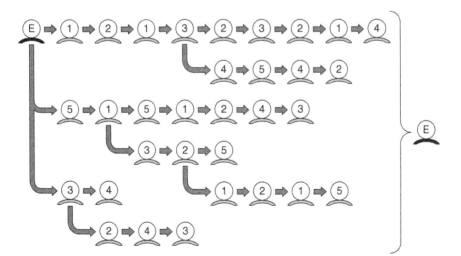

Figure 6.2 Dialogue Flow in Asynchronous Discussion.

96 Teaching Roles

and the type of online discussion envisaged. In MOOCs, to take an extreme example, the volume of asynchronous messages makes dialogue ineffective; more is said than can possibly be read and engaged with. All that might be hoped for is that students get a general sense of what the previous 20 or so students might have thought at the time they engaged with the same materials.

In distance education contexts, online discussion forums generally need to be well designed, compulsory and supported by dedicated tutorial staff to be effective. Compulsory asynchronous engagement is a recommended element of any DDE core, with flow-on dependencies on both the experts who teach, and the learning activity mix selected for each module. Asynchronous dialogue also assists with the relational element of DDE and provides valuable data for analytics. The remainder of this chapter assumes a core with compulsory asynchronous engagement in place, and a class or cohort size of approximately 20 to 25 students.[1] Decisions about the role asynchronous online discussion will take in the core are fundamental to the number, role and function of tutorial staff.

Different core approaches are certainly possible, even to the extent of having no deliberate cohort-based online discussion. Key to DDE is the bias towards asynchronous (as opposed to synchronous) engagement and the availability of tutorial support on that basis.

I suggest that a core with an active tutor role will assume asynchronous dialogue characteristic of Wegerif's dialogic education, which is made up of three principles:

1. Questions are carefully framed to encourage reflection and good answers.
2. Answers are not end points but a stimulus for further questions in a long chain of dialogue.
3. The teacher's role is to weave contributions into a coherent whole, leading [participants][2] to find meaning and helping them think of further questions. (2013, p. 14)

Wegerif is quick to acknowledge that what he terms monologic or transmissive means of educating still have a part to play; however, this must be in a context of dialogue.

Ultimately in DDE the teaching function is predominantly asynchronous, and both assimilative elements (readings, video and audio materials) and the design of facilitative activities are generally prepared before the module is released. What is designed in advance will seldom change, unless the learning activities require correction or need to be updated or improved. So, then, are all student learning encounters preordained? Fortunately, with reference to Table 6.1, facilitative activities can be designed to provide customisation and personalisation within the study period. Online discussion and assessment feedback, both asynchronous in nature, can be tailored to individual students. Everything else is predetermined.

The design and execution of effective asynchronous facilitative activities requires multiple skillsets working in harmony. Consider this example of two online discussion briefs:

Teaching Roles 97

1. What are the strengths of Davis's model? What are its weaknesses?
2. For the next 2 weeks we will be considering Davis's model and how well it works in practice.

- In Week 1, I'd like for you to explain in about 100 words how the model might apply in your own immediate context. Don't worry about what other theorists have talked about, just describe your own impressions.
- In Week 2 I'd like for you to reflect on all Week 1 contributions and explain the strengths and weaknesses of the model, drawing on others' experiences and whatever else occurs to you (introduce the theorists here, too, if you want to). Aim for about 150 words in this post.

I'll draw together the results in a summary post.

Clearly the two briefs are quite different. Let's imagine that both are compulsory. The first brief is difficult for students to engage with. What is expected? How will the posts be engaged with? Is the brief a discussion, or simply an opportunity for students to share their own independent thoughts? What will the tutor be contributing (indeed, is there even a tutor)? The second brief is much more detailed, and it's clear that there will be active tutorial involvement. The second activity will take more time but is far easier for students to engage with.

Drawing on these two sample briefs I'd like to make two observations. First, effective facilitative activities, particularly for online discussion, require a well-conceived brief. It's not enough to set a question; instead, online discussion requires a carefully framed *invitation* that brings together the expertise that both a lead academic and a learning activity designer can provide. The invitation also determines just what it is that the tutor role will contribute, and shapes what pastoral support staff might draw from in order to identify and assist students who either do not participate or struggle in their participation. Subject knowledge, an effective student brief, personalised facilitation and sympathetic pastoral support are all elements of success in online discussion. Seldom will a single academic have the requisite ability or opportunity to provide accessible, scalable and personalised online discussion engagement.

Second, because of the way facilitative activities (particularly asynchronous conversation) create specific expectations of the tutorial role, their use (or not) ought to be well defined in the core. Consistent expectations of the tutor role add to the simplicity and scalability of the DDE model. Should the use of facilitative activities not be well defined, their use across modules will likely vary, reducing scalability and changing the tutorial workload across modules. It is the role of the core to define how the roles of lead academic, learning activity designer, tutor and pastoral support staff interrelate. Agreeing the role of asynchronous online conversation in the core is critical for determining how teaching functions and the configuration of the operating model (see Chapter 8).

These observations force the question: who is the teacher in the DDE model?

98 Teaching Roles

Who is the Teacher?

In 2011, as already described in Chapter 2, I was challenged with the task of preparing a teaching and learning strategy for the Open Polytechnic, a dedicated distance learning institution. Traditionally the strategy had been prepared from the perspective of academic faculty. I was determined to take a more inclusive approach, as I was conscious of the considerable effort invested by learning activity designers and module writers (the latter not always academic staff) in what students experienced. A key question we needed to confront was 'Who is the teacher?'. In a distance education model, who does the teaching? In our cross-unit conversations it became apparent that traditional views were inadequate.

I draw from the resulting strategy here in some length, as it summarises the view of teaching central to DDE (note that the word *ako*, a *te reo* Māori term, combines the concepts of both teaching and learning).[3]

> *Ako* is at the heart of all that we do and aspire to at Open Polytechnic. *Ako* contributes to the success of our students, and provides them with quality education programmes which engage, enlighten and empower students to new challenges, new discoveries, and new potential through relevant and valued qualifications. Through teaching we transform learners, progress aspirations and improve livelihoods, which ultimately enriches our nation. Our graduates think and do as practitioners think and do.
>
> Our understanding of 'teaching' is distinctive because of our specialisation in distance education, whereby "academics and specialist general staff together form an integral part of the teaching system" (Evans & Nation, 2000, p. 3). **Teaching** is the design and use of intentional activities to bring about active participation by students, to develop understanding, knowledge, skills and attributes. At Open Polytechnic, teaching is an integrated activity that includes curriculum and course development, and student support.
>
> (Open Polytechnic, 2013, p. 3)

Teaching in DDE is more correctly considered an integrated system, a function more than a role. The emphasis is not so much on *who the teacher is* but rather *how teaching takes place*. Ideally the academic authority and subject voice, learning activity design, tutor facilitation and pastoral support activities all combine into a seamless, mutually complementary teaching experience for the student. In DDE, teaching is a shared experience of multiple teachers, each contributing their particular expertise. When considering pedagogy, it is more correct in DDE to emphasise teaching as a function rather than the role of a single teacher.

Teac*hing* over teac*her* is compatible with the Community of Inquiry (CoI) framework, an archetypal way of conceptualising online education illustrated in Figure 6.3.

In the CoI framework, the educational experience is a combination of social (identification with community), cognitive (construction of meaning) and teaching (overall design) elements. It is not the purpose of this book to expound the CoI,

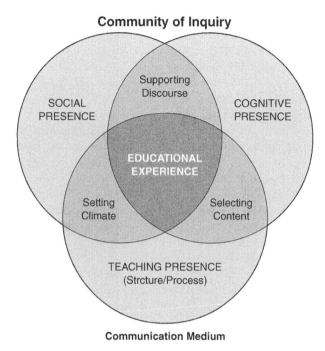

Figure 6.3 The Community of Inquiry Framework.
Source: From Garrison, 2017, p. 25. Copyright 2017 from *E-learning in the 21st century: A community of inquiry framework for research and practice* (3rd ed.) by D. R. Garrison. Reproduced by permission of Taylor and Francis Group, LLC, a division of Informa plc.

other than to point out that it considers teaching a presence rather than a role.[4] Teaching presence is associated with the design of instruction, facilitation and the overall shape of the intentional social and cognitive presence elements. It is referred to as the 'unifying force' (Garrison & Vaughan, 2008, p. 25) of the framework. Critically, the CoI does not refer to teach*er* presence because it is assumed that all participants, including students, are able to express an element of teaching in the learning community.

Teaching as Development and Dialogic

It is helpful to consider teaching in DDE as consisting of two interdependent activities: those that are designed in advance before a student studies a module, and those that take place as the module is studied. I term these the development and dialogic activities, respectively.[5] Dialogic takes us back to the term used by Wegerif mentioned earlier, a term emphasising the importance of students entering into dialogue rather than simply assimilating information. In Chapter 4 I described the 'Experttaught' principle with reference to Palmer's subject-oriented teaching. In keeping with this, the point of the dialogic is to encourage the student to become conversant with the subject. Sound development will encourage a dialogic experience for students. Figure 6.4 shows the relationship across the development and dialogic activities.

As in classic distance education, DDE recognises development and dialogic as discreet yet interdependent activities. The *development* of module materials is predetermined, prepared in advance by a team consisting of a lead academic and learning activity designer working in partnership and including tutor representation.[6] The *dialogic* takes place as students study a module. During the dialogic, the emphasis of teaching is on tuition and feedback, based on the learning activities prepared in development. Tutors and pastoral support staff are predominant in the dialogic, though the lead academic might also be involved. Teaching, then, is the domain of the lead academic and learning activity designer in development, and the tutor and pastoral support team in the dialogic (though a lead academic might – perhaps should – also function as a tutor from time to time, and might also be active in a pan-tutorial group role through webinars). A feedback loop, drawing on an evidence base made up of analytics, module evaluations and tutor comments, informs the further development of the module.

The partnership required for development is nicely illustrated by the TPACK framework.[7] TPACK is primarily concerned with how teachers might combine Technology (as enabler), Pedagogy (as how) And Content Knowledge (as what) in support of good digital education. There are three main elements to the framework, presented as forms of knowledge:

1. Technology Knowledge (TK): what is known about working with and applying technology.
2. Pedagogical Knowledge (PK): what is known about teaching method and practice.
3. Content Knowledge (CK): what is known about the subject.

Any one of the three components might provide the weakest link to DDE development. The quality of a DDE experience is determined by how well the components of TPACK intersect, illustrated in Figure 6.5.

The TPACK framework rightly identifies that there are three forms of knowledge brought to bear in module design in digital education: technical knowledge,

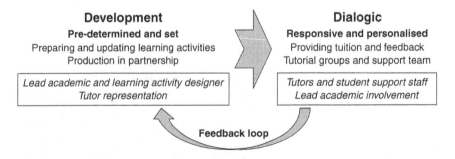

Figure 6.4 DDE Module Teaching Activities.

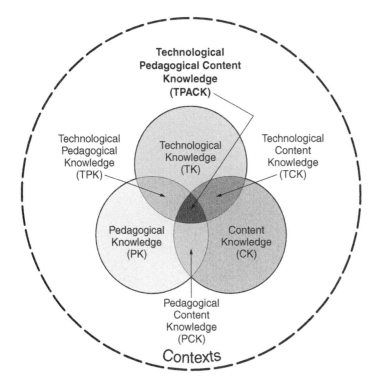

Figure 6.5 TPACK.
Source: © 2012 by tpack.org. Figure reprinted with permission.

pedagogical knowledge and content (subject) knowledge. In on-campus settings, the academic is assumed to be responsible for all three, so professional development and assistance becomes a focus for enabling digital education. In classic distance education settings, the three forms of knowledge are represented in the module design team with the academic responsible for all decision-making. In the DDE model, the lead academic provides the all-important Content Knowledge and valuable insight into Pedagogical Knowledge and (often) Technological Knowledge as it relates to the subject. A learning activity designer brings a more specialised perspective of Pedagogical Knowledge and Technological Knowledge, and acts as guardian of the core approach for consistency. Together, the lead academic and learning activity designer collaborate to develop a module (Figure 6.6).

In module development, then, the lead academic and learning activity designer collaborate in the teaching role. The challenges of collaboration in this way should not be underestimated, as both lead academics and learning activity designers tend to be highly motivated professionals with a strong sense of ownership of the student experience. Encouraging teamwork in module development is a key element of DDE's success.

In the dialogic experience, the tutor becomes much more prominent. From a student perspective, however, it is the module learning activities (pre-prepared in

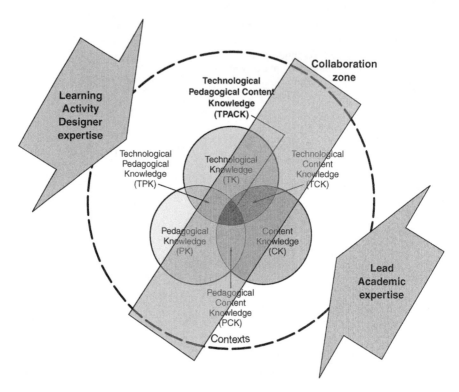

Figure 6.6 The TPACK Collaboration Zone for Module Development.
Source: Figure adapted with permission.

development) that are considered the primary means of learning. This is not to denigrate the role of the tutor, merely to make it clear that the tutor works as part of the overall teaching experience, much of which is predetermined in the development of the module materials. Most of the tutor's activity is shaped by the way in which the module is designed. The role of the tutor is to help each individual student relate to the subject, primarily through the module material and through personalised feedback to each student. The tutor becomes the direct human representative as a module is experienced by a student; the support team are more in the background. From time to time a lead academic might also become involved in the dialogic, as outlined below.

Teaching Roles in DDE

In DDE, teaching takes place before a module is experienced by students (in development) and during study activity (in dialogic). Teaching is largely asynchronous, in that students are not required to engage with ideas or one another in real time, even though there may be due dates for various activities.

Development requires an optimal combination of technology, pedagogy and content knowledge that benefits from learning activity design. Dialogic requires clear parameters for the tutorial and pastoral support functions, which complement the design decisions made during development. For the remainder of this chapter we will consider the four teaching roles of lead academic, learning activities designer, tutor and pastoral support. It is important to note that variations on the roles proposed here are certainly possible. Lead academic functions, for example, might be distributed across more than one individual.

Lead Academic

The lead academic role provides the academic rigour and the voice of the subject to the student experience. The lead academic represents the subject, and so is accountable for the development of learning objectives, the validity of assessment and the overall performance of the module. The role works with the learning activity designer in the development of module materials and assists with the dialogic. As the representative of the subject, it is important that the lead academic is concerned with research and, wherever possible, application and practice within their discipline.[8] This both maintains the lead academic's subject expertise and enhances their scholarly reputation.

Because the lead academic teaches as part of a team, there is no imperative that they become anything more than conversant with pedagogy or technology as it applies to digital teaching; the value added by their role is that of the subject's voice. As indicated earlier, this is a more confined role than that typically enjoyed by lecturers and on-campus academics. Importantly, though, the role still leaves room for innovation and expression for those lead academics who are energised teachers. The lead academic is part of a development team and works within the agreed core during module development. They are also able to propose and help design custom elements as part of the Consistent principle, providing plenty of scope for innovation alongside improving the access, scalability and personalisation of learning.

Depending on the core approach selected, the role of a lead academic may be concerned with:

- Assisting to define and enhance the core approach for the qualification they contribute to, on an ongoing basis.
- Collaborating with learning activity designers and tutors to develop the module associated with their subject and assisting in the analysis and decision-making associated with evidence of how well the module is performing.
- Contributing ideas for custom features within their module.
- Ensuring all marking is fair, consistent and provides useful and applicable feedback.
- Identifying and properly representing the key concepts relevant to the module's learning objectives.
- Keeping up to date with the latest developments within their subject, alongside research.

104　Teaching Roles

- Leading and supporting their tutorial team as an escalation point for all academic enquiries related to their module.
- Maintaining professional relationships with academic peers across the qualification they contribute to, and with other scholars related to their subject.
- Managing their tutor teams' performance and interaction with students.
- Monitoring their module's overall performance in terms of student retention and completion.
- Providing webinars, readings and updates to students and alumni as it relates to their subject and research.
- Researching their subject area, including applying their subject in practice.
- Updating module learning activities.

A lead academic can also serve as a tutor in their module, which is recommended so that they get a first-hand view of the student experience and become better able to assist tutors.

The ideal lead academic is:

- A committed team player, who respects and appreciatively engages with the pedagogical ideas and practice of others (particularly learning activity designers and tutors).
- Able to present their subject through webinar and small-group tutorial.
- Connected with other scholars in their subject area.
- Experienced in the application and practice of their subject area.
- Fluent in the application of evidence for improving student outcomes.
- Interested in the ongoing development of the tutor team accountable for the module's dialogic.
- Managerial in their monitoring and leadership of their tutorial team.
- Respected for their subject knowledge and how they represent their subject.
- Well-qualified in their subject area.

In DDE academics can focus on the subject area they are expert in. The extensive scholarship of teaching and learning and the ongoing development of technological knowledge makes it very difficult for lead academics to maintain expertise across all TPACK elements of development. Instead, the domains of pedagogical and technological knowledge are the domain of the learning activity designer.

Learning Activity Designer

The learning activity designer role is a tailored version of the instructional designer, educational designer, learning designer and TEL designer roles I have encountered across the years. Essentially the role contributes expertise in the areas of adult education, pedagogy, technology and to a certain extent project management[9] to the task of module development. The term 'learning activity designer' reinforces that the role is not solely an editing one, and neither is it concerned with preparing or formatting assimilative materials. Instead, the learning activity designer draws on a palette of learning activities (discussed in more depth in the next chapter) and the more specialised skills media developers contribute. In addition, learning activity designers serve as guardians of the qualification core and the champions of custom approaches agreed during module development.

The learning activity designer is not necessarily an expert in media development. Instead, their expertise is the art and science of learning in digital education. Their role involves identifying the key concepts of a module's learning objectives and designing effective learning activities to assist students to be educated towards those objectives. The learning activity designer assists with development of the students' learning journey across each module, and the ongoing improvement of that journey through the application of evidence to their craft.

Depending on the core approach selected, the role of a learning activity designer may be concerned with:

- Collaborating with lead academics to assist them in representing their subject to students through an effective education design.
- Complying with project management requirements related to how modules are designed and developed.
- Contributing to the core of the qualification they are associated with.
- Designing activities that lead students to fully understand the key concepts related to the module's learning objectives.
- Ensuring the production quality of all assimilative and facilitative materials and activities.
- Fully understanding the learning objectives and core approaches related to the module they are working on and ensuring overall module development is compliant.
- Identifying and understanding the key concepts of the subject, including the identification of common misconceptions as an aid to learning activity design.
- Integrating all learning activities into a coherent student experience.
- Interpreting evidence related to a module's performance and deciding on ways of improving student understanding.
- Maintaining and contributing to the knowledge base concerned with adult education, pedagogy and technology.
- Preparing module briefs for tutorial staff and the pastoral support team, and maintaining reference notes related to design decisions, copyright and updates.
- Proposing and championing agreed ideas for custom approaches.
- Researching and summarising the scholarship of effective teaching practice related to the subjects they contribute to.

The ideal learning activity designer is:

- A committed team player, who respects and appreciatively engages with the pedagogical ideas and practice of others (particularly lead academics and tutors).
- Able to gather and present evidence related to various pedagogical approaches.
- Actively researching adult education and pedagogical literature.

106 Teaching Roles

- Continuously seeking to innovate (propose custom approaches) in addition to the core.
- Fluent in the application of evidence for improving student outcomes.
- Media-development savvy, in terms of knowing how best to apply media in education.
- Part of a community of practitioners.
- Project-minded, fluent in project management and working to deadlines.
- Respected for their pedagogical and technological knowledge and how they represent them.
- Up to date with learning activity scholarship and methodology.

The crossover here with lead academic characteristics is intentional. A learning activity designer is very much an academic in their own right, with subject specialisms in adult education, pedagogical and technological knowledge. As with a lead academic, learning activity designers ought to be continuously learning and contributing to the ideas and evidence base of their subject. How lead academics and learning activity designers might best work together is considered in Chapter 7.

Tutor

The tutor role is an essential component of DDE, bringing personalisation at scale and facilitating the flexible accessibility that makes up the heart of the model. The tutor becomes the primary personal contact point for the student during the dialogic, making the tutor the teaching representative of the university across the student's period of enrolment. While tutors are subject experts in their own right, their role in the dialogic is largely defined by the learning activities that make up the development of the module. Typically, tutor activity will be based on dialogic activity, first-line academic support and providing feedback to students.

In DDE the tutor's predominant role is facilitative. Any assimilative contribution is made in response to student request; a tutor is not an online lecturer or presenter. Instead, their focus is on clarifying points already covered in the module materials and providing the facilitation required by the learning activities of the module. If module materials do not adequately facilitate students' understanding, tutors should intervene first by alerting the lead academic of the need for module materials to be revised, second by inviting the lead academic to intervene and, as a last resort, facilitating a brief presentation or making additional learning activities available. A tutor should complement and not seek to replace module learning activities.

Depending on the core approach selected, the role of a tutor may be concerned with:

- Aiding student success.
- Conducting one-to-one, one-to-few and one-to-many tutorials.
- Fulfilling the responsibilities of their module brief.
- Giving feedback to the lead academic related to the module's development and performance.

- Having complete familiarity with the module learning activities.
- Intervening personally to promote student engagement.
- Maintaining the CRM as it relates to their students.
- Monitoring each student's performance based on their interaction with students and their student dashboard.
- Promoting student understanding of module concepts.
- Providing extensive and personalised feedback to students through asynchronous dialogue and assignment marking.
- Welcoming new students.

The ideal tutor is:

- A lifelong learner, eager to maintain their subject knowledge and teaching skills.
- Approachable and available to the students they are responsible for.
- Comfortable in escalating student queries to a lead academic or member of pastoral support staff, and recommending a student contact pastoral support when necessary.
- Committed to the success of each student.
- Continuously aware of each student's progress.
- Consistent in their activity for the duration of their cohort.
- Fluent with the learning objectives and learning activities in the module.
- Part of the tutor and lead academic community.
- Reliable in their updating of CRM data related to their interaction with students.
- Responsive to feedback regarding their own performance.
- Systematised in their application of analytics data to their activity in student support.

In DDE a tutor is not a free agent. The role is heavily contextualised by the agreed core approach for the module and the requirements of tuition established in the development of the module. However, the tutor must apply their intuition, subject knowledge, tutorial and interpersonal skills to each engagement with students. The tutor role, though highly structured, must promote the application of judgement and discretion. This reflects the Consistent principle; the core approach determined for each module ought to include room for the custom elements of each tutor's strengths to also be expressed. In practice, there is often considerable overlap of the tutor role with those of lead academic, learning activity designer and pastoral support during the dialogic.

Pastoral Support Staff

The pastoral support team might be made up of both staff and those students especially invited and appointed to provide peer support. Pastoral support should be thought of as a package of support services that include administrative, enrolment, library, peer mentoring, personal, programme planning, study skills and technical support services. Ideally, all of these will be available through the same contact point, providing students with a single and comprehensive support service. Students should

108 Teaching Roles

also be properly briefed as to what to expect from their tutors and what to request from the pastoral support team.

While pastoral support staff work behind the scenes, their collective work is an essential element of what makes a university a university, and what makes students successful. All pastoral support team roles are highly service-oriented and are supported themselves through a well-maintained information base. Pastoral support is frequently taken for granted by both universities and students. The services it provides are typically hygiene factors, in that if all is well they are seldom praised, but if there is a glitch or a poor service experience it is keenly felt by students. Pastoral support staff must be as professional and supported as the tutorial team.

Delineation across all support service types must be clear, with no duplication of effort and with well-understood accountabilities for every element. The level of coordination required necessitates a matrix management approach, or else a single student-facing unit. Where pastoral support staff are not based in the same unit, all services should be accessible through the same interface and work to coordinated standards and protocols; from the student perspective, there should be one support team and not multiple units to deal with. The primary interface to support services should be online and available through a variety of services, but a well-staffed, generously available toll-free phone number remains a must at the time of writing.

Depending on the core approach selected, the role of pastoral support staff may be to provide a one-stop shop concerned with:

- Applying analytics and further evidence towards the improvement of all aspects of service.
- Maintaining all elements of the student experience outside of the dialogic.
- Maintaining CRM records as they relate to student requests and responses.
- Meeting clear and agreed student service levels.
- Making proactive contact with students based on the overall pastoral support mandate.
- Managing student handover when students change cohort.
- Offering between-module contact and advice.
- Offering enrolment and programme planning advice.
- Offering study skills advice.
- Organising and facilitating all-of-university and student body events, including online presentations from academics, student news and special events.
- Proposing and championing policy changes to improve student outcomes.
- Providing a full and complete service response to all student requests.
- Providing administrative support related to all elements of student policy.
- Providing technical support including resetting passwords, software troubleshooting and application orientation.
- Supplying an integrated support experience for all students.
- Tracking and closing student requests when escalation is required.
- Training and supporting a student peer-mentoring network.
- Updating automated and proactive messaging systems in response to feedback and analytics.

Proactive contact to all students is based on standard messages sent at key times; for example, an automated reminder of a self-paced referencing module 3 weeks before an essay assignment is due, information about local university-related events, motivational stories from other students, promotion of graduation ceremonies and reminders of the next module students are enrolled in 4 weeks before their cohort is due to finish (or else an automated reminder to enrol!).

In a well-designed DDE system, students will have access to their own personal information, with write access to elements including preferred email and contact details. An effective UX for online administrative systems will assist in freeing pastoral support time for those exceptions that represent the best use of the more specialised knowledge held across the pastoral support team. The design of pastoral support services requires intensive effort and top-level coordination. Ideally, a single point of accountability will exist across all pastoral support functions so as to present a coordinated and always-improving service.

The ideal pastoral support team member is:

- An active and inquisitive listener.
- An experienced student themselves, able to readily adopt an empathetic approach to student support.
- Capable of explaining things patiently and without criticism.
- Careful to document each student encounter.
- Dedicated to providing an efficient, professional and comprehensive outcome.
- Eager to learn about all elements of pastoral support, rather than their main area of expertise.
- Fully aware of their domain of expertise, and aware of where the expertise of others may be more useful.
- One who remains with the case until it is resolved to the student's satisfaction.
- Truly pastoral, in that they can have delicate conversations with students who might be distressed or aggressive and bring the conversation to a satisfactory conclusion.
- Up to date with the knowledge base related to their area of support.

It is good practice to provide support team members with revolving opportunities so that they become familiar with multiple service areas. While the pastoral support role is highly structured, even templated, there are always circumstances requiring an empowered and personalised response.

Accountability for Student Success

In all organisations it is good practice to have a single point of accountability for performance. Multiple accountabilities bring uncertainty and cloudiness to decision-making and improvement. So, where there are multiple teaching roles, who is accountable for student success?

Rather than considering student success as a single component, it is helpful to discern between the components that contribute to student success. For example, in

110 Teaching Roles

the DDE mix suggested in this chapter, immediate accountability is shared as follows.

- The academic integrity of the module: lead academic.
- The effectiveness of learning activities: learning activity designer.
- Module dialogic: tutor.
- Pastoral support: pastoral support team.

These accountabilities reinforce the role descriptions in this chapter. The development team of lead academic and learning activity designer must collaborate effectively; tutors must leverage the module materials, encourage student interaction and provide full and useful feedback; the pastoral support team must provide a comprehensive function. All have specific and interdependent accountabilities for overall student success and are designed to provide the level of teaching suggested by Biggs and Tang in this chapter's opening quotation.

The pastoral support team is accountable for multiple elements and might be considered a catch-all for accountabilities not explicitly addressed by the other three roles – albeit on an improvement rather than a blame basis. For example, if students are being enrolled in a qualification they are clearly not ready for, accountability for fixing the issue should rest with the pastoral support team; the issue is likely to be an inadequate policy related to enrolment standards (if it is a breach of policy, the breach can be traced to its source to be corrected!).

Management of these accountabilities must also be clear. Ultimately, in DDE lead academics are accountable for the performance of their tutor body, who are in turn accountable for the student dialogic experience. Depending on the size of the tutor group, a lead academic might employ the services of a tutor manager; however, the lead academic is still accountable for overall tutor performance. In turn, a head of school or dean will be accountable for the performance of their lead academics. A senior management lead will be accountable for all elements of learning activity designer work, and another will be accountable for all pastoral support activity. These overall points of accountability will themselves report to a single, top layer of management to ensure a coordinated and responsive approach to student success.

All of these roles and accountabilities function within an overall series of systems responsible for analytics, IT infrastructure, curriculum maintenance and accreditation, results processing, professional development, and so on. It is extremely difficult to try to neatly separate teaching roles from their underlying support infrastructure, as all of these elements are to some degree interdependent; we will return to this point and the importance of systems thinking in Chapter 8.

Teaching as an Interdependent Activity

Universities can be very politicised in how they operate. The necessity of academic and administrative staff to serve as partners for a university to gain and maintain its identity often leads to conflict, particularly in terms of where one's turf ends and another's begins. What constitutes teaching is at the very heart of the university endeavour; teaching in DDE is a shared, interdependent activity. The architecture of teaching proposed for DDE is a defining element of the model and is critical to a university's ability to achieve the access, scalability and quality benefits DDE can offer.

In DDE, teaching is, at the core, asynchronous – which has clear implications for teaching roles. In my description of teaching roles, I have assumed a core approach based on asynchronous discussion and a central role for module materials. Of course, it is perfectly possible for the principles of DDE to be applied differently and for variations of the four roles to be in place. The role most often adjusted is that of the tutor. Care must be taken, though, because if the roles vary too much, it may prove difficult or even impossible to maintain all the principles of DDE. If, for example, the learning activity designer role is subsumed into the lead academic one or learning activity services are made available on an as-needed rather than critical basis, the Consistent, Data-analytics-driven, Evidence-based, Expert-taught, Learning-activity-oriented, Relational, Success-driven and Systematic principles are likely compromised – in which case the model is no longer DDE.

The lead academic role as defined in this chapter, and the implications for what might traditionally be considered the sole charge of the academic, is central to DDE. Maintaining the traditional academic role as sole source of pedagogy risks taking a fragmented, academic-centric view of education that runs counter to accessibility, scalability and personalisation. For academics, the lead academic role presents opportunity rather than compromise and for students the lead academic role assists with having a consistent, constantly improving and educationally sound experience across their qualification.

As indicated earlier in this chapter, module development is central to the teaching roles of lead academic, learning activity designer and tutor. The next chapter, on learning activity design, describes how modules are best developed for DDE and provides further insight to the functions of these three roles.

Activities

1. Which of the four schools of thought as to what digital education (no change, blended addition, academic as designer or specialist-assisted) might mean for on-campus staff best describes your own university?
2. What role does Wegerif's concept of the dialogic already play in your teaching, or the teaching across your university? Are carefully framed, reflective questions leading to dialogue a central part of education?
3. How do development (the creation of pre-set activities) and dialogic (tuition and feedback) take place in your module, or at your university? How well is their interdependence managed?
4. How does your university's context shape the TPACK model at your university? How are the Technological, Pedagogical and Content Knowledge elements of digital education represented across the teaching function?
5. The four teaching roles of lead academic, learning activity designer, tutor and pastoral support team are designed to be interdependent. What challenges do

112 Teaching Roles

you foresee at your own university, should these roles be developed as proposed in the DDE model?

6. Where are accountabilities for the academic integrity of modules, the effectiveness of learning activities, module dialogic and pastoral support in your university? How well does the accountability work?

Notes

1. The ideal number of students in a single group or cohort depends on many factors. Some suggest cohorts of 200 are ideal; others, fewer than 10. The ideal number is the one that best aligns with the overall core approach.
2. Wegerif's original text here reads 'children'; however, the principle is the same.
3. The same strategy also introduced the principles of whakapiri, whakamārama and whakamana encountered in Chapter 2.
4. See https://coi.athabascau.ca/coi-model/ for more detail about the CoI and the scholarship surrounding it.
5. I deliberately avoid the term 'delivery' here, because it implies a one-way relationship from university to student and the assimilation of content rather than a participation in meaning-making. 'Dialogic' as a term may seem clumsy, but it is much more accurate.
6. The lead academic and learning activity designer work as part of an overall development team.
7. See http://matt-koehler.com/tpack2/tpack-explained/for an overview.
8. At the Open Polytechnic, a provider of vocational education, the lead academic function is often performed by respected practitioners who are expert in their vocation.
9. The Open Polytechnic has a dedicated project management role, and the Open University a commissioning role for project management. At the very least learning activity designers need an understanding of project management even if such roles are in place.

References

Biggs, J., & Tang, C. (2011). *Teaching for quality learning at university: What the student does* (4th ed.). Maidenhead, England: McGraw Hill & Open University Press.

Evans, T., & Nation, D. (2000). *Changing university teaching: Reflections on creating educational technologies.* London: Kogan Page.

Garrison, D. R. (2017). *E-learning in the 21st century: A community of inquiry framework for research and practice* (3rd ed.). New York, NY: Routledge.

Garrison, D. R., & Vaughan, N. D. (2008). *Blended learning in higher education: Framework, principles, and guidelines.* San Francisco: Jossey-Bass.

Kezar, A., Maxey, D. & Holcombe, E. (2016). The professoriate reconsidered: A study of new faculty models. Retrieved 29 January 2020 from www.nea.org/home/68481.htm.

Open Polytechnic. (2013). *Teaching and learning ako strategy 2013–2016.* Lower Hut, NZ: Author.

Sandeen, C. A. (2014). *Unbundling versus designing faculty roles.* Washington, DC: American Council on Education Centre for Education Attainment & Innovation. Retrieved 29 January 2020 from www.acenet.edu/Documents/Unbundling-Versus-Designing-Faculty-Roles.pdf.

Seelig, C., Cadwallader, A. & Standring, D. (2019). Transformational change in delivery at Open Polytechnic, New Zealand. *Journal of Learning for Development, 6*(1).

Wegerif, R. (2013). *Dialogic: Education for the internet age.* New York, NY: Springer.

Chapter 7

Module Development
Context, Direction and Practice

> Where online education does work, it shifts the center of attention from faculty to student, from enrollment to engagement, from content to experience.
>
> (Anand, 2016, Chapter 30, para. 16)

Let me start with two terminological bugbears, which will help to situate this chapter. The first is the term 'student-centred'; the second, 'content'.

I'm certain we would all agree that the term 'student-centred' has a reassuring, common-sense ring to it. But what does it mean? In the case of a conflict, does it favour student satisfaction over student outcomes? To what extent might being student-centred require us to abdicate what we know might be in students' overall interests and development? The problem with 'student-centred' is that it glosses over the complex trade-offs that will always require the application of judgement and evidence in education. Think of it in terms of trying to develop a driver-centred road code. Is it driver-centred to let drivers judge for themselves if their car is road-worthy, set their own speed limit and decide who to give way to, or is it more driver-centred to insist on a series of rules that everyone must follow for the safety of all? 'Student-centred' can also lead to simplistic dismissal of approaches that might be more effective if they were better implemented. After all, a well-conceived, expertly delivered and memorable lecture must surely be more student-centred than a poorly designed, loosely facilitated and vaguely implemented group project. In this chapter I will instead apply the term 'education-centred', particularly as reflected across the terms 'whakapiri', 'whakamārama' and 'whakamana' (engagement, enlightenment and empowerment) that we first encountered in Chapter 2. The criterion becomes whether students are engaged, enlightened and empowered; the extent to which this might overlap with student preference is not of primary import.

The second term, 'content', has always struck me as unfortunate shorthand for learning materials. Content implies something that can be transferred from one place to another, as if a student should gather, stack and reassemble knowledge-as-stuff from the raw material provided to them, as if education were some sort of construction project. Content implies assimilation and education as merely writing, recording and linking to stuff that students read, listen to or watch. I much prefer the term 'learning activities' as a much broader acknowledgement of what ought to be

114 Module Development

designed for students to participate in. Content implies consumption, filling the brain; activity implies exercise, stretching the brain.

Underneath my discomfort with both bugbear terms is that they imply a single point of reference (the student, the content) and indicate an inadequate philosophy of education. A student-centred approach suggests the student is a customer seeking satisfaction, whereas our role is to educate; 'education-centred' is a term that better describes our approach. Content suggests assimilation is the best means of teaching and so we ought to provide students with comprehensive *stuff*, whereas our role is to get students to think differently as the means of knowing more. 'Learning activities' is a much better term than 'content' for describing what we are concerned with here.

The DDE principle of being learning-activity-oriented recognises that there are many different levels of learning, diverse subject contexts and multiple learning activity options, which bring a rich variety of practice. We must focus on *education* and make use of the broadest possible learning activity palette in our quest to provide education that is accessible, scalable and personalised – and we must be cautious in giving simplistic solutions any space in that endeavour.

This chapter is concerned with module development and so we will be primarily considering learning design. There is a fragmented yet substantial literature on learning design; it is, after all, a design science, to draw from the title of a recommended and authoritative book by Diana Laurillard, cited later in this chapter. What follows here is a single pathway through the various models, frameworks, terminology and practice that should at least serve to illustrate how learning activity design is at the heart of DDE.

The Pedagogy of Education Outcomism

I have another bugbear, one more philosophical in nature. In learning design circles, it is not uncommon for an educator to be challenged as to their pedagogical colour: are you a behaviourist, constructivist, social constructivist? Or, depending on the inquisitor, might you alternatively be instructivist, cognitivist, connectivist? Such debates often generate simplistic posturing, argument over definition or (perhaps worse of all) the neglect of various educational approaches that might be, depending on the circumstances, highly effective. The question also runs counter to the simple truth that 'we do not know enough about human learning to be able to produce a single comprehensive theory' (Jarvis, 2006, Preface and acknowledgements, para. 3). I suggest a new term entirely, one which can be open-ended in actual practice and which aptly serves the goal of formal education: 'education outcomism' (making me an education outcomist), which better represents an education-centred orientation. The remainder of this chapter will unpack just what this term means as the basis of a learning activity orientation.

Returning to the ideas in Chapter 2, the purpose of education is to engage, enlighten and empower. Education is also an all-of-person activity, which takes place through an intentional series of experiences offered to the student. Jarvis notes that learning takes place when our inner self encounters the outer world, 'usually

Module Development 115

when the two are in some tension' (2006, Chapter 1, Section 2, para. 8). Jarvis terms this intentional tension 'disjuncture'; Mezirow terms the tension 'dissonance'. The objective and effect are the same, in that education deliberately attempts to jar the student's understanding of the subject such that emotions, thoughts and actions form a better perspective, informed by substantiated knowledge and within an intentional framework.

Table 2.1 in Chapter 2 models the form of education that serves as the basis for this book. Now, I'll repeat the same table (here labelled Table 7.1) and add that the table is a summary of education outcomism. As Table 7.1 indicates, education outcomism involves the application of any suitable pedagogical approach in the pursuit of course and graduate outcomes.

I define education outcomism as an orientation that intelligently and defensibly applies whatever learning activity will assist students to achieve the learning outcomes they are pursuing at any given time towards the qualification the student is pursuing. This definition is suitably open-ended enough to justify various approaches. In practice, education outcomism is oriented towards qualification level, credits and graduate outcomes, which in turn are applied to module outcomes and assessment. Ultimately, all of these give shape to the learning activity design students encounter in each module.

Education outcomism designs experiences for students that are appropriate for what it is the student is tasked to learn. Whatever is demonstrated to work in helping students achieve agreed learning outcomes, in the context of the overall university operating model, is what is used. Naturally this places a great deal of import on a university's operating model (next chapter) and learning outcomes!

My position as an education outcomist does not seek to sidestep the various pedagogical categories mentioned earlier. Instead, education outcomists recognise

Table 7.1 The Framework of Education Outcomism

Education Outcomes (Peters)	Education Elements (Durie)	Education Mechanisms in Practice
iii. Initiation into domains of knowledge and skill	Engagement	Learning activity design[a]
ii. Acquiring knowledge and intellectual skills, and development of understanding	Enlightenment	Module learning outcomes and assessment
i. Change for the better	Empowerment	Qualification level, credits and graduate outcomes

Note

a Table 7.1 provides a useful means of defining key terms in their educational setting. *Learning activity design*, for example, might be defined as the means by which educators seek to *engage* students as an *initiation into domains of knowledge and skill*, in the context of *course/module outcomes and assessment* in the pursuit of *graduate outcomes*. *Empowerment* describes how *engaged* and *enlightened* students achieve *qualification outcomes reflecting a particular level and credit value* as a *change for the better*.

116   Module Development

the part each pedagogical category might play in pursuit of the overall educational endeavour, depending on what it is the educator is deliberately and transparently seeking to accomplish in the student. Education outcomism is an ensign made up of the pedagogical colours (note, plural) I hold dear, which for the record would tend towards instructivism[1] based on cognitivism, naturally recognising that learning is always constructed (yes, even in social contexts with others) by the learner in response to the part-behavioural preferences (and implicit requirements) of the curriculum.[2]

If my definition of education outcomism does not convince you, perhaps its application may. We begin by reversing the order of Table 7.1, so that we follow Peters' education outcomes from i. to iii. While from a student perspective these activities are encountered from top to bottom, a university will design from bottom to top. To apply education outcomism we need to think first in terms of qualification (level, credit and outcomes), then module outcomes and assessment, then learning activity design, as shown in Table 7.2. As we will see, there is an interdependence across all these terms, though generally design decisions cascade from qualification level, credit and outcomes to module outcomes and assessment, and module outcomes and assessment to learning activity design. Each of these layers of design also have a reverse influence, such that learning activity design ought to also further refine module outcomes and assessment, and module outcomes and assessment ought to further refine qualification factors.

From an education outcomism perspective, the qualification provides the context within which learning activity design takes place. The design of a qualification must conform to particular expectations of accreditation and formal recognition, particularly the assigned level and credit values, which in turn influence the graduate outcomes. Graduate outcomes are those characteristics and capabilities achieved by a student who has successfully completed a course of study.[3] Qualification level, credit value and graduate outcomes are foundational to all that follows. Generally, these three elements are formally approved by academic boards and accrediting agencies according to strict rules. With reference to the observations about learning in Chapter 2, it is at the level of the qualification that the shape of the smudge representing the student's intended development is defined.

Table 7.2 Foundations of Education Outcomism

Factor	Provides	In Answer To
Qualification level, credit and graduate outcomes	Teaching *context*	How is the qualification formally defined?
Module outcomes and assessment	Teaching *direction*	What capabilities will characterise success for the qualification and each module?
Learning activity design	Teaching *practice*	What activities will students undertake to develop and demonstrate their capabilities?

Qualification considerations set the context for module outcomes (the characteristics and capabilities achieved by a student successfully completing a specific module) and assessment. Module outcomes and assessment go together because their relationship is symbiotic. Much of educational effectiveness relies on the quality of how graduate outcomes are expressed across module outcomes, and how well module outcomes are reflected in assessment; therefore, this relationship is critical in DDE. The effects of this relationship flow on to learning activity design and, ultimately, the tutorial role and student experience.

Thus, module development flows from formal qualification definition to the approval of outcomes to the preparation of assessment and learning activity design. Together, these form the curriculum of a qualification. This chapter will move from one development stage to the next, from teaching context at the qualification level, to the teaching direction set by each module's outcomes and assessment, to the level of learning activity design practice.

Context: Qualification Level, Credit and Outcomes

Chapter 3 introduced the offering of qualifications, subjects and disciplines as one of the four critical questions defining how a university operates. In the context of that critical question the matter of levels was addressed, and the New Zealand Qualifications Framework was provided as an example (Table 3.1).

The SEEC group (initially the South East England Consortium, though now with a broader mandate) maintains a useful set of level equivalency descriptors across the frameworks used across many countries, available from their website, www.seec. org.uk. The 2016 revision describes the setting, knowledge and understanding, cognitive skills, performance and practice, and personal and enabling skills that might be appropriate at each level of study.

Table 7.3, drawing from the summary descriptors in SEEC (2016), shows the SEEC summary descriptors for each level of study across some country qualifications frameworks. The levels and associated descriptors form the basis of qualification and module outcomes and are the touchstone of education outcomism. While the level numbers and specific wording across the Australian, Canadian, New Zealand and United Kingdom systems differ, they essentially work in the same way and are broadly equivalent once the level numbers are reconciled. Each system also includes a more detailed set of parameters useful for developing qualification and module learning outcomes.

From Table 7.3 we can see that a bachelor's degree (Level 6 United Kingdom, Level 7 Australia and New Zealand) will result in graduates who can 'critically review, consolidate and extend a systematic and coherent body of knowledge'. To achieve this overall expected knowledge outcome, the graduate has to study a certain number of credits (a currency made up of learning hours experienced in the form of modules) across Levels 4–6 (United Kingdom) or 5–7 (Australia and New Zealand), beginning with a broad understanding of the fields of work or study, becoming more specialised and adding more depth to their learning as they progress.

A country's educational system (or recognised accreditor) will dictate educational outcomes and credit requirements in some detail. In jurisdictions guided by the

118   Module Development

Table 7.3 SEEC Level Descriptors Showing United Kingdom and Australia/New Zealand Level Equivalence. Used with Permission

SEEC Level (Cross UK)	Australia & NZ Level	SEEC Summary Level Descriptor (2016 Revision)
3	4	Apply knowledge and skills in a range of complex activities demonstrating comprehension of relevant theories; access and analyse information independently and make reasoned judgements, selecting from a considerable choice of procedures in familiar and unfamiliar contexts and direct own activities, with some responsibility for the output of others.
4	5	Develop a rigorous approach to the acquisition of a broad knowledge base; employ a range of specialised skills; evaluate information, using it to plan and develop investigative strategies and to determine solutions to a variety of unpredictable problems; and operate in a range of varied and specific contexts, taking responsibility for the nature and quality of outputs.
5	6	Generate ideas through the analysis of concepts at an abstract level with a command of specialised skills and the formulation of responses to well-defined and abstract problems; analyse and evaluate information; exercise significant judgement across a broad range of functions; and accept responsibility for determining and achieving personal or group outcomes.
6	7	Critically review, consolidate and extend a systematic and coherent body of knowledge, utilising specialised skills across an area of study; critically evaluate concepts and evidence from a range of sources; transfer and apply diagnostic and creative skills and exercise significant judgement in a range of situations; and accept accountability for determining and achieving personal and/or group outcomes.
7	8	Display mastery of a complex and specialised area of knowledge and skills, employing advanced skills to conduct research, or advanced technical or professional activity, accepting accountability for related decision making, including use of supervision.
8	9	Make a significant and original contribution to a specialised field of inquiry, demonstrating a command of methodological issues and engaging in critical dialogue with peers and accepting full accountability for outcomes.

SEEC group, a qualification's stated education outcomes must be equivalent to the expected knowledge outcomes in Table 7.3: regardless of the discipline or subject area, graduates must meet the criteria set. This maintains the integrity of qualification type. The requirements for having a qualification formally recognised are often stipulated very clearly in order to maintain this integrity. For example, the New

Module Development 119

Zealand Qualifications Authority specifies that a bachelor's degree is required to have the following educational (graduate) outcomes:

A graduate of a Bachelor's Degree is able to:

- demonstrate intellectual independence, critical thinking and analytic rigour
- engage in self-directed learning
- demonstrate knowledge and skills related to the ideas, principles, concepts, chief research methods and problem-solving techniques of a recognised major subject
- demonstrate the skills needed to acquire, understand and assess information from a range of sources
- demonstrate communication and collaborative skills.

(n.d., Outcomes, para. 3)

The structure of a bachelor's degree in New Zealand requires a student to complete at least 360 credits of study. Of these at least 72 must be at Level 7 or higher; in the English QAA (Quality Assurance Agency) system a bachelor's degree culminates in at least 60 credits worth of achievement at Level 6. Each credit is notionally the equivalent of 10 study hours, a number that includes self-directed study and an allocation for students' assessment activity. These requirements in terms of intensity make the formal education system robust and broadly equivalent across all universities, giving confidence to students, employers and society as to the student investment of effort in their university education.

A bachelor's degree would normally consist of study at Levels 5–7 in the Australian and New Zealand system, which are equivalent to the modules students encounter in the first, second and final years of a 3-year programme of study. Ultimately, the graduate of the bachelor's degree must reflect the criteria expected of a Level 7 qualification; on the way, the student needs to attain the criteria stipulated at Levels 5 and 6. Critically, what constitutes effective pedagogy in a bachelor's degree qualification ought to reflect the expected criteria set for each level.

Important to any application of DDE is the identification of which level descriptors apply. The SEEC group outputs provide the basis for nation-specific criteria such as that of the Australian Qualifications Framework in Table 7.4.

With reference to the Australian Qualifications Framework, it is easy to see why a standard 3-year degree will tend to be based on different pedagogical emphases as a student advances towards graduation. The emphases will be roughly as follows.

- Year 1 – familiarity with: the range of a subject or discipline, specialised vocabulary and core ideas and concepts, to set a foundation for application (Year 2) and critique and extension (Year 3). In terms of Table 7.4, the graduate of this year will 'will have specialised knowledge and skills for skilled/paraprofessional work and/or further learning', the latter with what follows in Year 2 in mind.
- Year 2 – ability to apply the vocabulary, core ideas and concepts learnt in Year 1 alongside the introduction of further specialised vocabulary, and core ideas and concepts. The graduate of this year 'will have broad knowledge and skills

120   Module Development

Table 7.4 National Qualifications Framework Levels of the Australian Qualifications Framework (from Australian Qualifications Framework [AQF], 2013, p. 18)

Level	Qualifications	Summary of Criteria
1	Certificate I	Graduates at this level will have knowledge and skills for initial work, community involvement and/or further learning.
2	Certificate II	Graduates at this level will have knowledge and skills for work in a defined context and/or further learning.
3	Certificate III	Graduates at this level will have theoretical and practical knowledge and skills for work and/or further learning.
4	Certificate IV	Graduates at this level will have theoretical and practical knowledge and skills for specialised and/or skilled work and/or further learning.
5	Diploma	Graduates at this level will have specialised knowledge and skills for skilled/paraprofessional work and/or further learning.
6	Advanced Diploma, Associate Degree	Graduates at this level will have broad knowledge and skills for paraprofessional/highly skilled work and/or further learning.
7	Bachelor Degree	Graduates at this level will have broad and coherent knowledge and skills for professional work and/or further learning.
8	B. Hons. Deg., Grad. Cert., Grad. Dip.	Graduates at this level will have advanced knowledge and skills for professional or highly skilled work and/or further learning.
9	Master's Degree	Graduates at this level will have specialised knowledge and skills for research, and/or professional practice and/or further learning.
10	Doctoral Degree	Graduates at this level will have systematic and critical understanding of a complex field of learning and specialised research skills for the advancement of learning and/or for professional practice.

for paraprofessional/highly skilled work and/or further learning', the latter in preparation for Year 3.

- Year 3 – ability to critically engage with and evaluate specialised vocabulary, core ideas and concepts. 'Graduates at this level will have broad and coherent knowledge and skills for professional work and/or further learning.'

So, by the end of a 3-year degree programme in Australia,[4] the graduate is empowered to apply and critique the vocabulary, concepts and key ideas of the discipline they have been studying as the means of being ready for professional tasks and further study at Level 8. This empowerment is the result of ongoing and gradual enlightenment, facilitated by a series of engaging learning activities along the path towards graduation. Education is an intentionally gradual, purposeful and progressive experience, whereby module learning outcomes combine to develop a graduate who has achieved against universally agreed educational criteria.

The very first step towards developing a DDE module is to confirm the qualification reference point, which will be the accrediting agency of your university. These are broadly similar internationally though some level and credit value differences may be apparent. The reference point will determine the levels of study that will make up the qualification, which will in turn set the types of capability the graduate outcomes must reflect and the number of credits (learning hours) required. If the desired graduate outcomes are more (or less) ambitious than those required by the reference point, a higher (or lower) qualification is being designed. There is no point trying to develop master's level outcomes for a bachelor's degree, as master's level graduate outcomes are for master's level qualifications. Neither are diploma level outcomes entirely suitable for a bachelor's degree.

A second important step is to determine the number of credits that will be assigned to each module. This determines the size of each module in terms of notional learning hours. Typically, it is up to the university to decide as to how many credits might be allocated to modules, though in DDE it is recommended that a consistent size, neatly divisible into 120 (the standard full-time academic year) be chosen. The current trend towards micro-credentialing might suggest 3–5 credits as an ideal size, though for gaining degree qualifications of 360 credits and for coordinating discreet module outcomes into qualification outcomes – not to mention the need to effectively assess each module so that credit can be earned – a more substantial number of 20 or even 30 might be optimal. An overly fragmented curriculum consisting of multiple small-credit modules can be difficult to scale and result in a disjointed student journey. A larger credit value can also work towards a more judicious use of assessment, and a better continuity of subject-based asynchronous dialogic around a dedicated module tutor. Arguably, small-credit modules are best for those students seeking a knowledge top-up rather than a full qualification.

In the development of a curriculum or syllabus, level indicators are essential reference points for writing appropriate outcomes. Outcomes, you will recall, are the foundation for assessment and learning activity design practice. Additional formal regulations will dictate the number of credits at each level required for accreditation. Fortunately, universities tend to have specialised departments to assist with the development of curricula; the requirement of DDE is that curriculum documentation be sufficiently detailed to contribute to the development of a core, in accordance with the Consistent principle.

Credit Decisions

A credit is, broadly speaking, a unit of educational activity. Depending on the qualifications framework you are subject to, each credit notionally represents 10 hours of student activity consisting of module-related private investigation, reflection, revision and assessment. Credit value and the number of weeks a cohort runs for set the

122 Module Development

volume and pace of learning and the size of each module. A full-time annual study load is, again depending on the framework, 120 credits or 1,200 learning hours (the equivalent of 30 weeks of 40 hours) per year. A full-time on-campus student will typically do 60 credits per semester over two semesters per year, often requiring four 15- or three 20-credit modules to be completed in parallel. Summer schools add another opportunity for further study in case catch-up is necessary.

In DDE it is recommended that students work in sequence, one module at a time, in accordance with the overall Flexible principle. Accepting enrolments on a rolling basis and starting frequent study cohorts permits part-time students to achieve a degree at the same rate as full-time students, as illustrated in Figure 7.1. In the example, each 30-credit module is studied over 12 weeks (requiring around 25 study hours per week, noting that this time includes self-directed learning and assessment preparation).

There are several benefits to adopting a standard, substantial credit module size as illustrated in Figure 7.1. Part-time students can set up a regular study pattern suitable for ongoing part-time work and family responsibilities. Students are also free to concentrate on a single module's learning activities at any time. Depending on the university's qualification design, it may be possible for a DDE student to study full-time – either by doing two modules at a time in parallel, or individual modules in a compressed, rapid timetable, perhaps as an enrolment option with a compressed cohort and dedicated tutor. It may be possible for a student to complete a traditional, 3-year bachelor's degree in 2 years of full-time study, or 3 years' part-time study.

Key to setting the standard credit value size for each module is thinking about the number of modules a student needs to complete for their overall qualification, the estimated weekly study load, the breadth of subjects that need to be studied, compatibility with other universities, options for intake transfer and the administrative steps required for smaller credit values.

- 20 credits = 200 hours = 20 hours per week over 10 weeks; 14.25 hours per week over 14 weeks; 18 enrolments required for a bachelor's degree.
- 30 credits = 300 hours = 20 hours per week over 15 weeks; 25 hours per week over 12 weeks; 12 enrolments required for a bachelor's degree.

The United Kingdom's Open University has many 60-credit modules, requiring only six enrolment events for a bachelor's degree. The Open Polytechnic in New

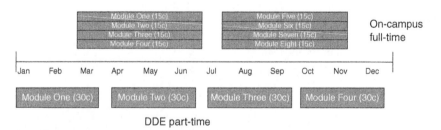

Figure 7.1 Conceptual Study Progress for 120 Credit Study, On-Campus and DDE Part-Time.

Zealand generally has 20-credit courses, which are at odds with the 15-credit courses that tend to be used across other polytechnics.

Providing further possibility under the Flexible principle, the absence of rigid study semesters would enable a student to take a month off when necessary. Figure 7.2 illustrates how the same module might be made available on a regular, monthly or bi-monthly basis depending on student demand.

The benefits to students of regular intakes include the ability to enrol and start anytime, as learning materials can be made available instantly in advance of the next actual intake. So, a student enrolling in mid-February can also begin their studies on that same day; they just join the underlying March cohort of students. The regular intake opportunities add structure to the education experience, with the added benefit that a student having to put their studies aside for whatever reason – as 'life gets in the way' – can do so by transferring their enrolment from one intake to the next. Clearly this is not to encourage students to never complete; what constitutes a valid transfer from one intake to another is defined by university policy.

Various teaching events might also be held at specific times across cohorts. For example, an online lecture featuring the latest research by the lead academic held in March might be available to all active cohorts at that time. A practical workshop might take place across different study regions in April and August, which students attend to complete their practicum requirements outside of cohort dates. Such events might enrich and complement, rather than displace, the module learning activities students are studying.

Conclusion: Setting Context Through Qualification Level, Credits and Outcomes

In determining and defining the shape of qualifications, many important decisions are made, which set the context for how each module is shaped and which learning activities are applied.

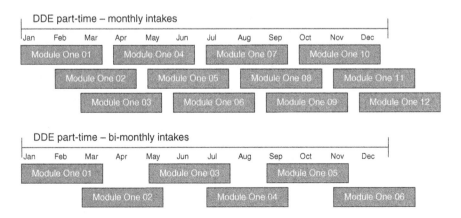

Figure 7.2 Overlapping Module Instances Providing Flexibility to Students.

124 Module Development

It is clear that:

- Graduate outcomes must reflect the expectations of the qualifications framework the university is subject to.
- Students will need to complete minimum numbers of study credits across different framework levels in order to meet qualifications requirements.
- Each level of a qualifications framework sets outcome expectations, which modules at that level are required to meet.
- Credit values determine module size and influence the level of flexibility available to students.
- Important operating model decisions related to the availability and pace of modules determine the amount of flexibility available to students.

To meet our three foundational objectives of providing accessible, scalable and personalised education, it is suggested that the following steps be taken.

1. Each qualification should have a defined set of entry criteria and pathway options for students who are not yet ready. In other words, a bachelor's degree may not be realistic for students with no previous school qualification. To be accessible to all, a bachelor's degree ought to include a lower-level certificate, diploma or bridging option.
2. Module credit sizes should be appropriate to the qualification on offer and be standardised. A bachelor's degree of 360 credits might be best served by modules of 30 or even 60 credits, allowing students to benefit from substantial modules and achieve their goal with fewer enrolments. Deciding the number of hours students are expected to commit to study each week will help to determine module credit sizes and cohort dates.
3. Qualifications should be based on monthly, bi-monthly or quarterly module enrolment patterns. Standard semester or trimester enrolments are inflexible and unnecessary in DDE and reflect a supply-driven approach to availability. Overlapping cohorts enhances student flexibility, as students who fall behind can transfer from one cohort to another without having to wait for months on end.
4. Cohort offerings should permit students to adopt a pace that suits them. For example, the same 30-credit module might be completed in 12 or 24 weeks (25 or 12.5 hours per week for study, respectively).
5. The first module of any qualification should be compulsory. If all new students are required to take a particular module as their first, that module can be especially designed to introduce students to the qualification they are enrolled in and provide additional tutorial support. Generic study skills can also be embedded within the module so that students are better prepared for the next modules they choose.

Such decisions, made as a qualification takes shape, provide the context for module and assessment design.

Direction: Course/Module Outcomes and Assessment

In order to gain a qualification, students will need to study and successfully complete a series of modules. Qualification level, credit and graduate outcomes, discussed above, provide the *context* for each module. Module outcomes and assessment give modules their *direction*, as it is these that shape the learning activities students engage with (see Table 7.2).

I have deliberately linked module outcomes with assessment. The link has long been foundational to effective education in an approach known as cognitive alignment, in which 'we systematically align the teaching/learning activities, as well as the assessment tasks, to the intended learning outcomes' (Biggs & Tang, 2011, p. 11). This alignment takes place in reverse order: the intended learning outcomes (ILOs) are decided upon first. These in turn shape assessment, then learning activity design (next section). To prepare assessment after the full module learning activity design has taken place risks assessing against the learning activities, rather than the ILOs.

The benefits of determining all module ILOs and assessments before designing each module are multiple. For a start, the advance work removes or reduces duplication of coverage. Confirming all ILOs and assessment in advance also helps ensure assessments are well aligned; as more than one critic has pointed out, there is no reason why a student doing a 360 credit degree made up of 15 credit courses ought to be required to do 72 assessments, many in the same test/essay/exam format! Finally, the dual work lends itself to shaping the consistency (core and custom) approaches to learning activity design, discussed later.

Setting Intended Learning Outcomes (ILOs)

John Biggs's SOLO (Structure of the Observed Learning Outcome) approach is an excellent starting point for setting effective learning outcomes. The SOLO taxonomy distinguishes between quantitative changes to a student's knowledge (that is, knowing more) and qualitative changes (that is, knowing differently). Importantly, qualitative change is built on the foundations of quantitative change just as empowerment relies on enlightenment, which in turn relies on engagement. This is like Illeris's escalation of learning described in Chapter 2, whereby cumulative (mechanical) learning, assimilative (additional) learning and accommodative (transcendent) learning are used to assist in transformative (significant or expansive) learning.

Writing effective learning outcomes relies on an appreciation of each module's level and a clear presentation format: 'One of the key criteria of a good ILO is that the student, when seeing a written ILO, would know what to do and how well to do it in order to meet the ILO' (Biggs & Tang, 2011, p. 119). An effective learning outcome will typically follow the format of verb, subject and context:

- To *describe* the basic working of a jet engine from the perspective of a mechanic.
- To *interpret* draft legislation as an informed citizen.
- To *generate* a research question with reference to previous published studies.

126 Module Development

Even from this list it is apparent that not all learning outcomes are equal. Some might be met through memorising a diagram. Others may require the application of a framework. Still others might require in-depth analysis. Fortunately, it is easy to calibrate learning outcomes with module level as will now be explained with reference to Table 7.5.

To begin with it is helpful to explain the four elements of the SOLO taxonomy, which are both quantitative (unistructural and multistructural) and qualitative (relational and extended abstract).

1. **Unistructural:** At the unistructural level, students are required to learn terminology and basic ideas, typically presented in factual form.
2. **Multistructural:** At this level, students are encouraged to see knowledge in relationship to other knowledge. Recall still plays an important part; however, the recall requires a deeper understanding.

In both unistructural and multistructural levels of the taxonomy the emphasis is on changing how much students know – that is, on quantitative change. It is easy to see the similarity here with Illeris's cumulative and assimilative learning. Arguably, the term 'content' finds its home at these levels.

The remaining two levels of the taxonomy instead focus on how students know – that is, qualitative change.

3. **Relational:** Biggs and Tang note that this is the 'first level at which "understanding" in an academically relevant sense may appropriately be used' (2011, p. 89), because students are required to manipulate and apply knowledge.
4. **Extended abstract:** At this level students are expected to develop and extend knowledge, going beyond what is already known.

Table 7.5 Change, SOLO Taxonomy and ILO Verbs (Biggs & Tang, 2011, Table 7.1, p.123)

Change	SOLO Taxonomy	ILO Verbs
Quantitative	Unistructural	Memorise, identify, recognise, count, define, draw, find, label, match, name, quote, recall, recite, order, tell, write, imitate
	Multistructural	Classify, describe, list, report, discuss, illustrate, select, narrate, compute, sequence, outline, separate
Qualitative	Relational	Apply, integrate, analyse, explain, predict, conclude, summarise (précis), review, argue, transfer, make a plan, characterise, compare, contrast, differentiate, organise, debate, make a case, construct, review and rewrite, examine, translate, paraphrase, solve a problem
	Extended abstract	Theorise, hypothesise, generalise, reflect, generate, create, compose, invent, originate, prove from first principles, make an original case, solve from first principles

Here we can see some similarity with Illeris's accommodative and transcendent learning. Clearly, universities are properly concerned with the relational and extended abstract levels. However, it is not right to assume students already enter their studies with appropriate *quantities* of knowledge. If a student is to learn how to engage with a subject or discipline, they must first know *more* about the subject, so as to be able to journey with the subject in abstract, qualitative ways. Practically, it is best to develop learning outcomes for modules drawing on a variety of SOLO levels as suggested by Figure 7.3. Each module might have a series of four to six discrete ILOs.

Figure 7.3 illustrates how SOLO emphases might shift, using the levels of the Australia and New Zealand Qualifications Frameworks. A student will start studying modules at Level 5 concerned primarily with multistructural and relational outcomes (though some unistructural outcomes may also be necessary). By the time they reach Level 7 and the last year of their undergraduate degree study, they will be wrestling more with relational outcomes, with a sprinkling of multistructural outcomes (and a dash of extended abstract). A student working towards a doctoral qualification (Level 10) will be focusing almost exclusively on extended abstract outcomes.

The SOLO framework nicely maps on to qualifications frameworks and also clearly demonstrates the educational journey proposed by Peters in Chapter 1: a student goes from an initiation into domains of knowledge and skill (unistructural and multistructural outcomes) towards acquiring knowledge and intellectual skills, and the development of understanding (multistructural and relational outcomes) towards a change for the better (relational and, eventually through post-graduate and higher study, more extended abstract outcomes).

Setting appropriate learning outcomes ensures the integrity of the education journey, making clear to students, teaching staff and accrediting bodies how each module makes an identifiable contribution towards the graduate profile. Far from being a mere administrative requirement, learning outcomes form the basis for

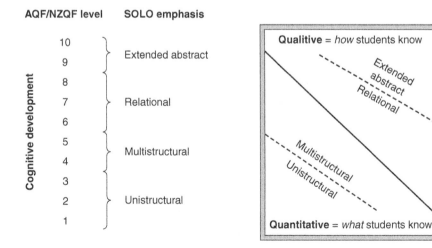

Figure 7.3 Suggested Emphases of SOLO Across Qualifications Level.

128   Module Development

assessment and learning activity design. All learning outcomes for all modules should be set before any learning activity design takes place.

In setting sound ILOs there is little unique to DDE. However, because DDE tends to rely more on predesigned learning activities with less (or no) synchronous contact, it is vital that ILOs are clear, deliberate and appropriate. It is extremely difficult to undo something designed in advance while students are engaged in study; while technical change is easy in digital media, pedagogical change is more fraught. In asynchronous DDE, students might be easily confused by a mid-course adjustment. In an on-campus class it is easier to change approach mid-stream because future lectures can be adapted and the reasons for change can be explained. In DDE, because of the upfront investment in designing and developing learning activities, major changes are much more difficult to facilitate. Getting ILOs right ensures that assessment and learning activity design are well formed by the various specialists who contribute to their development.

Assessment

Assessment is another terminologically difficult concept in university education. Many get fixated on the differences between formative and summative assessment, and between assessment *of* learning and assessment *for* learning. For the sake of brevity, here's my view: assessment is one of the most powerful means of education at a university's disposal. Assessment results might be centrally recorded (summative, for real) or unrecorded (formative, for practice); however, any assessment effort made by a student ought to receive feedback of substance and insight. Substantial feedback gives the student an opportunity to learn still more, and it provides evidence that the marker has properly engaged with the student's work.

Assessment is determined by the ILOs of each module, though such determination still brings educational opportunity. Assessment ought to provide an intentional learning experience. Designing assessment solely for compliance or evidence's sake misses an opportunity to contribute to a student's transformation. So, assessment is a form of education and not just a requirement of education. A student ought to *learn more as they are assessed* rather than *learn in preparation to be assessed*. Assessment in DDE is best considered a learning activity optimised for personalisation and reinforced with effective feedback.

As a compliance activity, assessment must be at least authentic (representative of the ILOs they are assessing), fair (realistic in terms of the level of the module), reliable (consistent across cohorts and able to be trusted) and valid (confirmed through cross-checking by an expert). Reliability ought also to consider the means by which cheating might take place. Any task students must perform ought also to be time-defensible; that is, the amount of effort required to complete the assessment activity should be formally stated and counted towards the overall credit hours of the module. Other requirements may be necessary depending on accreditation agency requirements.

By educational, assessment should be deliberately challenging, engaging and imaginative. Consider the first of the three sample ILOs listed earlier:

- To *describe* the basic working of a jet engine from the perspective of a mechanic.

This ILO might be assessed in various compliant ways. For example:

1. From the jet engine diagram, describe the internal workings and their function beginning with the intake fan and ending with the thrust nozzle (400 words).
2. In a 3-minute video clip and with reference to a cross-section diagram, describe the workings of a jet engine as you would to an interested member of the public (there is no expectation that you would include a member of the public in your presentation).

Both options here are certainly compliant; however, preparing a 3-minute video clip is a more challenging, engaging and imaginative task. By way of caution, though, it is in no one's interests to develop assessment tasks that are not properly focused on the actual learning outcome. It is no good to think of a challenging, engaging and imaginative task that requires the student to go well beyond the requirements of the outcome to demonstrate their attainment.

Key to effective assessment design is the transparency and marking consistency generated by a rubric. A rubric, or marking guide, is a clear outline of what is expected of the student and how marks or grades are allocated and used to ascertain whether a student's submission is a pass, a merit or excellence (or whatever other categories). A rubric makes the allocation of marks explicit; they can be provided to students in advance and can even be used as the basis for self-assessment and peer-marking.

A personalised assessment is one that draws on a student's experiences and perspectives, and that emphasises feedback. As much as possible, assessment should be tailored to what a student has already experienced and to the perspectives they already likely have. The assessment can then either recognise this previous understanding, or else draw on it to further challenge the student. For example, an assessment concerned with management might require a student to relate ILOs to their own workplace. In DDE, assessment is also prepared in advance of learning activity design to provide students with the opportunity to undertake assessment independent of the module itself. If, for example, the student already has the ability to explain the workings of a jet engine from their previous knowledge, they ought to be able to jump straight to the assessment and do it.

Feedback is one of the more critical elements of DDE. It is often said that students tend to ignore assessment feedback; this could be for a variety of reasons. First, for on-campus students studying multiple modules in parallel, there may be little time to effectively engage in feedback. Students may also find – as I frequently did in my undergraduate years – there is little meaningful feedback to reflect on! In DDE, providing meaningful feedback is a central element of the tutor role (remember Malcolm in Chapter 5, who talked about marking 'as my main activity'). Depending on the core, tutors will establish a great deal of insight about the students they are charged with. Malcolm's account is worth repeating here, as it demonstrates

130 Module Development

the various structures that must be in place to support the effective, educational use of assessment.

> We were trained to focus on ideas, assumptions and perspectives as much as on what students actually submit. Students upload their work into the online system, and their documents are automatically sent on to us electronically. The marking system works well. Full rubrics are provided, which makes grading much easier. We mark the student work in Word, tracking changes and adding comments. We are required to rewrite passages where argumentation could be better, correct referencing and annotate any insight we have that would help student thinking. All of this can take a lot of time. We're given a target of 500 words of comments per student essay, from in-text and overall summary comments.

The emphasis on feedback ensures student work is properly engaged with and that the student benefits from genuine, personalised attention into their achievement of ILOs. It is also good practice for DDE tutors to prepare post-marking summaries, outlining the class-wide performance of the assessment and outlining areas for improvement. This can also provide useful feedback to the module design team. Such feedback need not be overly detailed. Consider this:

> Well done everyone! You worked hard in describing how a jet engine works and I was impressed by the various presentations I received. The only thing I noticed across the board was some of you did not provide enough detail about the compressed gas expanding as the fuel-air mixture is burned. The expansion is critical for thrust, so the expansion rather than the heat is important to mention. All of you mentioned the heat, but it's the expansion – the result of the heat – that really needed emphasis. There were quite a few exemplary presentations that I'm going to ask permission to share.

From a student perspective this is useful additional information; I wasn't the only one to miss that! From the perspective of the module design team, this feedback repeated across various tutorial groups means the learning activities explaining the working of the jet engine need some tailoring, to make sure heat is more clearly explained as the means of expansion (and therefore thrust).

In DDE there are various options for assessment practice that enhance the accessibility and scalability of assessment. Depending on the core, the following examples might be applied.

- **Randomised assessment tasks unique to each student**: For example, deep question banks (not just multiple-choice, but short- and long-answer as well) could be drawn on for personalised tasks. Equation-based tasks – for example, in financial analysis – might be designed in advance with appropriate random-number ranges so that each student studies a financial statement unique to them from a pre-prepared bank of case studies. A marking guide might be automatically generated for the marker in each case, drawing from the same assessment bank.

Module Development   131

- **Evidence gathering based on analysis of results to each question**: Student grades and class-wide tutor feedback can form part of an ongoing evidence base, ensuring assessment becomes more finely honed and that question banks remain authentic, fair, reliable and valid.
- **Standard self- and/or peer review**: Students might be requested to reflect on their work as they submit, estimating how their work will be marked according to the rubric. This has the advantage of drawing attention to the rubric and encouraging engagement with eventual tutor feedback. Peer review has the same advantage.
- **Video-based assessment:** Rather than write an essay or have a demonstrated skill signed off by an assessor, students might be asked to provide video evidence. Such performances can be stored as evidence of achievement.
- **Viva voce as assessment and for confirmation**: Cheating is always possible with any assessment in which the student is not observed creating or participating in the assessment task. A viva voce test or exam, which may be recorded as the student engages with it, provides plenty of evidence of the student's ability to meet ILOs and might be used if there is any suspicion of cheating. A well-designed viva-based exam of, say, a half-hour might also provide a useful replacement for an otherwise paper-based, supervised exam of 3 hours.
- **Badging or profile updating**: Meeting a learning outcome by passing an assessment could automatically generate an electronic university badge, which the student might add to their online profile (possibly via LinkedIn). A badging regime might identify individual skills and bundle skills into larger recognitions.

Ultimately, assessment is based on ILOs. In DDE, the module development team designs assessment to emphasise educational outcomes and personalisation rather than simply compliance. Assessment practice relies on a series of sympathetic university processes and systems. Good assessment design is both an art form and science.

Practice: Learning Activity Design

By the time the qualification is defined, and all modules have confirmed ILOs and assessment developed, the *context* and *direction* for learning activity design is in place (see again Table 7.2). The *practice* of learning activity design across each module can then begin. Learning activity design relies on a clear and agreed approach in accordance with the Consistent principle (core and custom), which serves as the basis for team development and the tutor role.

Learning Activity Design and the 11 Principles

It is in this section that the Learning-activity-oriented principle is further explained. Of the 10 other principles of DDE, the most significant for learning activity design is that of Consistent. How a module is designed both reflects and determines a university's operating model. As a rule, less variability at the level of the module means less complexity for the operating model. The Consistent principle, then, seeks to keep module variability to a minimum without undermining effective education or closing the door to innovation. Choosing a core approach, extended through custom practice, helps to reduce variability while encouraging novelty.

In Chapter 3, consistency was described in terms of macro- (university-wide), meso- (qualification-specific) and micro- (module-specific) decisions. It is at the level of module learning activity design that these decisions are implemented, shaping the student study experience. At the level of module learning activity design, the macro-context sets the overall institutional constraints and opportunities available to the module team. In turn, the design of the qualification and its graduate outcomes serve the same function at the meso-level. In other words, by the time the practice of learning activity design is ready to begin, the substance of the core approach should already be in place.

The underlying learning activity design is set by the core, in accordance with the Consistent principle. However, that same principle also recognises the legitimacy of custom approaches that might be better than the core ones in specific situations. The purpose of the Consistent principle is not to enforce a bland conformity to the lowest common denominator of learning activities. Rather, it is to set a reliable foundation on which education can be achieved. As mentioned in Chapter 4, the goal isn't conformity but rather non-inconsistency. At module level, innovative approaches to learning activity design are certainly possible, and even encouraged. Consistency, then, is the combination of top-down, qualification-oriented core approaches and bottom-up, module-oriented customised approaches as shown in Figure 7.4.

This is not to suggest that the core is optional in each module, just that it can be reshaped using custom approaches where opportunity permits. Any variation to the core must be agreed to by the lead academic and learning activity designer, as custom approaches have implications for the operating model and the student experience. We will pick this point up again shortly, when we consider different approaches to learning activity design.

It is not the purpose of this book to outline what a specific, module-level core ought to look like. The DDE model does not insist on a single core model; rather, it provides the general framework for learning activity design to take place in the

Core set at university (macro) level,
refined for qualification (meso) level

Pedagogical expression –
learing activity design at module (micro) level

Custom set at module level

Figure 7.4 The Consistent Principle: Core at Qualification Level, Custom at Module Level.

context of the 11 principles. It is at the practice level, where learning activity design decisions are made, that the organisational decisions related to the principles – that is, operating model decisions – are brought together in the form that students will encounter them. It is here, to refer to the Anand quotation at the opening of this chapter, that the centre of attention shifts to the student's experience. We'll look now at how the 11 DDE principles determine the practice of learning activity design.

Data-Analytics-Driven: Continuous, Objective Improvement

If a DDE teaching model is to be driven by data analytics, learning activity design must support the gathering of suitable data for the purposes of student support and evidence-based practice. Sufficient data points are necessary for feeding the student dashboard to indicate progress and for informing support teams as to which students might benefit from proactive contact. Learning activity designers ought also to be familiar with analytics insight into the sorts of activities that best engage students and assist them in meeting learning outcomes, and the overall operating model must allow for the ongoing feedback loop of analytics insight to practice.

Digitally Agile: Built for the User and Reusable

In DDE, learning activities are digital. This makes study portable and embeds digital literacies. DDE does not recommend any particular virtual learning environment or learning management system, and neither does it propose any particular online learning activity application. However, it does promote an on-screen experience. All learning activity materials are digital, even when specific readings or articles are also made available in print.

Evidence-Based: Driven by Data

In applying DDE, a university will generate a strong evidence base of practice. This evidence base is a body of knowledge constantly updated and referenced by learning activity designers, who draw from such lessons each time a new module is developed and revised. The evidence base should override any individual's judgement, unless it is possible to apply that judgement as a custom development that might be used as the basis for gathering further evidence.

Developing an evidence base relies on effective data analytics, which in turn relies on digital agility.

Expert-Taught: Involving Specialists

Chapter 6 mentioned the various teaching roles recognised in DDE. It is not possible to be too prescriptive of the tutor's role. One university might choose to have a very active and highly interventionist tutor role serving small numbers of students, while another may prefer tutors be much more remote and intervene only where analytics indicate it may be necessary. Both approaches might be suitable in the same

134 Module Development

university in different qualifications and different levels of study. Rather than define the tutor's role, module learning activity design will be defined by the tutor's role. Importantly, the implications of any custom approach on the tutor's role should be considered. Consideration should also be given to whether the lead academic might feature as a presenter from time to time, perhaps across cohorts.

Flexible: Universally Open

The Flexible principle makes it possible for students to start and, to some extent, complete their module outside of concretised start and end dates. Synchronous events should not be set in stone unless unavoidable; even in such circumstances, alternatives need to be made available. This has implications for learning activity design, in particular for group work and practicum requirements. The DDE model is not prescriptive on the detail here, as flexibility is a relative concept. If group work and collaborative activity is a desirable element of a university's or qualification's core, it must be catered for – ideally within a universally open frame. Flexibility does not mean the end of cohorts or due dates, nor that collaboration is frowned upon. Learning activity design ought to always take place in a digital system optimised for universal accessibility, and identify discrete taster possibilities from the developed module.

Learning-Activity Oriented: Designed to Educate

Chapter 4 introduced the ICEBERG principles and the seven-fold learning activity design set used by the Open University. There are many frameworks and models available to universities to choose from for learning activity design. Two additional ones are mentioned here.

Perhaps the most prominent model is that of Laurillard (2012), whose book *Teaching as a Design Science* is highly recommended. Laurillard suggests six types, in Table 7.6.

There is a clear similarity to the Open University list in Table 4.1 of Chapter 4, which listed assimilative, finding and handling information, communication, productive, experiential, interactive/adaptive and assessment as seven learning activities (the Open University list branches from Laurillard's work).

Another useful perspective is provided by the Learning Activity Management System (LAMS) proposed by the LAMS Foundation.[5] LAMS is based on four activity types: Informative (provides information to learners), Collaborative (involves learners working together), Assessment (requires learner response) and Reflective (captures learners' thoughts). The LAMS online system can be used to generate online activities based on these four types.

Any such framework can be selected (or even customised) by a university. Key to effective learning activity design is ensuring it reflects evidence-based practice. With reference again to the ICEBERG principles in Chapter 4, design should be intentionally integrated, collaborative, engaging, balanced, economical, reflective and gradual (Weller, van Ameijde & Cross, 2018).

Module Development   135

Table 7.6 Types of Learning (Laurillard, 2012, Chapter 6, Table 6.3). Copyright 2012 from *Teaching as a design science: Building pedagogical patterns for learning and technology* by D. Laurillard. Reproduced by permission of Taylor and Francis Group, LLC, a division of Informa plc

Learning Through	Conventional Technology	Digital Technology
Acquisition	Reading books, papers; listening to teacher presentations face-to-face, lectures; watching demonstrations, master classes.	Reading multimedia, websites, digital documents and resources; listening to podcasts, webcasts; watching animations, videos.
Inquiry	Using text-based study guides; analysing the ideas and information in a range of materials and resources; using conventional methods to collect and analyse data; comparing texts, searching and evaluating information and ideas.	Using online advice and guidance; analysing the ideas and information in a range of digital resources; using digital tools to collect and analyse data; comparing digital texts, using digital tools for searching and evaluating information and ideas.
Practice	Practicing exercises; doing practice-based projects, labs, field trips, face-to-face role-play activities.	Using models, simulations, microworlds, virtual labs and field trips, online role-play activities.
Production	Producing articulations using statements, essays, reports, accounts, designs, performances, artefacts, animations, models, videos.	Producing and storing digital documents, representations of designs, performances, artefacts, animations, models, resources, slideshows, photos, videos, blogs, e-portfolios.
Discussion	Tutorials, seminars, email discussions, discussion groups, online discussion forums, class discussions, blog comments.	Online tutorials, seminars, email discussions, discussion groups, web-conferencing tools, synchronous and asynchronous.
Collaboration	Small group projects, discussing others' outputs, building joint output.	Small group project, using online forums, wikis, chat rooms, etc. for discussing others' outputs, building a joint digital output.

Learning activity design can take place using tools and approaches such as University College of London Knowledge Lab's Learning Designer set, developed as part of an Erasmus project, which consists of six activities based on Laurillard's six types (Young & Perović, 2018). LAMS is also an online module development system. Such approaches can be applied within an ADDIE (Analysis, Design, Development, Implementation, Evaluation) framework using Agile project methodology. What is important is not so much which is used, but what the core and custom tolerances are.

136   Module Development

Importantly, not all learning activities need be created from scratch. A multiplicity of materials can be curated from online sources. The decision to curate rather than create learning activities is not a binary one, but care must be taken with it. Too much curation, and valuable control and customisation is lost; too little, and flexibility and teaching opportunities are missed. Universities seeking to use curated materials must be alert to the copyright, licencing, broken link, privacy, digital format, extraneous content (advertisements and course-irrelevant links), narrative disruption and stylistic and contextual variation issues that come with them. It is wise to carefully manage curated sources, entering into licencing agreements as often as possible and deliberately using curated materials to complement one's own development.

It is useful for learning activity designers to develop and work within a core framework at the qualification level, for example, outlining the curated sources that best apply to the subject area and what proportion of learning activities will guide the core. For instance, a learning activity designer involved in a series of modules about engineering might choose to apply the PhET suite of simulations (https://phet.colorado.edu/en/about) as a standard source of interactivity, rather than use a variety of YouTube clips, websites and interfaces. Percentages might also be agreed in advance across each activity type, outlining the proportion of study time each should make up, such as in Table 7.7 (a suggestion for Level 6 engineering).

Any exceptions to these proportions would need to be agreed across the entire qualification development team so as to reinforce the Consistent principle.

Part-Automated: Applying AI

As suggested in Chapter 3 artificial intelligence can be applied to discussion forums and short-answer essay responses. Such activities might be added to provide feedback to practice and production activities, as well as in support roles.

Relational: Interpersonal

The Relational principle need not only imply mediated or moderated online discussion. Simply giving students opportunity to comment on a topic and see others' responses can be of educational benefit. There is a very broad scope in designing interpersonal activities in DDE, largely constrained by the role of the tutor. Learning activity design recognises the potential limitations of the tutor and learning support roles and the opportunities they offer for relational and interpersonal

Table 7.7 Suggested Proportion Core for Level 6 of an Engineering Qualification

Acquisition	20–30%	Production	20–30%
Inquiry	15–25%	Discussion	5–15%
Practice	20–30%	Collaboration	5–15%

Module Development 137

communications. These might range from students making optional comments on course materials for all to see, through to structured synchronous group events.

Success-Driven: Focused on Student Achievement

As proposed in Chapter 3 and mentioned above, the first module students encounter should feature a more supportive and scaffolded learning activity design. The first module's learning activity design ought to emphasise feedback and an overall orientation to the disciplines related to the qualification.

Systematic: Accessible, Scalable, Personalised

DDE relies on a systematic approach to learning activity design so that accessible, scalable and personalised learning can take place across the entire university. This underscores again the importance of the Consistent principle, and reinforces the importance of a clear and education-centric operating model. While learning activity design is rightly concerned with having students attain ILOs, it ultimately takes place in accordance with university systems and processes. Module-level learning activity design decisions will always be shaped by a university's overall operating model.

Developing Learning Activities as a Team

As outlined in Chapter 6, module learning activity design is a team activity that brings together the expertise of lead academics and learning activity designers. Recall the TPACK framework, especially the collaboration zone in Figure 6.6; it is in the collaborative zone that lead academics and learning activity designers develop the learning activities that constitute the module.

For actual module development it is best to use a project-based methodology. Depending on the urgency of development, the expertise and availability of project members and overall budget, the best methodology might be based on waterfall or Agile, part-time or full-time, remote or co-located activity. How this is done can vary; here is a generic approach that might serve as a starting point.

A series of roles might be involved in module design.

- A Lead Academic provides the subject's voice and ensures all relevant subject considerations are represented. The Lead Academic is the primarily source of Content Knowledge (recall, TPACK), and also advises on Pedagogical and Technological possibilities.
- A media specialist provides multimedia design advice and supervises the preparation of animation, audio, interactive and video assets for the module.
- Learning activity designers ensure consistency with the core as the module takes shape and support the potential of various custom learning activities that might also be beneficial to student learning. Learning activity designers provide

138   Module Development

Pedagogical and Technology Knowledge and serve to finalise learning activities ready for student use.

- Project Managers keep an eye on budgets and schedules and convene all steering and working group meetings. They also ensure that any risks to either budget, time or quality are escalated to the project steering group and are responsible for the finished module's progression towards being open for enrolment. Project Managers escalate any issues (including disagreement across the module team) to the project steering group for resolution.
- Subject Matter Experts (SMEs) might be contracted academics or vocational practitioners, provide additional and more specialised perspectives as required to ensure that learning activities are informed by current knowledge and practice.
- The project steering group, made up of senior university managers and academics responsible for the development of multiple modules across a qualification, provides ultimate oversight to the project and supervises budgets, timeframes and any risks arising until the project is complete.

So, how might teams best work together? A structured approach with clear responsibilities for each role is key. A clear core design, committed steering group and interdependent mindset across the development team goes a long way to managing expectations and focussing on a successful outcome.

Design of a module generally benefits from the following factors.

- **A team commitment:** Successful DDE module design relies on the bringing together of TPACK expertise, in the context of a development project. Regardless of project methodology, it is ultimately the way in which a module design team actually functions as an interdependent team that will determine achievement. For some lead academics and learning activity designers, working with others under DDE may bring about a clash of cultures (Cowie & Nichols, 2010). Such clashes are far from uncommon in universities where module development requires different roles to collaborate.
- **Clear project responsibilities:** Module design brings together a group of experts and is an expensive activity in terms of energy, time and money. Without a clear set of project responsibilities and accountabilities, module teams can become locked in disagreement. Having a clear RAPID (Recommend, Agree, Perform, Inform, Decide) matrix clarifying project roles goes a long way towards ensuring that conflict is minimised. The following project roles and accountabilities are broadly recommended:

  - assessment creation: learning activity designer, with the agreement of the Lead Academic
  - ILO alignment: learning activity designer, with the agreement of the Lead Academic
  - learning activity core: represented by the learning activity designer

Module Development 139

- learning activity design: learning activity designer, with the support of a media specialist, with the agreement of the Lead Academic
- project management: Project Manager, with steering group
- subject integrity: Lead Academic, supported by SMEs.

None of these roles work in isolation; however, the accountabilities are clear. Ultimately, the steering group intervenes where serious disagreement across the immediate project team occurs.

- **Early identification of custom opportunities:** In early development team meetings, any potential custom learning activities should be explored by the learning activity designer and, where appropriate, a media specialist. Any proposed custom developments can then be proposed and cleared by the project steering group. Because custom learning activities may be exceptional to the university operating model, opportunities must be carefully explored before being committed to.
- **Alignment with ILOs:** An early planning meeting should also define how the module being designed complements others through ILO alignment, and begin to define actual assessment tasks. These lay a firm foundation for actual learning activity design and development of the overall module.
- **Block or Topic outline:** Once ILOs and assessment are confirmed, planning of each block or topic takes place. This is generally in the form of headings, key resources and activities that help to further refine the development task.
- **Identifying taster opportunities:** In each module it should be straightforward to isolate a particular subtopic or sub-block that might be provided as a free or discrete course in itself. Such tasters might be made freely available to the public, as is the case with the Open University's OpenLearn initiative.
- **Completion, checking and warranty period:** It can take a long time for a module team to complete its task. However, it is a mistake to think that a new module can simply be put into service without follow-up. Ideally, a new module will be subject to careful analytics scrutiny during its initial delivery, with the module team on standby to provide immediate adjustment if necessary. At the completion of the first cohort, overall analytics insight should also be consulted and the module adjusted as the data indicates.
- **Evidence-based methodological improvement:** Each project will result in lessons and insight. A development debrief provides opportunity for the development team to compare experiences, leading to an evidence base for ongoing process and role improvement.

A good way to reinforce the sense of development team and begin defining a module's shape is through the use of the London Knowledge Lab's ABC workshop[6] or equivalent.

140   Module Development

From Top to Bottom, Bottom to Top

In Table 7.2 education outcomism was introduced as a process involving three questions:

1. How is the qualification formally defined? The answer is by determining qualification level, credit and graduate outcomes, which set the context for teaching.
2. What capabilities will characterise success for the qualification, and each module? The answer: module outcomes and assessment, which set the direction of teaching.
3. What activities will students undertake to develop and demonstrate their capabilities? The answer is learning activity design, which determines teaching practice.

At the completion of each module, and the development of the overall series of modules leading to the qualification, it is helpful to consider these questions in reverse. Just as the teaching context sets the overall teaching direction, which in turn sets teaching practice, so teaching practice engages the student, which in turn enlightens the successful completer of each module and, ultimately, empowers the qualification graduate. In considering learning activity design, we have come to the bottom of Peters' education outcomes and the beginning of each student's journey.

This chapter has outlined how modules take shape within DDE. Our final chapter will explore how universities can operationalise DDE and implement education outcomism in ways that are accessible, scalable and personalised.

Activities

1. Consider your own response to the question, 'What are your pedagogical colours?' How much does your answer resemble that of education outcomism as defined in this chapter?
2. Which accreditation scheme is your university subject to? How does your university formally interface with the agency responsible for the accreditation of qualifications?
3. Think about your own experience of assessment. What is the most profound assessment task you have ever done, and how did it change you? Which of the four schools of thought as to what digital education might mean for on-campus staff (no change, blended addition, academic as designer or specialist-assisted) best describes your own university?
4. Consider the education outcomism foundations of context, direction and practice. Using one sentence for each, describe how each of these three are set at your university.
5. Consider the ILOs of a module you are familiar with. How do the ILOs match the level at which the module is pitched? How well do the ILOs map back to the graduate outcomes?

Module Development   141

6.   Consider the different team roles proposed for module development. What might their equivalents be at your university? What roles at your university might need to change, should you seek to adopt a similar team approach?

Notes

1.   I agree with an assertion once made by Paul Kirschner, that anything less than instructivism is an abdication of the responsibility of the educator. Broadly, instructivism might be considered the application of the educators' expertise to the understanding of the student. Unhelpfully, at least for those always seeking to strictly categorise, even committed connectivists are being instructivist in their choice of promoting connectivist learning activities – but that is not really my point here.
2.   My stance here must be understood in the context of a university education because, for example, learning from experience clearly does not require an explicit instructivism.
3.   I avoid trying to distinguish between aims (overall purpose), objectives (more specific goals) and outcomes (student achievements), as a twofold granularity of outcomes across the qualification and module is generally sufficient. I am also assuming that any institutional outcomes (Biggs and Tang, 2011) – that is, any generic outcomes a university decides all of its graduates should achieve regardless of qualification such as leadership or ethical living – are included within qualification ones.
4.   The New Zealand and United Kingdom frameworks are broadly the same; the Australian one is used here purely for example's sake. Other jurisdictions such as Ontario, Canada have a 13-level framework (www.tcu.gov.on.ca/pepg/programs/oqf/); although the level numbers may differ from those in other Commonwealth countries, there is qualification-equivalence.
5.   See https://wiki.lamsfoundation.org/display/lamsdocs/WVI+LAMS+Primer.
6.   See https://blogs.ucl.ac.uk/abc-ld/.

References

Anand, B. N. (2016). *The content trap: A strategist's guide to digital change*. New York, NY: Random House.
Australian Qualifications Framework [AQF]. (2013). *Second edition January 2013*. Retrieved 29 January 2020 from www.aqf.edu.au/sites/aqf/files/aqf-2nd-edition-january-2013.pdf.
Biggs, J., & Tang, C. (2011). *Teaching for quality learning at university: What the student does* (4th ed.). Maidenhead, England: McGraw Hill & Open University Press.
Cowie, P., & Nichols, M. (2010). The clash of cultures: Hybrid learning course development as management of tension. *Journal of Distance Education, 24*(1), 77–90. Retrieved 29 January 2020 from www.ijede.ca/index.php/jde/article/view/607/1032.
Jarvis, P. (2006). *Towards a comprehensive theory of human learning*. New York, NY: Routledge.
Laurillard, D. (2012). *Teaching as a design science: Building pedagogical patterns for learning and technology*. New York, NY: Routledge.
The New Zealand Qualifications Authority. (n.d.). Bachelor's degree. Retrieved 20 November 2019, from www.nzqa.govt.nz/studying-in-new-zealand/understand-nz-quals/bachelors-degree/.
SEEC. (2016). *Credit level descriptors for higher education – 2016*. Retrieved 29 January 2020 from www.seec.org.uk/wp-content/uploads/2016/07/SEEC-descriptors-2016.pdf.

Weller, M., van Ameijde, J. & Cross, S. (2018). Learning design for student retention. *Journal of Perspectives in Applied Academic Practice*, 6(2). Retrieved 29 January 2020 from http://oro.open.ac.uk/57277/1/JPAAP%20weller.pdf.

Young, C., & Perović, N. (2018). *Introduction to the ABC LD workshop* (Vol. 1). Retrieved 29 January 2020 from http://blogs.ucl.ac.uk/abc-ld/files/2018/05/ABC_LD-Toolkit-Intro.pdf.

Chapter 8

Operating Models and Organisational Change

> Put bluntly, then, the rather limited sets of digital practices highlighted in our data are those that best 'fit' the rather limited expectations and processes that currently constitute university teaching and learning ... the lack of more active, participatory or creative uses of technology within our survey data suggests that only certain forms of digital practice are being legitimized through wider institutional regimes and systems of configuration.
>
> (Henderson, Selwyn & Aston, 2017, p. 1577)

Since 2004 the New Media Consortium (NMC) has released an annual Horizon Report suggesting how higher education might be influenced by emerging technologies. The 2019 edition (Alexander et al., 2019) lists 'Rethinking How Institutions Work' as a long-term trend. The same report also highlighted the evolution of faculty roles as a difficult challenge and rethinking the practice of teaching as a wicked problem impeding the adoption of technology in higher education.

The Horizon Report series seeks to identify the trends and issues associated with technology in education at particular points in time, drawing on a panel of international experts. Looking across the 2019 report, three themes relevant to this book are apparent.

- Organisational change: The report rightly identifies 'cost, access, and workforce readiness' (p. 7) and the emergence of the part-time, employed non-traditional learner, which 'requires faculty and academic advisors alike to act as guides and facilitators'. Despite this need for adaptation, panellists framed rethinking in terms of 'a gradual evolution rather than a disruption of current practices' (p. 7).
- The role of faculty in digital education strategy: The report recommends that 'faculty need to be included in the evaluation, planning, and implementation of any teaching and learning' (p. 16) as a means of assisting in adoption and scalability. Panellists noted that 'in order for faculty to fully engage in educational technology, training and professional development should be provided to facilitate incorporation of technology' (p. 16).
- The practice of teaching: The report notes that course design is playing an increasing part in student instruction, emphasising again a shift in the faculty

144 Operating Models and Organisational Change

role towards facilitation rather than direct instruction. Increasingly faculty are finding themselves as members of a course development team. Where this approach is not in place, 'instructors are challenged to create these experiences on their own' (p. 19).

These three themes immediately prompt some key questions:

- Organisational change: Is it possible for faculty to eventually evolve into a guide and facilitation role? Is a guide and facilitation role even desirable, given the potential for dedicated staff (tutors and dedicated student support staff) to provide these services, leaving faculty to focus on lead academic responsibilities?
- The role of faculty in digital education strategy: Are faculty best placed to critique a digital education strategy, given that internal consultation is evidence of a supply-side culture? Are the student voice and emerging student study preferences considered valuable? How likely is it that faculty will take access, scalability and personalisation as their starting point, or evaluate the potential of technology beyond the practices they are currently familiar with?
- The practice of teaching: Are individual course teams best placed to promote and influence organisation-wide initiatives in areas such as data analytics, digital agility and flexible access? Where are such systems and associated processes determined? How do we best bring about a faculty role that respects the subject knowledge and discipline authority, without limiting the significant potential for technology to make its contribution across the university?

These questions are not confined to teaching practice or roles. They are systematic, university-wide questions, which transcend immediate practice into questions of organisational structure and direction. We start to stray into the awkward territory of organisational change, strategy and structure – a territory where administrative and academic staff tend to roam with mutual suspicion. I have done my best to defend the perspective of 'university as organisation' and the joint responsibility academics and administrators have in determining the identity of a university in Chapter 2. In subsequent chapters I have sought to promote ways of thinking about digital education based on a particular organisational design.

Until we see educational technology – the subject of the Horizon Report – as being concerned with institutional configuration as well as classroom practice, we will continue to imagine evolutionary change as faculty gradually morphing into facilitators. Such a process will likely be painful, grinding and lengthy – and the end point will likely not be as desirable as the one proposed in this book. I argue instead for an intentional shift towards education-centred practice based on providing accessible, scalable and personalised education through engagement, enlightenment and empowerment. The education-centred approach, I believe, calls us to transcend current practices; this transcendence will, in most universities, require strong leadership and purposeful change management. The sort of education imagined in this book will not come about through faculty accord, gradual evolution or cosmetic changes towards team-based course design. The sort of education imagined in this book will instead be the result of intentional decision-making in pursuit of a specific vision of education.

If DDE as outlined in this book is to be achieved by a university, high-level and systematic decisions must be made. Certain questions must be answered: what is our core approach for teaching at the macro-layer? How will analytics inform teaching? How often will modules be made available to students? How will our course design roles work together? How will evidence direct change in our teaching practices? Who decides on teaching model change? Such decisions transcend the classroom or VLE course area: they should direct rather than respond to practice and assume an overall rather than module-based viewpoint. As reflected in Chapter 3 and with reference to SAMR, module-centred change will, at best, bring in digital education in ways that Substitute or Augment existing practices that likely fall short of the accessible, scalable and personalised vision of DDE. Bigger, systematic decisions are required to bring about the Replacement potential of DDE.

This chapter, then, is concerned with organisational change towards DDE, facilitated through operating model design. We will start with an overview of operating models and their development. With that foundation in place, we will examine organisational change.

Operating Models: The Basis for Systematic Change

Universities are, ultimately, organisations made special by their unique combination of social and academic goals. As organisations, the internal operations of a university reflect an operating model, even if that model is not formally articulated. An operating model, simply put, is a model of how functions work and interrelate. It is a description of the way things are done, concerned with how purpose, structure and strategy are brought about by the actual workings of the organisation.

An operating model might be designed to show the 'as is' and 'to be' states of an organisation. The former is an operating model view of the organisation in its current state, whereas the latter (also referred to as a target operating model or TOM) is representative of an aspirational future state. In many universities the operating model is not articulated at all; from experience, the concept of a university having an operating model tends to be politely dismissed. An operating model is not a wishful managerial theory: it is an everyday actuality. The question is to what extent an operating model reflects intent and design, rather than incidental practice. If 'the way things are done' does not match 'the way things ought to be done', the operating model is likely at fault.

Considering universities from an operating model perspective helps to understand the dynamics of why universities work as they do, and to demonstrate what might need to change for DDE to be applied. Our starting point, then, is the assertion that all universities have an operating model (whether it is accidental or intentional), and that those universities seeking to apply DDE (and thus achieve accessible, scalable and personalised education) must be deliberate in their adoption of a new operating model.

My coverage of operating models and their development is deliberately simplistic in this chapter. What I aim to provide is an overview of what operating models are,

146 Operating Models and Organisational Change

how they might be designed and how they can be used to help universities adopt DDE to make education accessible, scalable and personalised. So, my coverage here aims to link university strategy with university capability. The practice of aligning an organisation towards its strategic objectives really takes place under the banner of enterprise architecture. This term is helpfully defined by JISC, a United Kingdom not-for-profit dedicated to promoting digital solutions in higher education, as:

> ... a strategic management technique that links organisational mission and goals, processes, information and technology. It provides a way of representing and understanding functions that differ in essence and making sense of the interrelationships between them.
>
> (2014, 'What is enterprise architecture?', para. 9)

The overall complexity and fragmentation of the various models and approaches used across enterprise architecture is much too difficult to navigate here. What I will do instead is provide a taster of organisational modelling and change management to at least introduce how a university might embed DDE into its workings.

There are various ways of modelling an organisation. For example, a capability map can describe a university in terms of the various functions it needs to have, and the relationships across those functions. Figure 8.1 is an example of a top-level capability map, which shows how various parts and functions of a university interrelate in pursuit of four outcomes (commercial partners, educated graduates, improved society and research insight).

A university might also be modelled as a business, which would differ from a capability model in that purpose, structure and strategy would be included in the diagram. An operating model, as presented by Campbell, Gitierrez and Lancelott (2018), demonstrates how an organisation provides a value proposition in the context of its suppliers, locations, organisation, information and management system. An operating model is a visualisation or series of visualisations:

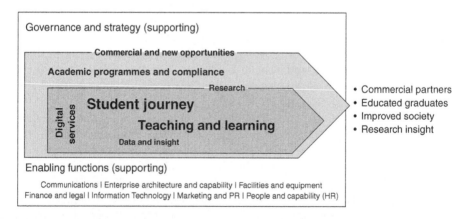

Figure 8.1 High-Level University Capability Map Reflecting DDE.

Operating Models and Organisational Change 147

... that show the elements of the organisation, such as activities, people, decision processes, information systems, suppliers, locations, and assets, that are important for delivering the organisation's value proposition(s) and how these elements combine to successfully deliver the value proposition(s).

(Campbell et al., 2018, p. 3)

It is unfortunate that much of the operating model and enterprise architecture literature available is steeped in such language. More helpfully, and in recognition of the objectives I have in mind for this book, an operating model might be defined as a visualisation or series of visualisations showing how all elements of a university work together to provide engagement, enlightenment and empowerment to students.

At the highest level, an operating model can be described in terms of a canvas as demonstrated in Figure 8.2.

The operating model canvas model proposed by Campbell et al. helps to present a single-page view of a university.

- The **suppliers** are collaborative partners who provide some form of input or regulation to the organisation.
- **Locations** are the places in which customers (personalised learners) experience and interact with the organisation.
- The **value delivery chain** provides an overview of the processes the organisation performs in order to provide its benefits (the benefits being commercial partners, educated graduates, improved society and research insight).
- The **organisation** is the departmental structure that coordinates personnel in support of the value delivery chain.

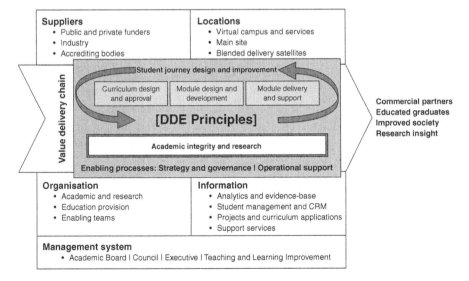

Figure 8.2 Operating Model Canvas Reflecting DDE.

148   Operating Models and Organisational Change

- **Information** summarises the IT applications and data systems that support the value delivery chain.
- The **management system** lists the various committees and groups responsible for decision-making and key performance indicators.

The operating model canvas in Figure 8.2 is somewhat generic and need not be taken as an ideal, though it will be used for illustrative purposes across the remainder of this chapter. Two points are implicit in the diagram: Organisation exists to support the value delivery chain, and Information serves a critical cross-delivery chain function. Typically, a university will need to adapt its Organisation to adopt DDE, and broaden its appreciation of Information beyond the supply of IT systems more towards strategic implementation of technological systems across the value delivery chain.

At the highest level an operating model is shown as a one-page canvas. At its most detailed and complex, an operating model might consist of multiple process and analysis documents running into thousands of pages. In general, good practice is to have a robust high-level view and go into detail only where it might be needed.

An operating model canvas is the starting point of more detailed documentation. Table 8.1 proposes four levels of operating model design for universities, beginning at the single-page operating model canvas and extending into more detail.

Table 8.1 Proposed Operating Model Approach to University Design

	Level	*Descriptor*	*Optimal Outputs*
High-level design	**1. Operating model canvas**	Overview of university, as an operating model canvas and student journey map	• Design principles • Student journey map • Operating model canvas
	2. Value delivery chain map	Overview of value proposition components showing processes (one page per value delivery chain)	• Business unit confirmation • RAPID analysis across value chain and student journey map • IT systems map • Governance map • Level 2 process maps
Detailed design	**3. Detailed value chain map**	Overview of operational flows (swim lanes; approx. 10 pages per value delivery chain map)	• SIPOC • Teams • Data flows
	4. Detailed processes map	Where needed, step-by-step tasks required per detailed value chain map (lists; 10 pages per detailed value chain map)	• Lists of process tasks performed by actors

Operating Models and Organisational Change 149

The activities at Levels 1, 2 and 3 represent the minimum requirement of an operating model for the purposes of planning organisational change. We'll now look at each of the four operating model levels, before summarising the contribution operating models make to university design, organisational change and DDE.

Level 1: The Operating Model Canvas

The canvas such as that shown in Figure 8.2 is the output of a series of decisions and consultation. Developing an operating model canvas is a group activity that begins with a desired future state, articulated in the form of a general strategy and a list of design principles. In this book I have assumed the general strategy to be education that is accessible, scalable and personalised. I have also proposed DDE as consisting of 11 design principles, as described in Chapter 4.

Before finalising an operating model canvas, it is useful to illustrate the desired student journey map. Imagining the university from the perspective of personalised learners adds the student dimension to design and helps frame important conversations that will later take place in operating model design. A student journey map describes the desired student experience from seeking a programme of study, finding out more and enrolling, through being oriented to the university, the first module of study and their subsequent study experience, to their eventual graduation and alumni relationship. Clearly the study experience is the major element of this journey, so sufficient detail of that component in particular should be provided to inform the value delivery chain. An example high-level map (not intended to be read) is shown in Figure 8.3 (note that the shaded central part is the module-by-module study experience).

A student journey map should locate every potential student encounter with the university at a glance and prompt high-level answers to the following questions:

1.   What does the student experience at this stage?
2.   What data is captured and used?
3.   What IT systems are involved?
4.   Who in the university (which departments and teams) are involved?
5.   What communications should a student experience, and when?

Answering these questions will help to check whether the operating model canvas is representative of what students will experience as they progress through their journey from initial inquirer through to successful graduate. The student journey map is also one of the major value delivery chain activities, which is revisited in more detail as the overall operating model takes shape.

The outputs of Level 1, once broadly agreed, set the stage for more detailed – yet still high-level – design.

Level 2: The Value Delivery Chain Map

Level 2 design involves showing the Level 1 value design chain map in more detail as a series of process maps. If Level 1 design is complex because of the level of consultation

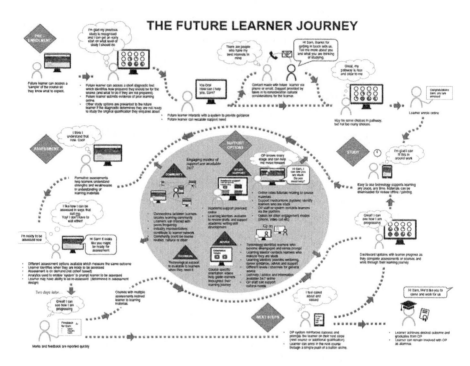

Figure 8.3 The Future Learner Journey Map.
Source: © The Open Polytechnic (2017).

and overall agreement required, Level 2 design is complex because of its comprehensive scope; each high-level process activity within the university must be included.

It is helpful for Level 2 process design to adopt a numbering system, so that supplementary documentation can be traced back to process diagrams. In the operating model canvas example in Figure 8.2, the numbering system might follow this pattern (noting that [DDE Principles] is bracketed to show its centrality to design and is not intended as an actual process):

1.0 Student journey
2.0 Curriculum design and approval
3.0 Module design and development
4.0 Module delivery and support
5.0 Academic integrity and research
6.0 Enabling processes: Strategy and governance
7.0 Enabling processes: Operational support.

For the purpose of illustration, a sample process map is provided as Figure 8.4. Note that the 'Enabling processes: Operational support' (7.0 in the list above) shown in Figure 8.2 might consist of multiple sub-processes including those associated with

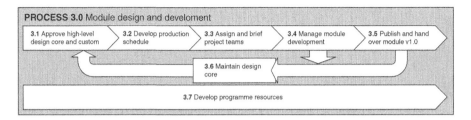

Figure 8.4 Sample Level 2 Process.

communications, finance, human resources, information technology and student records. The enrolments experience is more properly represented in the 'Student journey' process (1.0 in the list above).

Various iterations of design will be required to align the different outputs at this level, as each process map from 1.0 to 7.0 will need to accommodate every other map. This alignment is informed and challenged by the various descriptions accompanying each process map, as outlined in Table 8.2.

- **Business unit confirmation:** The completed process maps will further inform the optimal high-level university structure. The various Pro Vice-Chancellor level roles and teams required for the new operating model should be clear by the time Level 2 design is complete. For the purposes of illustration, I will assume five top-layer teams associated with Process 3.0 in Figure 8.4: Academic services, Academic team, Learning design and media development, Projects office and Strategy office.
- **RAPID analysis across value chain and student journey map:** RAPID is a popular framework used to communicate who, or which business unit, is involved with each part of a process. The 'R' unit or units Recommend activities within the process; 'A' units must Agree the output, with power of veto; 'P' units Perform the process; 'I' units Inform the output, but with no power of veto; finally, the 'D' unit Decides the output. There is only one 'D' unit, as otherwise the process will either suffer from stalemated disagreement, joint disinterest or deference to the most insistent (or to the budget holder). A RAPID is prepared for each Level 2 process. This activity is likely to be extremely controversial, as the aim is to define what is often taken for granted and may require difficult decision-making by university leadership. Examples of controversy are not hard to provide. Who, for example, ultimately decides the student journey (Process 1.0)? Coming back to my illustration, which of the five top-level units should decide the output to Process 3.0 (Module design and development)? For the latter, for various reasons aligned with DDE as described in previous chapters, I would argue for the Strategy office and suggest a RAPID as follows:

    - **Recommends**: Academic team; Learning design and media development
    - **Agrees**: Academic services; Academic team; Learning design and media development

152 Operating Models and Organisational Change

- **Performs**: Academic team; Learning design and media development; Projects office
- **Informs**: Projects office
- **Decides**: Strategy office

The controversy, tension and debate this RAPID might cause (yet also ease!) across a university will be obvious to you. Nevertheless, this is only a suggestion; universities may find it more prudent to maintain a faculty unit-centric approach alongside multiple, unit-based cores to provide consistency at the level of each faculty unit. Most important is that the RAPID clearly defines the roles each team plays across each process.

- **IT systems map:** An IT systems map lists all IT applications against their business owners and identifies which processes they contribute to. Integration with enterprise systems, local or cloud-based hosting, licenced or software as a service (SaaS) relationships should all be indicated as a Level 2 output.
- **Governance map:** A university will consist of various formal committees, sub-committees and informal groups. A governance map lists all the required formal committees and sub-committees, starting from a compliance perspective (that is beginning with the statutory and accreditation requirements the university is subject to). The governance map ought to reflect effective oversight of all Level 2 processes.
- **Level 2 process maps:** Figure 8.4 shows a sample map. Accompanying the map should be brief descriptions of each sub-process including its RAPID, any IT systems and data flows associated with the sub-process, and the high-level input and output of the sub-process (see Table 8.2 for an example).

By the time Level 2 design is completed, the 'to be' university has truly taken shape. The combination of process maps, business unit confirmation, RAPID decisions and IT and governance maps should provide a cohesive, clear and systematic view of the possibilities. A further benefit of a comprehensive Level 2 delivery chain map is that it becomes very easy to trace operational problems and mistakes to the precise process where they occur, meaning accountability is clearly assigned and solutions can be designed, agreed and integrated into the operating model.

Table 8.2 Sample Sub-Process Descriptor

3.2 Develop production schedule. The approved module(s) are added to the overall module production schedule, and team members and timeframes are agreed.

- **Inputs**: Core and custom specification, design brief, approved budget code.
- **Outputs**: Production schedule with team members and timeframes assigned.
- **Teams**: Academic team (R, A); Learning design and media development (R, A); Projects office (P, D); Strategy office (A).
- **IT and data flows**: Projects and curriculum applications, reports to all teams and Finance system.

Operating Models and Organisational Change 153

Level 3: The Detailed Value Chain Map

At Level 3, a swim lane diagram is used to demonstrate the actual workflows associated with each sub-process. It is at this level that detailed design begins. Swim lane diagrams are prepared and described alongside three additional elements: a SIPOC, team identification and data flows.

- A **SIPOC** (Suppliers, Inputs, Process, Outputs, Customer) identifies the relationship of the process with those surrounding it. The swim lane diagram provides the process element of SIPOC. Generating a SIPOC requires answering some simple questions: Which team leads into the process (Suppliers)? What do they provide to assist the process (Inputs)? What activities are performed (Process)? What does the process itself generate (Outputs)? Ultimately, who benefits from the process (Customer)? Answering these questions for each sub-process adds still more clarity to the operating model.
- **Team identification** is required for generating swim lane diagrams, because at Level 3 the process is described not only in terms of workflow, but also the team or teams involved at each stage. Figure 8.5 is an example of a swim lane diagram for Course (Module) and Assessment Development at Open Polytechnic. While the illustration is not intended to be clearly read here, the overall workflow and team swim lanes can be discerned (the team roles are in the far left of each row).
- **Data flows** from each process are also captured at Level 3, so that appropriate records are maintained and analytics opportunities mapped. Understanding data flows assists in identifying whether IT applications are adequate for operational requirements. New opportunities for data gathering and use are also identified through this analysis.

Level 3 documentation can run into the hundreds of pages. If seeking to fully transform a university's operating model, time should be spent preparing Level 3 documentation across the entire value delivery chain. Designing a full operating model at Level 3 provides full transparency and therefore confidence in the 'to be' state, and the discipline of preparation also has the effect of tying off loose ends. A full model at Level 3 has the added benefit of capturing the tacit knowledge and assumptions of each unit across the university and forcing conversations across teams that might otherwise view themselves as independent actors.

Level 4: The Detailed Process Map

Level 4 process maps are more detailed views of each process step identified in Level 3 (a colleague once referred to these as 'the screenshot by screenshot steps followed by each participant'). Level 4 analysis need only be done where job descriptions are being considered or where complex workflows require clarity.

154 Operating Models and Organisational Change

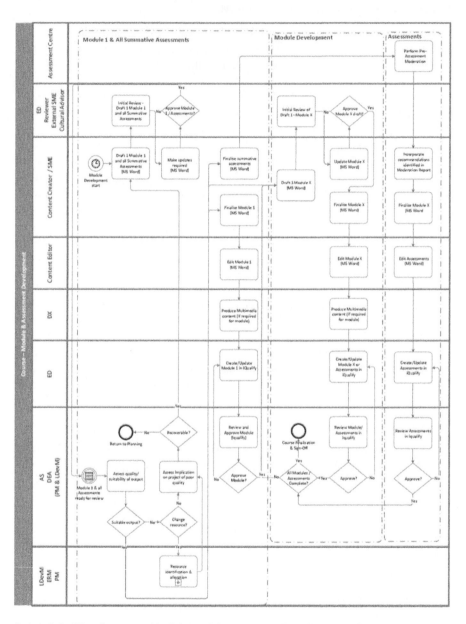

Figure 8.5 The Course – Module and Assessment Development Swim Lane.
Source: © The Open Polytechnic (2017).

Designing an Operating Model as the Basis for Change

The challenges associated with trying to prepare a comprehensive map of a university's internal workings have likely already occurred to you. Or perhaps you feel uncomfortable with the thought of trying to document the workings of a dynamic, interpersonal and academic system. Let me be clear here: a university is an organisation, and so can be mapped in the ways I have described. Admittedly it is folly to imagine that any documented description of a university's operating model can finally describe all its activities; however, a comprehensive design at Level 3 is a must reducing the risks of change.

At best, an operating model is a detailed approximation of reality, an approximation requiring constant attention and iteration to remain current and useful. The alternative to a detailed and documented operating model is a tacit and undocumented one, prone to failure. Designing an operating model to Level 3 provides the means of implementing DDE across a university, and of providing those 'wider institutional regimes and systems of configuration' required for 'more active, participatory [and] creative uses of technology' mentioned by Henderson et al. at the beginning of the chapter. A further benefit is that a well-maintained operating model enables performance issues to be traced to source, and improved. Indeed, any operating issues or problems ought to be traceable to a particular Level 3 element – and any fix applied can be implemented both at actual source and in overall context.

As the four levels of an operating model described above make clear, designing a 'to be' operating model is an involved task requiring multiple perspectives and many, many conversations. 'To be' operating models are best *designed*, rather than made. The distinction is an important one; creating an operating model is extremely iterative, even 'messy' (Campbell et al., 2018, p. 28). Multiple workshops, conversations, analysis and decisions lie behind the crafting of an agreed 'to be' operating model. Once the 'to be' model is designed to Level 3, the required IT and data systems and organisational chart can be finalised, and change implementation can begin. The documented operating model must be illustrative and comprehensive enough to be understood and serve as the basis for change. The operating model should, to Level 3, provide clarity about:

1. Where the core approaches (at macro-, meso- and micro-levels) are agreed, how they are maintained, and where custom decisions are agreed (Consistent).
2. Where analytics data is sourced, how it is stored and analysed, and how it is applied (Data-analytics-driven).
3. How student-facing systems are constantly improved to provide an ever more effective digital experience (Digitally agile).
4. How data is applied for the purposes of ongoing improvement across the entire student journey, including module design (Evidence-based).
5. The different functions performed across all teaching and support roles, across the entire value delivery chain (Expert-taught).
6. The mechanisms enabling anytime enrolment, cohort management, accessibility and the production of taster modules (Flexible).
7. How modules are designed and developed (Learning-activity-oriented).

156 Operating Models and Organisational Change

8. Where and how AI interventions are applied (Part-automated).
9. Where and how interpersonal communications take place across modules (Relational).
10. How students are intentionally supported through their first-module experience (Success-driven).
11. How the entire value delivery chain contributes to accessible, scalable and personalised education (Systematic).

So, the operating model should provide an end-to-end, enquirer-to-graduate view of how the 11 principles of DDE are applied.

Should you decide to prepare an operating model for your university in anticipation of applying DDE, the very first step you will need to take is to agree on the vocabulary and modelling framework you will be working with. You will also need to appoint a representative operating model project team (preferably assisted by expert advisors) and ensure top-level governance and sponsorship.

Towards Change: A Vision for DDE

This book has encountered many unhelpful terms; 'change' is yet another, unhelpful in that it spans a range including daily, incremental shift and entire reorganisation. I'm also certain that most experience of organisational change readers have had is largely negative. In general change is neither popular nor easy; the immediate response to the word 'change' in organisations is likely one of fear (Scarlett, 2016).

Throughout my career I have been involved in several large organisational changes in higher education settings. Most have gone well, but not all. Over the last 15 or so years I have learned that change is mostly about how little you get wrong, rather than how much you get right! Ultimately, though, success rests in whether the intended structural and procedural changes formally land or are rejected, and whether if rejected they were rejected for the right reasons.

Any change process begins with a vision. The vision for DDE is not the 11 principles, nor the educational characteristics of a university. The vision of this book is accessible, scalable and personalised higher education that engages, enlightens and empowers students. DDE is a proposed mechanism for realising that vision.

The terms 'accessible', 'scalable' and 'personalised' are relative terms rather than absolute ones. The accessible, scalable and personalised vision of DDE for higher education that engages, enlightens and empowers students is progressive. Think back to the perspective of the personalised learner offered in Chapter 1, and the challenge presented there of supply- and demand-oriented education. The typical university must change significantly if it is to become truly demand-oriented and so cater for the personalised learner.

The Challenges of Change

It is useful to think about change in terms of scale. We certainly do encounter change all the time. At work colleagues change, budgets change, students change.

Ideas and practices change. Such incidental change is usually expected and viewed as inevitable. Change becomes problematic when it is the result of decision toward large-scale intent, and where those decisions have significant implications. The objectives of change, the implications of change and the structure of change all determine how it will be greeted and engaged with.

- **The objectives of change:** Most fundamental to how change is received is the future state it is aiming to bring about. All change models are based on a vision or desired end state; the extent to which this is desirable and understood will set the tone for whether the proposed change is considered sympathetically.
- **The implications of change:** The extent to which the future state has implications for jobs, whether through redundancy or adjustments to responsibility and control, will determine the level of engagement and resistance associated with the proposal.
- **The structure of change:** There are substantial differences between a team-based, ground-up approach and a formal, top-down one. The former is effective where the desired changes are within the span of control or influence of staff. The latter is more effective and appropriate where more fundamental, organisation-wide changes are called for, or where the desired outcome is considered important, strategic or clear enough to warrant it.

Regardless of the objectives, implications and structure of change, change is hard work that requires effective and honest engagement with all staff. The form of change needed for adopting DDE is likely to be complex and large-scale, which, in any estimation, requires a formal approach. Though difficult, this sort of change is far from impossible; complex and ambitious change can be successful, provided it is well conceived, effectively planned, appropriately resourced and skilfully led. Change management has a significant literature (see, for example, the Management Institute Body of Knowledge at www.change-management-institute.com/cmbok) and, for the most part, the steps are obvious (Smith, King, Sidhu & Skelsey, 2014).

The scale of change likely required to bring about a DDE 'to be' operating model will be determined by the gap between the current, 'as is' operating model and the aspiration. Typically, the perspectives of learning activity design, data analytics, student journey and student support services are missing around a Vice-Chancellor's executive team; where this is the case, change management is likely to be especially difficult as the Vice-Chancellor's own team will likely need reconfiguration as part of the change process.

Diagnosing and Prioritising Change Towards DDE

The 11 principles of DDE are designed to work interdependently. Universities seeking to implement DDE should consider how well their current practice aligns with each principle. Table 8.3 suggests how a university might determine whether its alignment is ad hoc, coordinated or already achieved.

Table 8.3 Diagnosing Organisational Alignment with DDE Principles

Principle	Ad hoc	Coordinated	DDE
Consistent: based on a common core, and customisable to requirement and opportunity	Each module and student experience varies	A house style is used, which serves as the basis of all practice	A defined core provides consistency, and innovation is supported through custom provisions
Data-analytics-driven: objectively and continuously improved by data	VLE data analytics used at faculty discretion	Data analytics beyond VLE reports are made available, with guidelines for use; informs student support	Data analytics used across student support and module design functions; data dashboards are available to all
Digitally agile: driven by the user experience, and extensible	VLE and associated technologies are in place, supplementing other teaching forms	VLE and associated technologies form the basis of teaching forms	Digital services are ubiquitous and encourage students to adopt digital workflows
Evidence-based: reflecting proven practice, with feedback loops	Student evaluation returns are analysed for improvements	A broad range of student evaluation and analytics data is available to be drawn on as required, and is formally noted	Analytics and pre-enrolment surveys customise student support and lead to changes to core practices
Expert-taught: combining the work of specialists as a complementary team	Academics are responsible for all elements of teaching and module development	Academics are able to draw on the efforts of learning activity designers and tutors	Lead academics, learning activity designers and tutors have collegial and interdependent roles
Flexible: open and responsive, available to all	Traditional semesterised offerings, with modules available for enrolment two or three times per year	Students are able to enrol in some modules multiple times each year	Students can enrol at any time, and can also pause or speed up their study activities within appropriate parameters

Learning-activity-oriented: pedagogically sound, with education at the centre	Learning activities are developed based on the best judgement of the academic	Learning activities benefit from the perspective of learning activity designers	Learning activities comply with ICEBERG and the evidence-based core, with custom elements appropriate to ILOs
Part-automated: AI-assisted	No agreed approach to AI exists, and it is not encouraged	Experimentation with AI is evident across student-facing activities	Weak AI is routinely used in the form of chatbots and feedback on formative student work
Relational: tutor-supported and peer-assisted	Peer support is possible and encouraged	Reactive tutors monitor discussion forums and respond to email	Lead academics, tutors and peers engage with one another in accordance with defined core
Success-driven: outcome-oriented, in the sense of student achievement	Students can enrol in any first module they choose	Students are advised to enrol in a specific first module and have the option of orientation or bridging courses	First enrolment modules are especially designed to embed core skills, study behaviours and give a meta-view of the qualification
Systematic: deliberately accessible, scalable and personalised	Systems problems are addressed only when they become critical	Systems are frequently audited and reviewed, with a view towards improvement	All systems are purposefully aligned and improved in accordance with evidence

160 Operating Models and Organisational Change

I'm certain that comparing your own university with DDE will see a great deal of variability. Where to begin, should DDE be your objective?

In major change activity it is never wise to try to achieve too much in parallel if things do not need to be changed all at once. To achieve DDE, there is a recommended order of alignment by which DDE gradually emerges. The order is:

1. Systematic, with DDE alignment as the goal
2. Consistent
3. Digitally agile and Data-analytics-driven
4. Expert-taught, Learning-activity-oriented and Relational
5. Flexible and Success-driven
6. Evidence-based
7. Part-automated.

The first change step is towards Systematic, which sets the foundation for systems alignment and commits the university towards accessible, scalable and personalised education in accordance with the 10 remaining principles. The move towards Systematic will commit to operating model design in order to ensure the overall outcome resembles DDE and that each subsequent change event complements those that follow. The Systematic principle sets the foundation and framework for subsequent alignment.

The second step involves designing the Consistent core and custom approaches, which are foundational for all educational decisions of DDE. This is a critical stage, as the core and custom define the detail required of all subsequent change activity. Decisions about the core will determine the role of teaching roles, particularly that of tutor.

The third step is establishing a technical infrastructure suitable for the Digitally agile and Data analytics-driven principles. It is unlikely that any specific VLE will by default have the dashboards or systems links required for the full DDE experience, so design and investment will be necessary for customising IT systems.

The fourth step is likely the most difficult, in that it directly affects teaching roles and responsibilities. Expert-taught, Learning-activity oriented and Relational appear side by side because all three are inseparable. Arguably, traditional faculty have much to gain from the Expert-taught principle in that their role becomes much more specialised and discipline-based, and their influence is vastly extended by the accessibility, scalability and personalisation possible through DDE. In DDE teaching, traditionally the sole domain of the academic, becomes a shared function. Such sharing might be perceived as a threat – a loss of autonomy – rather than an opportunity to extend quality education. If the change activity related to the Consistent principle results in a core and custom of broad appeal, this fourth step will be much easier to navigate.

The fifth step, introducing the Flexible and Success-driven principles, will likely require some changes to curriculum and a commitment to design as indicated in Chapter 7. Developing a process for designing modules is an important part of an operating model.

The sixth and seventh steps are performed in the final stages and stretch from one end of the alignment model to the next, as demonstrated in Figure 8.6.

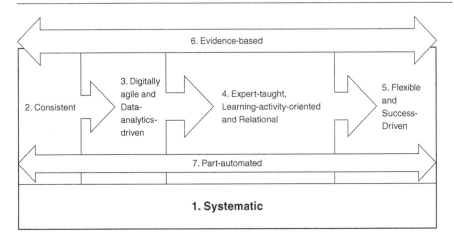

Figure 8.6 A Step-by-Step Alignment Model for the DDE.

In the diagram, the Systematic principle is demonstrated as the essential foundation for DDE. On this foundation, from left to right, Steps 2 through 5 are built. Once these are in place, the processes required to make the Evidence-based principle possible can be built in, as can the Part-automated principle. Symbolically, the Evidence-based principle overlaps the hard border of the model to show that the search for evidence must transcend the evidence DDE develops within itself. External scholarship is also keenly sought to improve how things are done.

It's difficult to see teaching and learning represented here, or the work of the academic, the role of research or the experience of the student. Diagrammatically, the student is not at the centre and neither is pedagogy. I trust that the careful reader will immediately understand why; these are all implicit. The model assumes accessible, scalable and personalised education based on engagement, enlightenment and empowerment for the student. Teaching and learning, the work of the academic and the role of research are the means by which all of this takes place. Anyone who has jumped to this part of the book or has a sense of discomfort in having universities described in this way might benefit from a refresher of Chapter 2.

Clearly DDE requires more than just adopting a few new approaches or adjusting some current practice. For most universities, achieving DDE requires a Transformation in terms of SAMR: the redesign of many tasks (Modification) and the creation of others (Replacement). Importantly, the Transformation should not change the educational quality or mission of the university. Instead, it is aimed at the processes and systems hindering the university from realising accessible, scalable and personalised education.

In change management terms, moving towards DDE is a transformative (paradigmatic) activity rather than an incremental (additional) one. Incremental change thinking assumes gradual movement towards a goal over time, and such change tends to take place within existing units or across a few units; as such, it is not broad enough as a mechanism for achieving DDE. Small improvements agreed across

162   Operating Models and Organisational Change

departments are well and good and indicate a healthy future-orientation; however, incremental change does not typically address core structural or operational issues across the entire university. The Systematic principle requires universities to undertake a deeper, comprehensive and ambitious programme of change in pursuit of DDE.

Managing Change

Successful transformative change relies on a sound method. Most change models suggest three phases similar to those proposed by Lewin (1951, as cited in Smith et al., 2014):

- Unfreeze: consider the current situation, identify the need for change and identify how the change might be best advanced.
- Change: implement the change plan, expecting confusion and challenge.
- Refreeze: establish the new patterns of activity as new processes become locked in.

Lewin's model nicely describes the dynamics of transformational rather than incremental change; the former requires a great deal more effort, in that it more directly challenges ingrained activities. Metaphorically, transformational change requires a thawing; incremental change, by way of contrast, moves at a glacial pace. Once transformation has refrozen, as it were, incremental improvements can and should continue (recall the Evidence-based principle, for example).

Another way of considering change is offered by Beckhard and Harris (1987, as cited in Smith et al., 2014), who propose a change formula:

$$C = [A \ B \ D] > X$$

- C = change
- A = level of dissatisfaction with the status quo
- B = desirability of the proposed change or end state
- D = practicality of the change (considering risk, disruption and change plan)
- X = the perceived cost (in terms of effort and personal impact) of the change.

The model provides clues to improving the prospects of a planned change. Success requires clear and convincing messages highlighting the importance of the change (both in terms of negative consequences of not changing [A] and the benefits of changing [B]); developing a clear, logical and transparent plan (C); and minimising the adverse outcomes related to job and process changes. An effective communications function is essential for managing all variables of the formula. The Beckhard and Harris formula also warns against starting from a sense of complacency (A), or a half-hearted view of the benefits (B). Universities are extremely complex, politically charged organisations where relationships across academics and administrators (managers) can easily become adversarial. I have written this book to demonstrate how

Operating Models and Organisational Change 163

the university as a whole might benefit from DDE, attempting to portray the benefits to both these stakeholder groups in better educating students, who, ultimately, ought to be considered the primary benefactors of all that a university does.

Variables A, B and D of the Beckhard and Harris formula rely on an effective change model. Fortunately, one exists; that proposed by Kotter (1996), whose book *Leading Change* remains contemporary. Kotter proposes an eight-stage process for implementing major change.

1. Establish a sense of urgency.
2. Create the guiding coalition.
3. Develop a vision and a strategy.
4. Communicate the change vision.
5. Empower broad-based action.
6. Generate short-term wins.
7. Consolidate gains and produce more change.
8. Anchor new approaches in the culture.

Kotter's eight stages nicely reflect Lewin's unfreeze, change, freeze model. Stages 1–4 relate to unfreeze, the number of stages underscoring the importance of pre-work before change takes place; Stages 5–7 bring about the actual change or shift in systems and structures; Stage 8 refreezes the university into its new operating model. It is worth spending some time now to consider Kotter's model, as it specifically relates to changes in a university.

1. **Establish a sense of urgency**. As mentioned in Chapter 1, education has remained remarkably unchanged by the digital revolution. Some practices have changed, but fundamental ways of operating have not. Complacency is a serious barrier to change for universities moving towards DDE. Until competitive dynamics do result in a 'burning platform' requiring DDE, it is best to highlight the benefits of a more accessible, scalable and personalised approach.
2. **Create the guiding coalition**. A strong, united and dedicated leadership team is required for change to be successful. This will naturally include a university's executive team and Vice-Chancellor but should also extend to the university Council. Senior management and stakeholder representatives should also be included, based on Kotter's four key characteristics of position power, expertise, credibility and leadership. The coalition must be able to consider the university informed by, but not limited by, individual responsibilities.
3. **Developing a vision and a strategy**. To some extent I have endeavoured to provide a vision and strategy in this book. Naturally much will need to be translated into the specific challenges and ways of working for any specific university.
4. **Communicating the change vision**. This is a vital and ongoing element of all change management programmes. In universities, where audiences are highly intelligent and trained to be both critical and articulate, a confident, well-informed, honest and straightforward communications team is a must. Clear and

164   Operating Models and Organisational Change

consistent communications are required reflecting Stages 1–3; frequent and reliable communications are also needed across Stages 5–8.

5. **Empower broad-based action**. Foundational to this stage is establishing the correct structures and roles. As is clear from previous chapters, DDE challenges the incumbent structures and decision-making centres of most universities and proposes different roles for teaching staff. Broad-based action is only possible once structures sympathetic to DDE are in place.

6. **Generate short-term wins**. Creating and visibly recognising improvements in performance (in terms of access, scalability and personalisation) is meant here. Kotter suggests this stage as a good opportunity for promoting the benefits of the change and for learning more about what the change is leading to. Fine-tuning plans is also an activity of this stage, as unanticipated challenges or unintended results begin to be encountered.

7. **Consolidate gains and produce more change**. At this stage, immediate managers ought to be able to bring about the final elements of change within their own areas of responsibility – and develop the processes needed for ongoing improvement. In Kotter's view, this is the stage where further structural and policy change takes place.

8. **Anchor new approaches in the culture**. Critically, Kotter points out that cultural change comes 'last, not first' (1996, p. 157). In this final stage, the change is still underway; Kotter cautions that this stage 'requires a lot of talk' and 'may involve [employee] turnover' (p. 157).

There is a critical point in change activity where the change becomes irreversible; that is, where the momentum of effort reaches a tipping point whereby it is easier for the change activity to be completed than it is to return to the starting point. It may be the formal ratification of new senior roles, the completion of a review of teaching activity, the formal adoption of a core approach or top-level sign-off of a new, agreed operating model. This tipping point is not just before Stage 6 of Kotter's model; it is just before Stage 5.

It is here my perspective differs from that of Kotter, at least where change in universities is concerned. Kotter suggests that the change vision is best expressed within existing structures (Stage 5), with structural changes following to consolidate the gains made (Stage 7). However, given that universities consist of highly interdependent systems and the scale of change DDE demands, I am of the view that structural changes are required as part of empowering broad-based change (Kotter's Stage 5). My reason is simple: universities are typically managed along school or faculty lines, rather than consolidated lines. Unless the elements of DDE are agreed across all academic units, structural shift is a likely requirement.

A structural shift based on student-oriented processes, rather than academic disciplines, is fundamental to DDE. Fortunately, universities are not necessarily bound to a full, disruptive and chaotic shift in configuration while existing students are being catered for. Many universities are also not yet quite uncomfortable enough to establish a sense of true urgency, hence the option of developing a parallel university alongside the existing one (Figure 8.7).

Operating Models and Organisational Change 165

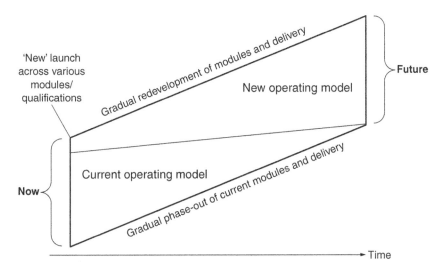

Figure 8.7 A Gradual Adoption of a New Operating Model.
Source: © The Open University (internal presentation, 2017).

It is possible, arguably even more desirable, to bring about DDE Systematisation principle across one new qualification at a time. While the gradual adoption demonstrated in Figure 8.7 would have two operating models co-existing – with its subsequent tension across the current and the new ways of working and the costs of duplication of processes – it has the advantage of minimising disruption and enabling new systems and processes to be redesigned from scratch. New systems can also be trialled and mature as more qualifications are carried across.

Conclusion: Transforming Universities for DDE

There is a vital need to emphasise the benefits for *all* from DDE. It is a mistake to portray DDE and the change it may require as being managerial or consumerist. Instead, DDE is a means by which an accessible, scalable and personalised student experience, culminating in authentic education, might be offered to many more students without compromising the core tasks of the academic or the nature of the university itself.

Transforming universities for DDE rests upon the successful completion of 10 major activities.

1. Initiate a transformation activity. This might start as an exploratory exercise. It is important that the activity has top-level buy-in and sponsorship. Should the activity gain traction, a formal change management plan will be needed.
2. Understand the current state, the 'as is' operating model. This need not be mapped to Level 3; a simple, high-level operating model canvas complemented

166   Operating Models and Organisational Change

by some Level 2 analysis will be sufficient. The diagnostic provided in Table 8.3 will assist.

3. Articulate a vision for a new, 'to be' state. This book articulates 11 elements of DDE, which might serve as the basis for designing an accessible, scalable and personalised education.
4. Conceptualise the desired student journey. Consider what the new student experience might be, perhaps articulating it as in Chapter 5 and in the form of a student journey map.
5. Develop the new 'to be' operating model canvas. This should be a public, collaborative and well-led endeavour.
6. Develop the 'to be' operating model to Level 3. This should be a careful, detailed and consultative activity guided by careful change management. The gradual adoption approach (Figure 8.7) is recommended over a single point transition.
7. Determine the new university structure. This will be the first actual activity of change. Once complete, the transformation will have passed its tipping point.
8. Design the 'to be' operating model to Level 4 where required. Where actual tasks and required roles are not clear enough for job descriptions to be finalised, perform Level 4 analysis.
9. Develop change plans and implement with new structure teams. Figure 8.6 suggests an order in which the various elements of DDE might be addressed.
10. Confirm the means by which the operating model will be continuously updated. The operating model will always require adaptation as the result of operating friction. Maintaining the operating model provides a clear means of ongoing improvement, both to diagnose operating problems and as the basis for regular operations review.

Beneath the 10 steps lies a great deal of effort, risk and complexity.

As mentioned in Chapter 1, there is no apparent urgency for universities to confront the challenges of change.

At least, not yet. As learners increasingly demand a more personalised experience, and as a few universities position themselves as accessible, scalable and personalised providers of sound education, the opportunity for differentiation described in this book will instead represent the necessary means of competing.

In this book I have endeavoured to present a model for digital distance education, along with design elements to bring it to life. Education need not change; the 'what' of universities will endure. Universities engage, enlighten and empower students; my hope is that they will, eventually, do so in ways unencumbered by the supply-side dynamics so common today. Taking a demand-side, personalised learner perspective can enrich and extend the university endeavour. It is my hope that university leaders across the globe will rise to the challenge of change based on a vision for improvement.

Activities

1. Consider your university's 'as is' state and prepare an operating model canvas. How does it differ from that in Figure 8.2?
2. Prepare a RAPID analysis for the different components listed below. How well are the departments you've identified aligned across them?

   a. The student study experience
   b. Course design
   c. The online experience
   d. Student retention and completion

3. This chapter confronts the challenges of change.

   a. Which are the most pronounced challenges in your own university, from your perspective?
   b. What would need to happen at your university to begin the journey towards the scale of change suggested in this chapter?

4. Consider the diagnostic in Table 8.3. How does your university align with the principles of DDE?
5. Think about the day-to-day operations at your university. What are the top three areas that do not seem to be functioning optimally? How well are the underlying processes understood?
6. The conclusion of this chapter outlined 10 major activities underlying change towards DDE. Which strikes you as the most challenging?

References

Alexander, B., Ashford-Rowe, K., Barajas-Murphy, N., Dobbin, G., Knott, J., Mccormack, M., ... Seilhamer, R. (2019). *EDUCAUSE Horizon Report | 2019 Higher Education Edition*. Retrieved 29 January 2020 from www.educause.edu/horizonreport.

Campbell, A., Gutierrez, M. & Lancelott, M. (2018). *Operating model canvas: Aligning operations and organization with strategy*. Zaltbommel, Netherlands: Van Haren.

Henderson, M., Selwyn, N. & Aston, R. (2017). What works and why? Student perceptions of 'useful' digital technology in university teaching and learning. *Studies in Higher Education*, *42*(8), 1567–1579. https://doi.org/10.1080/03075079.2015.1007946.

JISC. (2014). Enterprise architecture. Retrieved 29 January 2020 from www.jisc.ac.uk/guides/enterprise-architecture.

Kotter, J. P. (1996). *Leading change*. Boston, MA: Harvard Business School Press.

Open Polytechnic. (2017). ODFL Operating model: Blueprint, (October).

Scarlett, H. (2016). *Neuroscience for organizational change: An evidence-based practical guide to managing change*. London: Kogan Page.

Smith, R., King, D., Sidhu, R. & Skelsey, D. (Eds.). (2014). *Effective change manager's handbook*. London: Kogan Page.

Appendix

Am I Ready for Distance Learning?

Based on the 'Am I ready for distance learning?' questionnaire used by Laidlaw College, New Zealand. Reprinted and adapted with permission.

You have a unique set of circumstances.

Research has shown that different circumstances can affect how prepared you are for success in your study.

You can control or work on some of your circumstances, especially if you know that they are important.

If we have some idea of your learning context then we can better support you into success with your study.

MUST BE RETURNED WITH YOUR APPLICATION

Circumstances *The reason we ask the question is given in italics below*	Please circle the option that applies				
	A	B	C	D	
Are you self-disciplined, able to construct and work to a schedule? *You must take responsibility for finding out and managing your deadlines.*	Not really	Sometimes	When I set my mind to it	Yes, absolutely	
Which statement best describes how well you can study on your own? *You will need to sustain your own effort, without being regularly inspired by others.*	Not good	Unsure	Good	Excellent	
Would you describe yourself as motivated for study with us? *If you are studying because you have been told to by someone else, or in the absence of other ideas, then it may be hard to persist when difficulties arise.*	Not really		Yes	Highly	

Appendix: Am I Ready for Distance Learning? 169

How would you best describe your reading and writing skills? *You will need to spend quite a lot of time reading, and also writing essays and assessments. Some readings may be challenging to understand.*	Not practiced	Practiced	Proficient	Excellent	
How old will you be when you start your first paper(s)? *Older students often have informal experience which helps with their study.*	18 or under	19–23	24–44	45+	
What is your highest level of previous qualification? *Prior qualifications prepare students for further tertiary study. Because you are enrolling in a 'humanities' type subject, if your qualification is a technical one you may not find it has prepared you well for this type of study.*	None or low	University Entrance or Certificate	Diploma or Skill based/ Technical Degree	Humanities Degree or Post-graduate	
What are your family's expectations? *If your family is supportive then they are more likely to give you time and resources for your study.*	Not supportive	Mostly supportive		Fully supportive	
Are you the first of your family to study at a tertiary level? *If someone in your family has studied at tertiary level, then you are more likely to have seen the necessary study habits/ attitudes.*		Yes	No		
Which of these statements best describes your internet access? *Having less online access will limit the time you can spend on the online learning and library sites.*	At friends, work, or library	Unreliable, at home	Reliable at home		

continued

170 Appendix: Am I Ready for Distance Learning?

Which of these statements best describes your ability to use a computer? *Less familiarity with computers will be a barrier when you want to find resources, fill out forms and explore for information.*	Not at all confident	Can use all common apps	Confident and able to explore		
Add the number you circled in each column.					
	Multiply the above number by 1 =	Multiply the above number by 3 =	Multiply the above number by 5 =	Multiply the above number by 10 =	TOTAL

Please turn over to see what your score means for you …

What does my score mean?

Here is our suggestion – if you would like to discuss this further, please contact The Centre for Teaching and Learning.

Your score	What you can expect:
Greater than 70	You should have no difficulty with distance study. You will need to allow about 10 hours per week per course.
51–70	You can approach your distance learning study with confidence, but expect to work hard! Plan well and maintain consistent study habits.
21–50	You are likely to find distance learning study quite a challenge. When you enrol, please make sure you are doing a manageable number of courses (see below) and that you develop a solid study plan. If you are able to place some good boundaries around your time and develop good study habits, you have a good chance of success.
Less than 20	It doesn't seem as if you are ready to begin your distance learning study yet. We recommend you change your circumstances in some way before studying with us. Call us for advice on how best to prepare.

Have I Selected the Right Number of Courses?

How many courses are you planning to take at once?		x 10 =	
How many hours per week will you be employed (paid or voluntary) while you are studying?			
How many hours a week are you typically involved in community and hobby activities?			
How many hours a week do you have family or other commitments?			
How many hours a week are you involved in other study with another institution?			
Total: Add the five boxes above:			

If your total from the above table is more than 60, then please reduce your courses. If you cannot reduce your courses, then call us for advice on alternatives (e.g. summer school, campus-based classes).

While it may be possible to do intense study on top of a busy workload when you are studying on campus, it is much harder when studying through distance learning. This is because of the intense learning activity required.

Need Some Help?

If you wish to discuss anything from this questionnaire, or to get help in choosing programmes or courses (papers), please contact The Centre for Teaching and Learning.

Index

Page numbers in *italic* denote figures and in **bold** denote tables

academic as designer model 91
academic freedom 21
academic leads *see* lead academics
Academics For Academic Freedom 21
accessibility 4, 14, 92, 137, 156
accommodative learning 26
accountability for student success 109–110
ADDIE (Analysis, Design, Development, Implementation, Evaluation) framework 135
additional learning 26
Agile project methodology 135
ako 98
Anand, B.N. 41, 113
Archibald, R.B. 8, 9
Aristotle 17
artificial intelligence (AI) 61–63, 71, 136, **159**, 160, 161, *161*
assessment design **115**, 116, **116**, 117, 128–131
assimilative learning 26
assimilative learning activities **60**, 93, **93**, 96, 106
asynchronous teaching 63–64, 93, **93**, 94–97, **94**, *95*, 111
Australia, qualifications framework 117, **118**, 119–121, **120**, 127, *127*

back office systems 71
badging 131
Barnett, R. 16
Bates, B. 24
Beckhard, Richard 162–163
big data analysis 51–53
Biggs, John 90, 125–126, **126**
blended distance model 37–38, **39**, 40, 91, 93

blended on-campus model 37–39, **39**, 91, 93
bridging modules/qualifications 59, 60
business unit confirmation 151

Campbell, A. 146–147
campus-based model *see* on-campus model
capability maps 146, *146*
change management 162–165, *165*
Chantelle (student narrative) 77–80, 87
Coaldrake, O.P. 35, 42
Collini, Stefan 19
Community of Inquiry (CoI) framework 98–99, *99*
compliance 11–12, 20, 22, 152
consistency of practice 49–51, 92, 131–132, *132*, 137, **158**, 160, *161*; *see also* core approaches to education
content, use of term 113–114
content knowledge 100–101, *101*, *102*
continuous improvement 55–57
core approaches to education 44–46, **45**, 49–51, 71–72, 132, *132*
Course Experience Questionnaires (CEQs) 55–56
Creative Commons licences 54–55, 59
credit decisions 121–123, *122*, 124
cumulative learning 26
customer relations management (CRM) systems 57–58, 71
customisation 49–51

data analytics 51–53, 133, **158**, 160, *161*
data dashboards 52
data flows 153
data warehouse systems 71
DDE model *see* digital distance education (DDE) model

Index 173

demand-orientated education 11–13, 21–22
detailed processes map **148**, 153
detailed value chain map **148**, 153, *154*
development activities 99–101, *100, 101, 102*
dialogic activities 99–100, *100*, 101–102
dialogic education 94, 96
digital agility 53–55, 133, **158**, 160, *161*
digital distance education (DDE) model
42–44, **43**, 48–67; Consistent principle
49–51, 92, 131–132, *132*, **158**, 160, *161*;
core approach 44–46, **45**, 49–51, 71–72,
132, *132*; Data analytics-driven principle
51–53, 133, **158**, 160, *161*; Digitally agile
principle 53–55, 133, **158**, 160, *161*;
Evidence-based principle 55–57, 133, **158**,
160, 161, *161*; Expert-taught principle
57–58, 91, 133–134, **158**, 160, *161*;
Flexible principle 58–60, 122, 123, *123*,
134, **158**, 160, *161*; Learning-activity
oriented principle 43–44, 60–61, **60**,
134–136, **135, 136, 159**, 160, *161*; Part-
automated principle 61–63, 136, **159**, 160,
161, *161*; Relational principle 63–64, 136,
159, 160, *161*; Success-driven principle
64–65, 137, **159**, 160, *161*; Systematic
principle 66, 137, **159**, 160, 161, *161*;
see also module narratives
digital education 30–32, **32**
digital learning 30–31
digital literacy 53
digital rights management-free (DRM-free)
55
discussion forums *see* asynchronous teaching
distance education models *see* digital distance
education (DDE) model; traditional
distance education model
Drucker, Peter 1, 10
Durie, Mason 28, **29, 115**

education: vs. learning 16–18; linking
learning to 23–27, *26*; *see also* higher
education
education outcomism 114–117, **115, 116**,
140
Ellen (lead academic narrative) 84–87, 88
enrolment patterns *123*, 124
enterprise architecture 146, *146*
Epictetus 17
ePortfolio platforms 32, 51, 77
ethical considerations 4; artificial intelligence
62; data analytics 52
Evans, P. 7–8
evidence-based practice 55–57, 133, **158**,
160, 161, *161*; assessment design 131

expert teaching 57–58, 91, 133–134, **158**,
160, *161*; *see also* lead academics; learning
activity designers; pastoral support teams;
tutors and tutorial role

face-to-face tutorials 40, 43, 46, 50
facilitative learning activities 93, **93**, 94–97,
94, *95*, 106
feedback: assessment 129–130; student 55–56
Feldman, D.H. 8, 9
flexibility and openness 58–60, 122, 123,
123, 134, **158**, 160, *161*
flexible starting dates 59–60, 64–65
Forbes, Malcolm 17

governance map 152

Harris, Reuben T. 162–163
Henderson, M. 143
higher education: benefits of *3*; costs and
funding 2–3; demand orientation 11–13,
21–22; as engagement, enlightenment and
empowerment 5, 7, 22–30, **29**, 113, **115**;
as an industry 8–9; linking learning to
23–27, *26*; redesigning 4–7; resistance to
technological change 9–11; role of
universities 18–20; supply orientation
11–12; universities as social constructs 19,
21–22; as a wicked problem 4, 55, 143;
see also models of university education
Horizon Report series 143–144

ICEBERG design principles 61, 134
Illeris, Knud 24, 26, 125, 126, 127
incumbent practice 10
informative learning 25, *26*
initial modules 64–65
intellectual freedom 21
intended learning outcomes (ILOs) **115**, 116,
116, 117, 125–128, **126**, *127*; assessment
design and 128–131; learning activity
design and 137, 139
internet connectivity 87–88
interpersonal communications 63–64, 136
IT systems map 152

Jacques, Jeph 17
Jarvis, P. 27, 114–115
JISC 53, 146

Kearsley, G. 21, 40
Kegan, R. 25, *26*
Kettering, Charles 17
knowledge 23

174 Index

Kotter, John 163–164

Laurillard, Diana 1, 114, 134, **135**
lead academics 56, 57–58, 91–92, 103–104; accountabilities 110; data analytics 53; development activities 99–101, *100, 101, 102*, 111; dialogic activities 100, *100*, 102; module narrative 84–87, 88; systematic approach and 66
learning: accommodative 26; assimilative 26; cumulative 26; defined 22–23; digital 30–31; vs. education 16–18; informative 25, *26*; linking to education 23–27, *26*; transformative 25, 26, *26*, 27
learning activities: assimilative **60**, 93, **93**, 96, 106; facilitative 93, **93**, 94–97, **94**, *95*, 106
learning activity design 43–44, 60–61, 66, **115**, 116, **116**, 117, 131–140, *132*, **159**; DDE principles and 131–137, *132*; frameworks and models **60**, 61, 134–136, **135**, **136**; project- and team-based approaches 137–140
learning activity designers 56, 57, 58, 61, 91–92, 104–106, 136, 137; accountabilities 110; data analytics 53; development activities 99–101, *100, 101, 102*; systematic approach and 66
Learning Activity Management System (LAMS) 134, 135
learning theories 22, 23–27, *26*
lecture-based model *see* on-campus model
Lewin, Kurt 162

Malcolm (tutor narrative) 81–84, 88, 129–130
marking guides 129, 130
Massive Open Online Courses (MOOCs) 6, 31, 39, 63, 65, 96
mechanical learning 26
Mezirow, J. 25, 115
micro-credentialing 6
Miller, G.E. 70
mobile device optimisation 54
models of university education 27–30, **29**, 35–42; blended distance model 37–38, **39**, 40, 91, 93; blended on-campus model 37–39, **39**, 91, 93; on-campus model 37, 38–39, **39**, 91, 93; core approaches 44–46, **45**; qualification decisions 37; roles involved 41–42; subjects and disciplines 37; traditional distance model 37, **39**, 40–41, 91; who to educate 36; *see also* digital distance education (DDE) model
module design: bridging modules 59; initial

modules 64–65; taster units 59, 60; universal design 59, 60; *see also* learning activity design
module development 99–101, *100, 101, 102*, 113–131; assessment design **115**, 116, **116**, 117, 128–131; credit decisions 121–123, *122*, 124; education outcomism perspective 114–117, **115**, **116**, 140; learning outcomes **115**, 116, **116**, 117, 125–128, **126**, *127*; qualification design **115**, 116, **116**, 117–124, **118**, **120**, *122, 123*; *see also* learning activity design
module evaluation 55–56
module learning outcomes **115**, 116, **116**, 117, 125–128, **126**, *127*; assessment design and 128–131; learning activity design and 137, 139
module narratives 70–88; core features of 71–72; lead academic 84–87, 88; management student 77–80, 87; social work student 72–77, 87; tutor 81–84, 88, 129–130
Montaigne, Michel de 17
MOOCs *see* Massive Open Online Courses (MOOCs)
Moore, M.G. 21, 40

neural networking 62
New Media Consortium (NMC) 143
New Zealand: Open Polytechnic 27–28, 50, 98, 122–123; qualifications framework 37, **38**, 117, 118–119, **118**, 127, *127*
Nipper, S. 63

on-campus model 37, 38–39, **39**, 91, 93
online discussion forums *see* asynchronous teaching
online library services 61
Open Polytechnic, New Zealand 27–28, 98, 122–123
Open University, UK 40, 49, 60, **60**, 61, 70, 122, 134
open-access courses 59, 60
openness *see* flexibility and openness
operating models 42, 145–156, 165–166; business unit confirmation 151; capability maps 146, *146*; data flows 153; designing as basis for change 155–156; detailed processes map **148**, 153; detailed value chain map **148**, 153, *154*; governance map 152; IT systems map 152; operating model canvas 147–148, *147*, **148**, 149; process maps 150–151, *151*, 152, **152**; RAPID analysis 151–152; SIPOC 153; student

journey maps **148**, 149, *150*, 151; swim lane diagrams 153, *154*; team identification 153; value delivery chain map **148**, 149–152, *151*, **152**
organisational change 143–145, 156–166; alignment with DDE principles 157–162, **158–159**, *161*; challenges of 156–157; change management 162–165, *165*; implications 157; objectives 157; structure 157; *see also* operating models

Palmer, P.J. 23–24, 57
pastoral support teams 56, 57, 58, 91, 107–109; accountabilities 110; data analytics 53; dialogic activities 100, *100*; scaffolding first-time students 65; systematic approach and 66
pedagogical approach 114–117, **115**, **116**
pedagogical knowledge 100–101, *101*, *102*
peer review 131
peer-to-peer activities 63
personalisation 5, 11–13, 14, 92, 137, 156
personalised assessments 129
Peter, Laurence 17
Peters, R.S. 23, 24, 25, **29**, **115**, 116, 127
pre-enrolment surveys 59, 64, 65, 71; example 168–171
printed learning materials 10, 44; *see also* traditional distance education model
process maps 150–151, *151*, 152, **152**
profile updating 131
Project Managers 138, 139
Publilius Syrus 17
Puentedura, Ruben 32, **32**

qualifications 37, 117–124, *122*, *123*; bridging 59, 60; credit decisions 121–123, *122*, 124; design of **115**, 116, **116**, 117–124, **118**, **120**, *122*, *123*; frameworks 37, **38**, 117–121, **118**, **120**, 127, *127*

randomised assessment tasks 130
RAPID analysis 138, 151–152
real-time data warehouse systems 71
Relational principle 63–64, 136, **159**, 160, *161*
resource-based education model 37, **39**, 40–41, 91
rubrics 129, 130

SAMR model 31–32, **32**, 39, 66, 145, 161
scaffolding first-time students 65
scalability 4, 14, 40, 92, 137, 156

SEEC group 117–119, **118**
self-review 131
Siegel, H. 4
SIPOC (Suppliers, Inputs, Process, Outputs, Customer) 153
Skinner, B.F. 17
SOLO (Structure of the Observed Learning Outcome) approach 125–128, **126**, *127*
specialist-assisted approach 57–58, 91; *see also* lead academics; learning activity designers; pastoral support teams; tutors and tutorial role
Stedman, L. 35
student debt 3, 4
student drop-out 65
student feedback 55–56
student journey maps **148**, 149, *150*, 151
student narratives: management student 77–80, 87; social work student 72–77, 87
student retention 41, 61
student success 49, 52, 64–65, 137; accountability for 109–110
student support data 56–57
student support/counselling 41, 64, 65; *see also* pastoral support teams
student-centred approach 113, 114
Subject Matter Experts (SMEs) 137, 138, 139
subject-oriented teaching 57
success-driven approach 64–65, 137, **159**, 160, *161*
supply-orientated education 11–12
swim lane diagrams 153, *154*
synchronous teaching 63–64, 93, **93**, 94–97, **94**, *95*
systematic approach 66, 137, **159**, 160, 161, *161*
systems approach 21, 40, 92

Tang, C. 90, 125–126, **126**
target operating models (TOMs) 145
taster units 59, 60
teaching 57–58, 90–102, **93**, 143–144; accountability for student success 109–110; assimilative learning activities **60**, 93, **93**, 96, 106; Community of Inquiry (CoI) framework 98–99, *99*; development activities 99–101, *100*, *101*, *102*; dialogic activities 99–100, *100*, 101–102; facilitative learning activities 93, **93**, 94–97, **94**, *95*, 106; as interdependent activity 110–111; synchronous and asynchronous 63–64, 93, **93**, 94–97, **94**, *95*, 111

176 Index

teaching roles *see* lead academics; learning activity designers; pastoral support teams; tutors and tutorial role

team identification 153

technology 66; artificial intelligence (AI) 61–63, 71, 136, **159**, 160, 161, *161*; back office systems 71; digital agility 53–55, 133, **158**, 160, *161*; last-mile constraints 87–88; resistance to 9–11; SAMR model 31–32, **32**, 39, 66, 145, 161; students' devices 53–54, 87–88; TPACK framework 100–101, *101, 102*

TEL (technology enhanced learning) 30–31

TPACK framework 100–101, *101, 102*, 137

traditional distance education model 37, **39**, 40–41, 91

transcendent learning 26

transformative learning 25, 26, *26*, 27

tuition fees 3, 4

tutors and tutorial role 40, 41, 44, 56, 57, 58, 63–64, 91, 106–107; accountabilities 110; data analytics 53; dialogic activities 99–100, *100*, 101–102; face-to-face tutorials 40, 43, 46, 50; facilitative learning activities 93, **93**, 94–97, **94**, *95*, 106; module narrative 81–84, 88, 129–130;

scaffolding first-time students 65; systematic approach and 66

United Kingdom: degree awarding power (DAP) 19–20; Open University 40, 49, 60, **60**, 61, 70, 122, 134; qualifications framework 117, **118**

universal design 59, 60

universities: role of 18–20; as social constructs 19, 21–22; *see also* higher education; models of university education

University College of London Knowledge Lab 135, 140

user experience (UX) design 54, 66

value delivery chain map **148**, 149–152, *151*, **152**

video-based assessment 131

virtual learning environments (VLEs) 66, 71

viva voce tests 131

W3C compliance 54

Wegerif, R. 94, 96

wicked problem, education as 4, 55, 143

Wurster, T.S. 7–8

Yasmin (student narrative) 72–77, 87